Britain and the American Cinema

Britain and the American Cinema

Tom Ryall

SAGE Publications
London • Thousand Oaks • New Delhi

© Tom Ryall 2001

First published 2001

 SAGE Publications Ltd
6 Bonhill Street
London EC2A 4PU

SAGE Publications Inc
2455 Teller Road
Thousand Oaks, California 91320

SAGE Publications India Pvt Ltd
32, M-Block Market
Greater Kailash - I
New Delhi 110 048

British Library Cataloguing in Publication data

A catalogue record for this book is available from the British Library.

ISBN 0 7619 5447 3

Library of Congress catalog card number available

Printed and bound in Great Britain by Athenaeum Press, Gateshead

Contents

Acknowledgements

A considerable amount of the work for this book was done during a period of study leave in the academic year 1998/99, financed by Sheffield Hallam University and by the Humanities Research Board of the British Academy. Thanks are due to both institutions for this support and to Mick Worboys and Chas Critcher of the University's Cultural Research Institute. Thanks are also due to colleagues in the Film Studies group, Michelle Atherton, Catherine Constable, Gerry Coubro, Sheldon Hall, Sylvia Harvey, Angela Martin, Steve Neale, Jeff Perks and Jonathan Rayner, and to past colleagues Richard Maltby, Robert Murphy and Geoffrey Nowell-Smith. I am grateful to John Baxendale and Chris Pawling who commented on parts of the manuscript, and to Clare Abson and the staff of the University library and Janet Moat of the British Film Institute's Library for help in the matter of research material. Finally, I would like to thank the staff at Sage including Sophy Craze, my original commissioning editor, Seth Edwards who provided technical advice, and to Julia Hall who inherited the project and saw it through to completion.

Tom Ryall

1 American Films and National Cinema

Most nations have been obliged to negotiate a relationship with the American cinema both in their home market and in the wider international world of film. It might be argued that Britain has enjoyed a 'special relationship' with its transatlantic neighbour especially in respect of their shared history and language but also because of the key importance that the British market assumed for the Hollywood film industry as it developed on a global scale. At times, the British market has been completely dominated by the American picture while, in America, its British counterpart has had to make do with the odd high-profile hit film, from *The Private Life of Henry VIII* (1933) to recent examples such as *Notting Hill* (1999), or with a niche position as 'art cinema' as happened with the Ealing films in the period after the Second World War. If the traffic in British films to America has a patchy history, the traffic in actors and directors from the British theatre or cinema to Hollywood is more impressive. This is especially the case during the classic era of cinema and includes some of the most significant names in the history of the American film such as Chaplin and Hitchcock, Cary Grant and Ronald Colman, Vivien Leigh and Greer Garson. While there has been some traffic in the other direction, the list is not long and not as impressive, although it would include Joseph Losey, who fled from the Hollywood blacklist in the 1950s, Stanley Kubrick and Richard Lester. Beyond the exchange of films and personnel, American companies have set up distribution and production companies in Britain, as well as investing in British firms such as Gaumont British and the Associated British Picture Corporation, while some British firms have tried to establish footholds in the American market. In most respects the relationship was, and indeed is, uneven with the American industry dictating the terms of the relationship either through financial muscle according to some arguments, or through the popularity of its films according to others. However, there is one dimension in which the relationship favours Britain and that is in the adaptation of British material for the American film. British subject-matter drawn from history, literature, drama and biography has enjoyed a prominent place in the American film since the earliest days of cinema, culminating in the 1930s when Britain's rich cultural and historical heritage provided the basis for several of Hollywood's most prestigious films of the period. In contrast to the numerous 'British-American' films, American subject-matter has figured rarely in the British cinema.

This study chronicles aspects of the relationship between the two nations and their cinemas spanning the economics of domestic and international film production and the forms and content of cultural exchange, predominantly in the period of cinema's heyday as the principal form of leisure and entertainment for the mass of the population from the First World War until the 1960s. All dimensions of the British cinema – the production industry, the business structures of the distribution sector, film exhibition, the development of a diverse film culture – were touched in some way by the powerful American industry. The British cinema, film-making and cinema-going, together with the business and cultural frameworks within which films circulate and prompt reflection and comment, was obliged to define itself in the context of Hollywood and the popular appeal of American films. British cinema, of course, is not unique in this respect and the global strength of the American film industry established in the 1920s meant that most national cinemas had to position themselves in relation to Hollywood and its films, and to grapple with its appeal in order to create indigenous alternatives. In Britain, as elsewhere, this asymmetrical relationship has been construed as an impediment to the development of an indigenous film production industry and 'national cinema', a threat to national cultural sovereignty, and is an unvarying backdrop for several somewhat tortuous and agonized discussions of the state of the British film. The rest of this chapter is devoted to comment on the notion of 'the British film', the related notion of national cinema and the cultural response to the Hollywood film as an example of 'Americanization'. Subsequent chapters deal with the extent to which the American film industry has played a role in the development of the British industry, the ways in which the British industry has sought to register in the American market and the impact of British culture on the subject-matter of American films.

The British film

The British film has long been on the agenda of discussion as a feature of the national culture in a spectrum dominated by the traditional, verbally based arts of literature and drama. Such discussions are frequently conducted in terms of its problematic status and uncertain identity, and its perceived inferiority compared with its foreign counterparts whether from continental Europe or from the USA. Indeed, the critique of indigenous production can be traced back to the late 1890s. In their detailed study of the British Mutoscope and Biograph Company, Brown and Anthony suggest that

> it was at the beginning of 1899 that the first complaints began to appear about the content of some of the Mutoscope reels. That it was the British, rather than American, films that were involved in at least some cases can be irrefutably proved by a comparison of the backdrops used in subjects such as *Studio Troubles* and *Why Marie Blew Out the Light* with those in more respectable productions such as *Why Papa Can't Sleep* and *The Black Cat and the Dinner for Two*, which are known to have been produced by the British company at this time. (1999: 65)

The unfavourable comparison with the American film is a theme which persists In 1931, Norman Marshall, writing in *The Bookman*, suggested that British film-makers suffered from a dependence on stage material and he characterized British films in terms of a 'muddled slow-moving compromise between the conflicting techniques of the American film and the English stage' (1931: 71–2). Marshall also suggested that 'film is a form of art which is fundamentally unsuited to the expression of the English character and temperament', anticipating later comments by prestigious international film-makers such as Satyajit Ray and François Truffaut which effectively dismiss the British cinema as a serious cultural possibility (Barr, 1986: 1-6). For Marshall, Alfred Hitchcock was the 'only director who has made any real attempt to overcome the unsuitability of the film as a medium for expressing the English temperament'. It is worth noting that Hitchcock acknowledges that his films were modelled in part, at least, on lessons derived from the American cinema and from the work of D. W. Griffith in particular, and that his early career was spent 'in an American studio that happened to be located in London'. 'I certainly was deeply entrenched in American film', as he commented to Truffaut in the course of the famous interview marathon from the 1960s (Truffaut, 1978: 172).

The American film as exemplar, however, is only one dimension of the context in which the British film was obliged to define itself. Lindsay Anderson, in the course of an article on Hitchcock, positions the British film as tending to waver between the sophistication of the European film and the popular appeal of Hollywood:

> As geographically, Britain is poised between continents, not quite Europe, and very far from America, so from certain points of view the British cinema seems to hover between the opposite poles of France and Hollywood. Our directors never–or rarely–have the courage to tackle, in an adult manner, the completely adult subject; yet, they lack also the flair for popular showmanship that is characteristic of the American cinema. (1949: 113)

The notion of a cinema 'hovering' or wavering between powerful exemplars of film-making has been taken up more recently by Christopher Williams, who suggests that 'British film-making is caught between Hollywood and Europe, unconfident of its own identity, unable to commit or develop strongly in either direction' (1996: 193). Although 1940s critical comment did identify a new maturity in the British film represented by the 'quality' film, on the whole British criticism has either ignored the indigenous film or subjected it to vituperation for failing in terms of the polarities offered by Anderson and Williams. In the late 1920s the journal *Close Up* dismissed the British cinema for its failure to match the ambition of the European 'art' cinema of the time, while in the 1960s *Movie* attacked the British film for failing to match Hollywood's popular successes.

However, despite the adverse effects of the 'cultural marooning', and the hesitancy between 'art' and 'entertainment', there are a number of instances of

British films succeeding on an international basis and defying the gloomy pronouncements both of indigenous commentators and critics and of distinguished Indian and French film-makers. For the British film, 'succeeding on an international basis', of course, is more or less synonymous with success in the American market and there is a history of such success flagged by a small number of films which can be traced back to the 1930s. In 1933, Alexander Korda's *The Private Life of Henry VIII* was a huge hit in America, 'the first British film to break box-office records in America' (Street, 1986: 162), and an Oscar winner for its star Charles Laughton. It stands as the historical landmark which appeared to suggest that British films could compete with their Hollywood counterparts in the American market and that the production industry, which had revived since the catastrophic mid-1920s, had an export future. Subsequently, many companies have sought to emulate Korda's success. In the 1930s Gaumont British tailored their films for the American market by making 'epics' and importing American stars, while in the following decade, the Rank Organization made a determined pitch for American success, setting up its own international distribution company. More recently, the American success of *Murder on the Orient Express* (1974) led to lavishly budgeted programmes of 'mid-Atlantic' films by EMI, the media conglomerate, and Lord Lew Grade's Associated Communications Corporation. Though those attempts ended in failure and crises for the firms involved, the subsequent isolated success of films such as *Chariots of Fire* (1981) and other 'heritage-orientated' films, the romantic comedies *Four Weddings and a Funeral* (1994) and *Notting Hill* (1999), and the surprise performance of the ostensibly parochial *The Full Monty* (1997), have revived optimism about British cinema as an international force.

The national cinema

Despite the intermittent successes, the American hegemony over cinema in Britain has frequently been blamed for preventing the development of an authentically indigenous cinema, a body of films which could be regarded as a key component of the national culture. Although a domestic economy dominated by European and American cars, Japanese technological products and Swedish furniture may be considered undesirable on economic grounds, a cinema dominated by American films has been construed as far more threatening to the indigenous culture and politics, to the very life of the nation in a fundamental way. National cinemas have been seen as an important ideological bulwark linked intimately to the formation of a national self-consciousness, and an important source of national identity. The general significance of cultural production to the formation of national identities is suggested forcibly in Benedict Anderson's now widely quoted definition of nation as 'an imagined political community' (1983: 15). The sources on which that imagination of community, that sense of national identity, depends include the conventional discursive practices of politics and history – written and oral, formal and informal – which address national identity in an explicit fashion; the public display of nation (ceremonial state occasions, royal pageantry including weddings and funerals); the activities of the press and broadcasting; the personal world of social intercourse and friendship; and the private world of domestic and family influence.

However, also important to a sense of national identity are the imaginative worlds created by art and literature, and in the twentieth century most notably by cinema and television with their potential for reaching the mass audience. What is referred to as the individual and collective national self-consciousness was, and is, dependent, in part, on the somewhat volatile world of fictional film and television as it addresses or fails to address political and social realities. While many of the sources of national self-consciousness – political speeches, public ceremony – are directed towards the consolidation of national identity, the routine business of producing entertainment in the form of fictional films and TV drama is subject to a range of other determinants. It is in the context of the unpredictable world of fictional entertainment that Colin McArthur has drawn attention to the 'fundamental instability of "national identity", to its being a *process* rather than an *essence*, a process which has to be constantly reworked and restated in order . . . to offer identity positions from which social and political judgements are made and actions taken' (1984: 55). National identity, in this understanding, is not a matter of the fixed and immutable characteristics of the media stereotype (phlegmatic Anglo-Saxons, volatile Latins), or the reflection of notions of identity established in the official discursive sources. It is the temporary product of the fluid intercourse between a range of discourses fixed momentarily in response to circumstance but ready to shift and change as circumstances shift and change and new definitions enter the discursive arena. The elusiveness of 'national identity' is summed up by Richard Kuisel writing about France and 'Frenchness' in terms of 'the fabricated or artificial quality of the notion of a national community':

> What has defined and continues to define (Frenchness) is complex, changing, subtle, contested, and arbitrary rather than fixed, distinct, consensual, and given. It is not a matter of geographical space, history, language, the state, or even culture, though all of these contribute. None of these criteria provide precise impermeable, or permanent boundaries for the (French) nation because much of what defines its identity is imagined. (France) is an invention, a conceptualization. Like other nations, it is to a large extent a collective subjective perception. (1993: 4)

National identity is 'arbitrary rather than fixed' and it is this 'fundamental instability' which makes the imaginative and discursive world so important in social, political and cultural terms prompting governments to concern themselves with questions of the control of art and media products, especially those such as film and television drama with their capacity for making key interventions in the thematic rendition of the 'national' which are available to the mass of the population. In this context, the powerful presence of the

American cinema in Britain can be seen as a problem in so far as it has played an organizing role in the very definition of cinema, controlling its cultural development, constituting a significant determinant on the efforts of British film-makers to construct a national cinema.

At one level, the idea of 'national cinema' is relatively straightforward. French films are films made in France, Danish films are those made in Denmark and so on. Demarcations based on geo-political realities are well established for other art forms and promote an expansive approach to the writing of a national film history in which, for example, 'made in Britain' or 'made in France' entitles a film to be included in the account. Indeed, some would argue that such inclusiveness is a virtue. The task of the cinematic historian, according to Christian Metz, is 'to *save* as many films as possible; not *qua* copies, *qua* celluloid, but the social memory of those films' (1975: 23). Many cinema histories have been written in an expansive spirit providing invaluable inventories of films produced within national boundaries, incorporating 'as many films as possible' into their accounts and alerting readers to the span and scope of a cinema, to the range of films which should, at least, be candidates for inclusion in a work which purports to define a national cinema. The price paid for inclusiveness, however, as Metz acknowledges, is a conceptual promiscuousness in which

> various and sometimes contradictory criteria are called on, in a disparate and gossipy gathering: one film is 'retained' for its aesthetic value, another as a sociological document; a third as a typical example of the bad films of the period, a fourth is the minor work of a major film-maker, a fifth the major work of a minor film-maker. (1975: 23)

If we regard 'national cinema' as a critical concept, a term which denotes a number of film titles but also connotes qualities common to those films by virtue of their common national origins, the multiplicity of films entitled to be included in a national cinema history must, at least, be organized in some way. Critical terms require some discriminatory power and, as many recent historians of national cinema have acknowledged, for a coherent history-writing project, the significance of the term 'national' needs elucidation, both in general terms and in terms of the specific national history under scrutiny (Hayward, 1993: 1-17; Sorlin, 1996: 4-7).

The notion of national cinema requires some effort at synthesizing at various levels and in various ways, the actual films cited as instances of a national culture. As Philip Rosen has suggested:

> The discussion of national cinema assumes not only that there is a principle or principles of coherence among a large number of films; it also involves an assumption that those principles have something to do with the production and/or reception of those films within the legal borders of . . . a given nation-state. That is, the intertextual coherence is connected to the socio-political and/or socio-cultural coherence implicitly or explicitly assigned to the nation. (1984: 70)

Films are produced in specific places and, although they may share certain characteristics with those produced elsewhere, there is a strong common-sense assumption that such films mean something in terms of their national origins, that they cohere into a national cinema because they share a range of national characteristics. In this sense the critical term – 'national cinema' – is both descriptive and evocative. The term 'French film' affirms geographical location and geographical origins, but it also evokes qualities of style and theme, perhaps the mixture of romance and tragedy, the 'mists of regret', in the words of Dudley Andrew (1995), which capture the sensibility of French cinema or, at least, of a significant trend in a particular period, as is the case with the characterization of the 'poetic realist' cinema of the 1930s. Such evocations are, of course, selective and reflect the evaluative dimension of critical activity. In particular, critical writing on national cinema often involves quite radical selectivity privileging certain films, or film trends, above others; certain genres which appear to the critic to embody national characteristics rather more than others. Writing on genre criticism, Rick Altman has drawn attention to the distinction between 'inclusive' and 'exclusive' definitions of particular genres (1984: 6-7). Inclusive definitions have minimal membership conditions, with films loosely related to one another; exclusive definitions, by contrast, nominate a select body of films comprising a genre and imply strong and significant interrelationships between the individual films. National cinemas as well as film genres may be approached in this fashion. To take a familiar example, the Italian cinema of the immediate post-war period is frequently defined in terms of the neo-realist films of Rossellini and De Sica rather than the other films – Italian, American and so on – which made up some 96 per cent of the films which appeared on Italian screens of the time (Sorlin, 1996: 93-4). The Italian cinema is defined, that is, in exclusive terms by a small number of films chosen for their aesthetic and artistic affinities and for their specific stance in relation to Italian politics and culture.

The above remarks suggest that a national cinema is coterminous with a body of films but, as Andrew Higson has pointed out, the term 'national cinema' is used in a variety of ways, incorporating a range of elements over and above films themselves. As he suggests, the concept can be anatomized into four perspectives based on the institutional character of the film industry within a nation; on its typical exhibition and consumption patterns; on the cultural/critical accounts of its films; and on their textual-representational qualities – style, themes and genres – which can be linked to notions of the nation and with national identity (Higson, 1989). Accordingly, British cinema can be defined in terms of the specific business/industrial configuration organized for the production, distribution and exhibition of films. This has varied through history but for the period of the cinema's greatest success as an entertainment form the industry was characterized by a duopoly comprising two large vertically integrated combines, Gaumont British and the Associated British Picture Corporation, a range of smaller production firms, some independent cinema circuits and a powerful phalanx of American-owned distribution companies representing the interests of the Hollywood. In addition, a definition within the parameters of organization would involve a specification of the role of the state in matters such as legislative support, censorship and trade and business regulation. British cinema, however, if examined from the perspective of exhibition and consumption, is defined by the American pictures which have constituted the majority of films screened in British cinemas since the 1920s. As Geoffrey Nowell-Smith has pointed out, the 'hidden history of cinema in British culture, and in popular culture in particular, has been the history of American films popular with the British public' (1985: 151-2). Although the notion of a national cinema being made up of 'foreign' films sounds resoundingly wrong, going to the pictures for most people in Britain, as in many other countries, meant going to see an American film. For cultural commentators, on the other hand, a national cinema is often based on a filtered view of national production in which certain aspects of a cinema are presented as constituting the 'national cinema'. This is especially the case in relation to 'art' cinema where a specific culturally esteemed selection of a country's films is used to define that cinema. In Britain this has often meant documentary films, or documentary-influenced fiction films such as *Saturday Night and Sunday Morning* (Woodfall Films,1960) or the work of Ken Loach. Finally, in the approach which probably conforms to the usual understanding of what 'national cinema' means, British cinema may be defined as a body of films or film genres originating in some way from within the national boundaries, which offer a discourse of sorts on the character and qualities of the nation. A national cinema, then, is more than a corpus of films produced within a national territory. It is also the industrial and business infrastructure from which the films emerge and the cultural superstructure within which the films circulate and are discussed and written about. Indeed, the term 'cinema' itself is often used to refer to the amalgam of texts, industrial and cultural institutions which together constitute a larger object of study than simply films alone, but one more clearly related to society and history and one capable of addressing the term 'national'. Although it is understandable that films are the centrepoint of interest for 'film' historians, a national cinema can only be understood and defined on the basis of a range of empirical data of which films are only the most obvious.

The discussion above provides sufficient indication that defining and writing the history of a national cinema is anything but a straightforward task. Many national cinemas including the British have been defined by the state in legal terms. Quota and subsidy arrangements depended upon such definitions and governments have been obliged to formulate conditions for films to meet in order to be regarded as 'British', 'French' and so on. Such definitions were necessary in order to implement the protection of indigenous film production industries in the face of threatening competition from imported American films. Accordingly, in Britain, under the terms of the 1927 Cinematograph Films Act, for a film to be registered as British 'the author of the scenario had to be a British subject, the studio scenes had to be filmed in a studio in the British Empire' (Hartog, 1983: 64). A 1960s definition of French film, formulated to determine eligibility for subsidy qualification, required such films 'to be made by French producers in an original version recorded in the French language using French authors, technicians, productions personnel as well as principal actors' (Guback, 1969: 157). Also in the 1960s, Italian films were similarly defined requiring 'that the scenario comes from and Italian author or is revised or adapted by an Italian author', 'that the director, and the majority of the scriptwriters, must be Italian', 'that at least two-thirds of the principal roles, and at least three-fourths of the secondary roles must be given to Italian actors' (ibid.: 158). In addition, as the Italian example makes clear, the personnel nationality requirements were often couched in proportional terms enabling foreign personnel to work on Italian films, acknowledging the international character of the film industry. But legislative definitions are of the most minimal kind and fall short of what is usually understood as indicative of the substantive national credentials of a film. Their application, as John Hill has noted, can lead to the anomalous situation in which 'films like *Flash Gordon*, the *Superman* movies, and *Full Metal Jacket* have qualified as 'British' films while, conversely, such a typically British film as *Shirley Valentine* is registered as American' (1992: 11).

Other considerations need to come into play as well as the legal and financial context in which films are made. Writing on Danish cinema from the national perspective, Mette Hjort offers a cultural definition of national cinema, isolating factors such as the use of the native language, the translation into film of indigenous 'cultural monuments' including literature, the exploration of 'the shared practices of an imagined community located within the borders of the nation-state' and the 'important task of thematizing (the) community's past and projecting its future' (1996: 225). Hjort's definition requires that a national cinema, or a nation's films, must connect in some way with the social and cultural life of a nation, with its language and literature, and have an active and discursive involvement with its history and its contemporary social organization. It is in factors such as these that the national specificity of the cinema inheres rather than in the satisfaction of legal requirements. In this context, a film such as *Moulin Rouge*, made at British International Pictures in 1928, directed by the German film-maker, E. A. Dupont, starring the Russian-born actress Olga Tschechova, and set, as the title suggests, in Paris, fails to make the social and cultural contacts necessary to qualify as 'British' in Hjort's sense of the term. It did, however, satisfy the minimal requirements for registration as a British film in the legal sense. Other writers have indicated further factors which may be taken into account in the definition of a national cinema. Susan Hayward (1993: 8-17) has provided a series of typologies including genres, acting performance styles and stars as some of the ways in which a sense of 'the national' can be inscribed within a film. Pierre Sorlin, on the other hand, moves away from film-based definitions, suggesting that 'a national cinema is not a set of films which help to distinguish a nation from other nations, it is a chain of relations and exchanges which develop in connection with films, in a territory delineated by its economic and juridical policy' (1996: 10), a perspective which moves much closer to the notions of 'film culture' as definitive of a national cinema. The identity of a national cinema, from that perspective, becomes a matter of defining the constellation of ideas, institutions and films as it relates to the overall culture of a nation (Lovell, 1972: 5-15). The project of writing a history of a national cinema then embraces each of the dimensions that Higson isolates – the film industry and business, the film culture as incarnated in journals, academies, archives and so on, as well as the films produced within particular national boundaries. As Tom O'Regan has suggested, it is a 'messy' project, requiring a range of analytical strategies involving 'neither the analysis of a film text nor policy discourse; neither film industry journalism and economic analysis not film reviewing, but a mixture of each' (1996: 3).

Stephen Crofts (1993) has provided a lucid and comprehensive account of the options for national cinematic definition in the context of an international film industry dominated by Hollywood. The options cover a range of strategies in respect of mode of production, audience address, narrative and stylistic attributes, with Hollywood film acting as a reference point, from the imitation of American films as happened in Britain in the 1930s, to attempts at differentiation from Hollywood, through the creation of distinctive 'art' cinemas' as in France and Italy. They also include the example of the domestic industries of Hong Kong and India which have effectively ignored the American example in favour of films based on successful indigenous formulae. The British industry has, at various points in its history, produced and distributed films which try to establish a firm foothold in its own market through the exploitation of indigenous strands in the popular culture with established appeal in a range of other media and presentation forms. Examples of this trend would include the films of Gracie Fields and George Formby based on music hall, or the Hammer horror films of the 1950s and 1960s with their roots in Gothic literature. Some of these 'parochial' endeavours – the Hammer films for instance – have enjoyed international success but the industry has also sought to design films more consciously for the American market through the imitation of American genres in films such as *Evergreen* (1934) based on the Warner Bros. backstage musicals of the early 1930s such as *42nd Street* and *Gold Diggers of 1933* (see Higson, 1995: 135), or by using American stars such as Sylvia Sidney in Hitchcock's *Sabotage* (1936) or, more recently, Julia Roberts in *Notting Hill* (1999). Films such as *A Room with a View* (1984) and *Howards End* (1991) offer an 'art cinema' variant, the 'heritage' film, drawing upon strands of 'high culture' and particular historical periods – the nineteenth-century novel, Edwardian Britain – and devising a formula which has been relatively successful in penetrating a particular market segment in the United States. Debates on the identity of the British film have taken place within the framework of such different solutions to the problems of creating a national cinema with both an economic viability and a cultural relevance. British films emerge from an industry sometimes competing with Hollywood and adopting variants on its styles and techniques, sometimes retreating to parochial issues and themes concentrating upon the indigenous market both in terms of cultural identity and financial reality, sometimes blending aspects of British life and culture effectively for an international market.

Americanization

The attitude towards Hollywood, towards the American film, in the wider cultural community was formed in the context of a discomfort with the general 'Americanization' of British culture. The appearance of new communication forms at the end of the nineteenth century, the popular press, film and recorded music, prompted cultural commentators to express a range of concerns about their significance for culture both in its broad sense – 'a particular way of life' – and its narrower sense of 'the works and practices of intellectual and especially artistic activity' (Williams, 1965: 57; 1976: 80). The changes to be wrought by the new technological media were to have profound implications for the general life of the societies affected by them and were to construct new forms of intellectual and imaginative activity to supplement and subvert the existing worlds of artistic activity and information exchange. In terms of Britain, as Le Mahieu has suggested,

> the development of popular national daily newspapers, the cinema, the gramophone and other forms of mass entertainment threatened to upset traditional patterns of British culture. Attracting an audience of unprecedented size, this 'mass' or 'commercial' culture – no single term unambiguously defines the phenomenon – was created for profit, dependent upon new technologies, and often dominated by individuals outside the mainstream of British cultural life. (1988: 2)

Many argued that the changes had negative consequences – social, moral, political – for the very fabric of society, for culture in its broadest sense as well as for shape and character of cultural production, art and entertainment, as it moved from the traditional to the technological. The concerns are embodied in a number of general headings including technology, mass society, mass communication, urbanization, modernization and democratization, identified from the late nineteenth century onwards by numerous writers concerned about the impact of such changes on social and moral as well as cultural and artistic life. In many respects the phenomenon of caution in the face of new and different forms of art and entertainment was neither new nor specific to the late nineteenth century. Duncan Webster has drawn attention to the 'long history of the fears provoked by new cultural forms, with novels, plays, melodramas, music hall, newspapers, films, comics, rock/pop songs and videos, all in turn being seen to encourage crime or disorder or, at least, declining moral and social standards' (1988: 179). The key distinctions in this period, however, concern the interrelated phenomena of technology and urbanization and their complex relationship to the emergence of key cultural and communicative components of twentieth-century life – the cinema, the popular newspaper, radio and television. Concern deriving from the form and content of literature and theatre could be tempered by the limited accessibility of such forms; the mass character of the audiences addressed by the new media – partly though not wholly a function of urbanization – literally multiplied the fears and concerns for traditional culture evident in earlier times because of the dramatically multiplied audience for the new art and culture. The other characteristic and enduring concern which emerges with the advent of the new media, and one which proved to be central to a consideration of the British cinema and its development, was the identification of America with the 'new era dominated by the realities of city life and a technologically defined environment' and with the problems associated with the changes (Bigsby, 1979: 6). America and American culture became the focus for criticism and the term 'Americanization', although previously on the agenda in terms of political and cultural discourse, was to become a key concept in the cultural discussion centred on the new media. C. W. E. Bigsby has suggested two main reasons for the identification of America with the cultural shifts and the emergence of the new forms of culture: America 'was a society whose cultural identity was forged in an industrial age' and America lacked 'any established tradition and . . . the structures necessary to the validation of such a tradition, it had no resources with which to counter what (was seen) as a pernicious democratic mediocrity' (ibid.: 7). American culture embraced and incorporated the informational and artistic forms consequent upon technology and urbanization and, during the course of the twentieth century, managed to export its own incarnations of this culture – films in particular – to most corners of the globe. Such tokens of a rapidly changing way of life drew the attack of cultural commentators in Continental Europe and Britain whose stance seemed to suggest that resistance to them was part of the struggle to retain the traditional literary and artistic cultures in the face of technological barbarism. America's embrace of the new media forms was sometimes construed as an immature grasp of a rudimentary culture developed in the absence of the substantial traditions of art and culture characteristic of European countries. The consequences – popular newspapers, films, jazz – reflected the lack of tradition and their export to Europe either in exemplar form as models to be emulated, as happened with the press, or in actual form as imported products, as happened with films, became the focus of increasingly agonized and vituperative comment among the indigenous cultural elites.

It is possible to distinguish between two broad senses of 'Americanization'. The first pinpoints the various ways in which the international film and media industries have been dominated historically through patterns of finance, ownership and control by American companies and, although patterns of ownership have changed in recent years with, for example, Japanese high technology companies and Australian media magnates becoming more prominent in the world of international film, the American hegemony still persists. Also, associated with large-scale capital is the mode of production incorporating standardization, the division of labour and other characteristics deriving from the mass production of commodities but employed to an extent in the production of culture as well particularly in the context of the American cinema. The second sense concerns the actual products of American culture which circulate internationally – the films, television programmes, books, consumer items, cars, fashions and lifestyles – which the American capital and industrial infrastructure generates and which embody 'Americanization' in terms of cultural impact. The two are, of course, interrelated, with the mass circulation of American-originated products made possible, in part at any rate, by well-financed international distribution and marketing systems.

The mass culture configuration that had settled in Britain by the late 1920s prompted literary critics such as F. R. Leavis to renew the misgivings expressed by Matthew Arnold in the 1860s about the influence of America. Arnold had cast a critical eye on American culture and had argued that 'in the things of the mind, and in culture and totality, America, instead of surpassing us all, falls short' (quoted in Webster, 1988: 180). In *Mass Civilisation and Minority Culture* (1930), Leavis following Arnold's scepticism, outlined what came to be known as the 'culturalist' case against the American-influenced mass art and communication of the twentieth century. The popular forms generated by technology – the popular press, the cinema, advertising – constituted an attack on traditional culture, effecting a levelling down of cultural and moral standards which, in his view, were intimately intertwined. In short, their influence was a threat to the established cultural and social authority. However, as John Storey has pointed out, the selfsame new media were later attacked by the Marxist Frankfurt School of sociologists and cultural commentators for their role in the maintenance of social authority in the democratic West. As Storey suggests, 'Arnold and Leavis had worried that popular culture represented a threat to cultural and social authority, the Frankfurt School argue that it actually produces the opposite effect, it maintains social authority' (1993: 105). Suspicion of the popular press, films and popular music has united a number of traditions of criticism across political perspectives in a condemnation of popular and mass culture especially in its American variants, but also in the indigenously produced culture in so far as it reflected the American hegemony in form and style, in content and ideology.

The substantial presence of American films in the British context made such arguments about 'Americanization' sharp and relevant, with Hollywood both defining cinema's identity as a mass art for the audience and dictating to an extent the terms under which British film-makers tried to construct a national cinema of their own. Hollywood provided implicit models for film-makers in the specific forms, styles and genres, while it also defined the spaces in which films could be viable in a domestic production industry which found it difficult to compete with American films for screentime. One of the most formidable problems posed lay in the contradictory nature of this presence in which the American film industry defined films in terms of high production values, while ensuring that the space available for the domestic picture failed to provide the financial returns that enabled production values to be sustained at such levels.

2 The 'American Invasion':1895–1928

American film companies have been involved with the British film industry since the very earliest days of cinema, exporting film equipment and films to Britain, using Britain in the days before the First World War as a base from which to organize the European distribution of their films and later setting up branch companies staffed by Americans primarily for distribution purposes but, on occasion, for production purposes as well. The picture of involvement is uneven: sometimes direct with branches of American firms established in Britain; sometimes indirect with British firms acting as agents for American interests; sometimes the result of corporate decisions taken in America; sometimes the consequence of individual entrepreneurial initiative. Whatever the character of the involvement, Britain by the mid-1920s emerged as the principal foreign market for American pictures (Thompson, 1985: 126-7). The shape of the industry which developed during the formative years bore the imprint of the American industry in various ways and can be seen as a negotiation with the fact of growing American power in the international film industry during this period.

Britain like other industrial nations had a number of inventors and entrepreneurs working on the development of the moving picture and by the late 1880s, when Edison was registering patents for his Kinetoscope (peep-show) equipment in the United States, William Friese-Greene was claiming the invention of the 'Machine Camera' which would enable the projection of moving photographs on to a screen. Indeed, he was communicating with Edison on this very subject (Robinson, 1996: 28). However, Friese-Greene was declared bankrupt in 1891, his experiments and demonstrations coming to nothing despite the claims made on his behalf in the following years. His work is now regarded as largely derivative, dependent on the work of others; his status, according to John Barnes, 'just one of the several 19th century inventors who made unsuccessful attempts to construct a practical apparatus for taking and reproducing photographs in motion' (1996a: 44; see also Rossell, 1998: 107-9). Eventually, of course, it was Edison's Kinetoscope which introduced moving pictures to the American and European public, with the first British Kinetoscope parlour opening in London's Oxford Street in October 1894 by Edison licensees, Maguire and Baucus (Rossell, 1998: 89). The peep-show format, however, was short lived and was soon superseded by projected film shows on machines such as the Lumière Brothers' Cinématographe in France and elsewhere, Robert Paul's Theatrograph in Britain, Max Skladanowsky's

Bioscop in Germany and the projector invented by Thomas Armat and Francis Jenkins that the Edison company finally used to introduce projected films in the United States – the Vitascope. In Britain the first projected film programmes happened early in 1896, with the exhibition of Lumière films at the Polytechnic Institution in Regent Street on 20 February 1896 usually regarded as the first. However, British films were actually being screened on the same day by Robert Paul on the Theatrograph projector in a private meeting at Finsbury Technical College and Birt Acres had projected films to a meeting of the Royal Photographic Society more than a month before the Lumières' show (Barnes, 1976: 93; Coe, 1981: 74). The Regent Street show was the first commercial performance, the first public screening to an audience, but of more interest is the fact that the films screened by the Lumières, Paul and Acres were French and British not American. Indeed, the Americans were being left behind by developments in Europe and, as John Barnes has suggested:

> The rapid growth of the cinema in England in 1896 put her temporarily ahead of any other country, with the possible exception of France. America, which had been the birthplace of cinematography, was momentarily left behind. The hullabaloo over the debut of the Armat-Edison Vitascope at Coster & Bial's Music Hall on 23 April was confined to America, for in Europe successful film performances were already well established by that time. (1976: 171)

The Lumière programme at London's Polytechnic Institution may be regarded as 'the birth of the film industry in Britain' (Hunningher, 1996: 41). By that date, however, there were a number of indigenous companies working in some way or another in the nascent industry and their activities were undoubtedly given shape and purpose by the Regent Street event. The earliest firms to establish themselves in Britain, often started by individuals with a background in photography and the magic lantern, were concerned with the manufacturing of film equipment and the production of films as well as their promotion and sale, and their circulation to the public through a range of exhibiting outlets. These included Kinetoscope parlours for the early 'peep-show' versions of moving picture entertainment, music halls, 'penny gaffs' (storefront cinemas), travelling showmen and so on. They were small-scale concerns often family owned yet some of them made films which had a substantial international impact and which must be regarded as important contributions to the early development of the medium. The films of R. W. Paul, Birt Acres, Cecil Hepworth, and the Mottershaw family among others have a firm place in the early history of cinema and constitute an early rebuff to notions that Britain was an uncongenial home for the medium. As testimony to the early significance of British film-making, despite the fact that other foreign titles were available and listed in the programme, the only one included in the first American public exhibition of moving pictures in April 1896 was a British film. The Edison show included *Rough Sea at Dover* shot in 1895 by pioneer film- maker Birt Acre for Robert Paul's company. The rest of the programme consisted of 'films of dancing girls and excerpts of plays that had long been available for peephole viewing' but the short actuality picture stood out from the vaudeville influenced pictures and 'became the hit film of the opening night' (Musser, 1990: 118).

American companies in the first decade

There were a variety of interchanges between the pioneer film-producing nations in these early years. Equipment and films circulated around the globe, and machines were adapted and copied, as with Paul's work on the Edison Kinetoscope which exploited the fact that Edison had failed to patent his machine in Britain. In addition to this, films were screened without particular importance being attached to their national origins. The international circulation of films required an international infrastructure with parent firms needing to establish foreign bases of their own, or to work with indigenous firms using them as agents in the complex business of distributing films to a wide and disparate range of outlets. No film-producing country remained sealed off from others. This is clearly demonstrated in the ways in which American companies set up subsidiary operations in Britain during the 1890s. Two of the three leading American firms – the Edison Manufacturing Company and the American Mutoscope and Biograph Company – established bases in London both to distribute equipment and films and to make films to feed the fast-increasing demand for film material in America itself. The firms associated with the American pioneer companies rapidly moved into prominent positions to become the 'two commercial giants of the British film industry' by the late 1890s (Barnes, 1996b: 159). The Edison company interests were handled initially by one of their associate American firms, Maguire and Baucus, and a London base – the Continental Commerce Co. – was established in 1894 to sell Kinetoscopes and films. The company soon established a number of Kinetoscope parlours in London, made plans for openings in other European cities and, with the rapid development of the projected film, became a leading agent for a number of film manufacturers, American and European, including the Lumière company (Barnes, 1983: 155; Musser, 1990: 82). However, the company failed to secure rights to the Edison Vitascope projector and relations with the inventor deteriorated to the extent that they became involved in litigation with him towards the end of 1898. Although Edison continued to sell films through Maguire and Baucus, they lost their exclusive rights and subsequently Edison was to set up a London subsidiary – the National Phonograph Co. Ltd. – to organize direct sales of films in Europe instead of working through agencies (Thompson, 1985: 3). The company was effectively deprived of its original American rationale and, as Richard Brown has suggested, their 'future in the film business now depended largely on the performance of their business in England' (1998: 22).

The new directions for the company were presided over by Charles Urban, an American with experience in the entertainment industries – kinetoscope and phonograph parlours, travelling film shows – who was appointed as manager in 1897. He was also involved with Walter Isaacs in devising a projector adapted from existing machines which he introduced to the British film industry in 1897 and marketed under the name that soon became a generic term for any kind of film camera or projector – 'the bioscope' (Barnes, 1996a: 145. Cosandey, 1996: 83). Urban reorganized the Maguire and Baucus London branch in 1898 and renamed it the Warwick Trading Company after Warwick Court in Holborn where the firm had its premises. Early advertisements for the company indicate that equipment trading was a central activity. This included the Bioscope projector, Lumière's Model B cinématographe and a number of innovations in lighting, developing and printing equipment credited to British film pioneer, Cecil Hepworth, who had joined the company in 1898 (Barnes, 1996a: 146-7). However, the Warwick Trading Company also handled films, acting as selling agent for a number of prominent film 'manufacturers', including the Lumière Brothers and Georges Méliès together with British producers such as G. A. Smith, R. W. Paul and the Riley Brothers. The firm also developed its own production programme specializing in documentary and topical subjects, such as royal and state ceremonial both in Britain and abroad (*Gladstone's Funeral, The Coronation of the Queen of Holland*), sports (the University Boat Race), war and associated military and naval subjects including South African material both before and during the Boer War. It was soon to become one of the most significant production companies in Britain, particularly for its topical and news output (Barnes, 1996b: 159). Some fiction films were made, mostly comedies, and some films featuring music hall artists, but the production energies of the company were directed at non-fiction material from both Britain and around the world.

Urban left the Warwick Trading Company in 1903 under somewhat acrimonious circumstances involving complicated business manoeuvring between him and his erstwhile employers, court cases alleging libel and slander on both sides and bankruptcy proceedings against him. Matters came to a head in 1904 with a court case alleging illegal use of the 'Bioscope' trade mark by Urban (Brown, 1998: 24-34). Both parties were to survive these proceedings and to continue to play significant roles in the development of the British film industry. Urban established his own company – the Charles Urban Trading Company – with collaborators including G. A. Smith and Alfred Darling, associates from the Warwick Trading Company days and important figures in the film industry of the time. Urban's interests lay in educational and scientific film-making and, although the company's activities included the distribution of French and American dramatic films and some Urban-produced British examples of the genre, the company's catalogues contained numerous indigenous examples of films with botanical and zoological subjects as well as travel films. His collaboration with G. A. Smith led to the development of Kinemacolor, an early colour film process which was patented in 1906 and is acknowledged by historians to be the first commercially viable photographic system for the production of colour motion pictures (Kindem, 1982: 136; Usai, 1994: 13). Non-photographic colour effects had been a feature of the earliest films through the manual application of colour to individual film frames, the use of stencils and eventually a mechanized process involving dye transfer which was used on a number of prominent films of the 1920s including *Greed* and *The Big Parade*. Also, during the silent period, films were toned and tinted to produce generalized colour effects (Coe, 1981: 112-16). Kinemacolor was based upon photographic principles outlined in the mid-nineteenth century by James Clerk Maxwell which specified a three-colour additive process. Smith's innovation was to base the system on two colours thereby avoiding the considerable technical difficulties of the three-colour system (Kindem, 1982: 138). In 1909 Urban set up a company to exploit the process – the Natural Colour Kinematograph Company – and some successful films were produced, including footage of spectacular state occasions such as the Coronation of 1911 and the *Delhi Durbar* newsreel of 1911 with its two and a half-hour running time. The process was marketed abroad in France, Japan and the United States where it enjoyed a brief period of popularity. The system eventually foundered for a mixture of reasons including technical problems in both recording and projection, legal problems including the loss of the Smith/Urban patent rights in 1914 and, perhaps, a failure to exploit the process sufficiently in relation to the long narrative fiction film which was fast becoming the global film industry norm. Some fiction titles were made both in Britain and America but the most successful were documentary and news pictures like *Delhi Durbar,* and it has been suggested that Urban's own interests lay in the 'travel, educational and topical films' which figured prominently in his early career in the industry rather than in the burgeoning fiction film (Low, 1949: 99). The Kinemacolor episode brought Urban's British career more or less to an end. As Gorem Kindem has suggested:

> The loss of Smith's patent appears to have been catastrophic to Charles Urban. Within one month he voluntarily initiated the liquidation of the Natural Color Kinematograph Company, Ltd.'s assets to pay off his creditors. Urban then left England for America just before the outbreak of World War 1. (Kindem, 1982: 141)

Urban's career was to continue in America rather than Britain and included handling distribution of a government-sponsored propaganda film – *Britain Prepared* – for the American market, yet he had left a substantial imprint on the British film industry during its formative years. Described by Terry Ramsaye as 'the most aggressive factor in the British film trade' (1926: 562), his role in the early development of moving pictures or 'animated photography', as it was sometimes called, was recognized by contemporary commentators as of central importance. The first edition of *The Optical Lantern and Cinematograph Journal* proclaimed him as inventor of 'the bioscope, which has perhaps done more to popularise optical lantern entertainments than any other invention' (1905: 1:13), and a few years later the British *Stage Year Book* was to place him above Edison in the ranking of pioneers with the comment suggesting that 'the idea of living pictures . . . is generally credited to Edison, but to Mr. Charles Urban as its real pioneer all the real credit is due' (quoted in Harding and Popple, 1996: 216). In relation to the British cinema in particular, Low and Manvell have written:

It was to his initiative and remarkable grasp of the film's potentialities that the early British film industry owes such ambitious achievements as the scientific film, Kinemacolor, and the travel and war films of first the Warwick Trading Company and then the Charles Urban Trading Company – films which are outstanding in comparison with their contemporaries. (1948: 17)

It might be considered somewhat ironic that the various genres of factual film which subsequently were to be closely identified in British film culture as a key dimension of the distinctiveness of British film owed their early development to the endeavours of an American entrepreneur. Subsequent contributions to the factual film – the British Instructional films, Percy Smith's *Secrets of Nature* series, the Grierson project which brought considerable critical kudos to British cinema – might be said to have their origins in the activities of early film-makers including Urban.

Edison's major rival in America, the American Mutoscope and Biograph Company, also established a British base – the Mutoscope and Biograph Syndicate – in 1897 as part of its development strategy as a transnational organization. The United Kingdom was an appropriate base from which to develop an international profile with its highly developed financial service sector, its proximity to other European territories, its empire and the convenience of the shared language (Brown and Anthony, 1999: 11). The British base and its successor – the British Mutoscope and Biograph Company – was to become the largest British company of its time and 'its issued capital probably exceeded the total working capital of all the other film companies in the UK during the 1890s and early 1900s' (ibid.: 5). London's Palace Theatre of Varieties was hired to showcase its 70 mm gauge films and 'the Biograph's smooth running and enormous projected image immediately marked it out as a high-quality product' (ibid.: x). The company also built what is now regarded as the first studio in Britain, in London, where it filmed the first Shakespeare film, *King John* (Warren, 1995: 185). It was also closely involved with the 'peep-show' sector and its Mutoscope machines, superior to Edison's Kinetoscope, were an important part of its business operations in the early years. It differed from other companies in so far as its operation was self-contained. As Barnes has written:

The firm . . . held a unique position in the industry since none of its films or equipment (apart from Mutoscopes) were available on the open market, but remained the property of the company which employed its own cameramen and exhibitors. At this moment in its history, all its film, both negative and positive, was 70 mm wide and was therefore suitable only for its own equipment. (1996b: 134)

The uniqueness of the equipment employed by British Mutoscope and Biograph was a mixed blessing. The 70 mm film format used in the Biograph camera provided image quality which was superior to its competitors, and this was reflected in very favourable press comment on their shows. This technical superiority, however, limited their capabilities in some respects. 'The large gauge and speed of projection' note Brown and Anthony, 'which made the quality of the Biograph so impressive, limited the length of films to such an extent that it was difficult to produce anything but the most basic narrative episodes' (1999: 232). The company did adopt the 35 mm format but restricted its film production in favour of other areas of activity including picture postcards and domestic motion picture viewers such as the Kinora. By contrast, its American counterpart's move to 35 mm production led to its distinguished contribution to the development of the American cinema with the short films of Edwin S. Porter and D. W. Griffith.

The establishment of outposts in Europe, however, reflected only a small part of the American film industry's concerns during the early years of cinema. For the first fifteen years or so of its existence, from 1895 until just before the outbreak of the First World War, the industry was involved in a dual struggle. While ventures such as the Continental Commerce Company and the British Mutoscope and Biograph Company reflected the objective 'to establish agents and subsidiary offices abroad for the sale of American films', another objective closer to home was 'to reduce the foreign share of the US market' (Thompson, 1985: 2). The ways in which the American industry achieved both objectives had consequences for the British film industry. As indicated above, American companies had established some footholds in Europe in the 1890s and continued to establish bases as the industry developed with, for example, Vitagraph setting up branches in Paris and London in 1906. However, the relationship between such companies and the American parent-firms was unstable as demonstrated by the activities of Charles Urban in particular. The other objective for the industry, its position in its own domestic market, was the major preoccupation as American film producers focused upon the problem of supplying films for home audiences in the context of a rapidly growing demand for film and in the face of competition from the leading European producing countries including Britain. The establishment of American outposts in Europe took the international struggle to the competitor countries but some of these countries were themselves operating effectively as international forces in the American market itself. French film-makers especially had played a major role in supplying both equipment and films to the American industry and, by 1907, it has been estimated that two-thirds of the films released in America were from Europe, with a French company – Pathé Frères – 'being responsible for over a third of the films shown on American screens' (Musser, 1990: 488). Around 1905, the exhibition of films in the United States underwent an important change. At first, the moving picture had established its popularity in the American entertainment environment through a variety of outlets including Kinetoscope parlours, the vaudeville theatres, amusement parks, makeshift storefront theatres and the travelling exhibitors who were particularly important in bringing movies to rural audiences. The advent of the Nickelodeon – 'a small and uncomfortable makeshift theatre, usually a converted cigar store, pawnshop, restaurant, or skating rink' (Gomery, 1992: 18) – changed things significantly, inaugurating a significant shift in the social and leisure habits of a nation and establishing an important base for the development of a new cultural phenomenon. In the words of one film historian:

> In its short heyday, the nickelodeon theater was a pioneer movie house, a get-rich-quick scheme, and a national institution that was quickly turned into a state of mind. Its golden age began in 1905 and lasted scarcely nine years, but during that time it provided the movies their first permanent home, established a durable pattern for nation-wide distribution, and – most important – built for the motion picture an audience that would continue to support it for another forty years. (Merritt, 1985: 83)

The Nickelodeon network expanded rapidly and, with the introduction of frequent programme changes ranging from twice a week to daily, required an increasing amount of film material which American producers found it difficult to supply. The industry as a whole was internally divided with a succession of patent disputes and lawsuits which had begun in the late 1890s, hampering progress especially in the production sector. As one historian has written, the patent disputes 'stymied growth and prevented the industry from reaching its full potential. Only a handful of producers existed, whose energies were devoted more to protecting their patent claims than to the business at hand' (Balio, 1985: 103). In this context, French and Italian firms were able to compete very effectively and to supply the films for the burgeoning nickelodeon sector.

However, when the major patent holders – the Edison Manufacturing Company and American Mutoscope and Biograph – agreed to pool their interests along with a number of smaller patent holders to form the Motion Picture Patents Company in 1908, a measure of stabilization was brought to the industry. Its development proceeded apace, and the share of the market won by foreign companies began to decline. Although relatively short lived, the company

> radically altered, upgraded and codified American film production, distribution and exhibition. The Patents Company was responsible for ending the foreign domination of American screens, increasing film quality through internal competition, and standardizing film distribution and exhibition practices. But, and perhaps most significant, by licensing manufacturers, the MPPC succeeded in transforming the fledgling American motion picture business into an internationally competitive industry. (Anderson, 1985: 133-4)

This was an important step in the achievement of the twin objectives mentioned by Thompson for, as Kerry Segrave has argued, before 'the U.S. was ready to take on the world, it was necessary for the domestic industry to become "rationalized" in capitalist fashion' (1997: 6). This re-organization, in conjunction with the rise of the nickelodeon, led the American film industry away from its dependence upon imported films and whereas in '1907, 60 per cent of the subjects released on the American market were of foreign origin, by the last six months of 1909, foreign productions represented less than 50 per cent of films released and the percentage was declining' (Bowser, 1990: 23). The objective of establishing the American film in the domestic market was on the way to being achieved in the years preceding the First World War, but the trend was consolidated by the events of 1914–18 and their effect on the European production industries. Although the Motion Picture Patents Company was to exclude most foreign film producers from the American market, with Pathé Frères the important exception, foreign films were still to exercise influence in the pre-First World War American film industry. Indeed, the longer films from Italy and France provided exemplars for film-makers such as D. W. Griffith, but the numerical advantage that European and particularly French films had enjoyed over American films in the formative period of the industry was all but extinguished by the war.

While the American film industry in the period before the First World War began its move to a position of international dominance, the British industry, according to Low, was moving into a period of consolidation, at least in certain sectors of the industry (1949: 129). While it is true that the methods of distribution and exhibition consolidated into successful enterprises, the production record is another matter. At times during the first decade of cinema, British pioneer film-makers equalled if not surpassed their American counterparts in terms of invention with the Kinemacolor process and innovations in film form and content with the early narratives. During the second decade, however, Britain began to fall behind. Films from the formative years such as *A Daring Daylight Burglary* (Sheffield Photographic Company, 1903) and *Rescued by Rover* (Hepworth Manufacturing Company, 1905) compared favourably in terms of advances in narrative techniques with their American and European counterparts. Indeed, one historian of British cinema has suggested that *Rescued by Rover* is a 'clear precursor of the short films made by D. W. Griffith for the Biograph Company in America between 1908 and 1913' (Barr, 1997: 8). By contrast, during the subsequent years of consolidation in the other sectors of the industry, British film-makers seemed not able to produce films which stood against either the Griffith Biograph short films or the longer feature pictures coming from France and Italy which were to influence the future shape and structure of the industry throughout the world. However, it has been suggested that historiographical biases have distorted the judgement of the films of the period and that different critical perspectives would have presented such films in a different and more favourable light:

> a certain injustice has been done to British films of the immediately post-
> 'pioneer' period. Where there was innovation, it has been overlooked, or
> interpreted in the light of later developments, notably those that came to be part
> of the dominant Hollywood mode from 1913 onwards. In fact, British film of the
> period were often quite sophisticated, particularly in the comic and actuality
> fields. Narrative editing, too, was often innovative – but, unfortunately, the
> innovations tended to be in directions which went against the grain of what was
> to prove the dominant approach. (Hawkridge, 1996: 131)

As in America, the major growth in the British industry during the period was in exhibition. Makeshift cinemas known as 'penny gaffs' – a term for a low-class music hall – had been in existence since the late 1890s . These were often converted shops, although architectural historians have noted that a number of different kinds of buildings were adapted for film shows in the early years of the century, including country corn exchanges, workhouses, chapels, railway arches and skating rinks, existing alongside the more ephemeral venues of the street cinematograph and the tent shows (Atwell, 1981: 5, Barnes, 1996a: 71, Gray, 1996: 14). From around 1908 onwards, specially designed buildings – cinemas – began to appear alongside the conversion of music hall theatres for film shows. Historians differ in their identification of the earliest cinemas, citing, for example, venues in London such as Bromhead's 'Daily Bioscope' in Bishopsgate (1906) and the Balham Empire (1907) with its Pathé Frères films, and in Lancashire, the Central Hall, Colne (1907); another account suggests that the date is much earlier with the construction of two purpose-built venues for Robert Paul's Theatrograph shows at London's Olympia in 1896 (Brown, 1977: 520).

In terms of numbers, however, the key period is from around 1909 onwards. The Cinematograph Films Act of 1909 introduced strict safety standards to which exhibitors had to conform and provided a stimulus to new building. As Harding and Popple suggest: 'The days of the hastily converted chapel or skating rink were at an end. Cinemas now had to be purpose-built and, for the first time, architects had to put their minds to designing buildings specifically for film exhibition' (1996: 208). The new cinemas had projection booths and raked seating in acknowledgement of the special needs of the medium and in compliance with the government regulations. The public demand for films had become well established and the exhibition enterprise became a sound financial prospect attracting substantial investment capital during the pre-war period. As Rachael Low has noted:

> between 1908 and the First World War a transformation took place. The fixed show, with the specially built picture theatre following hard on its heels, was to draw millions of pounds into the exhibiting side of the industry at a time when British production was falling behind that of other countries. From 1908 onwards began a financial boom in exhibition which incidentally scattered England with a new type of impersonal community centre, as well as a new and distinctive architecture. The penny gaff was to give way to the age of the Bijou Palace. (1949: 15)

As in the United States, the cinema in Britain firmly established a significant place in the social and cultural life of the nation, with the number of cinemas in Britain by the early 1910s estimated by a number of historians as 3,500–4,000. The films supplied to this growing market came partly from British companies such as Paul, Hepworth, Urban and so on but by the First World War, British films had settled into their familiar position as minority fare on the schedules, with a substantial number of films coming from France and the United States.

Roy Armes has suggested that 'in 1910 foreign domination of the industry amounted to 85 per cent, with France (40 per cent) and the United States (35 per cent) in the forefront' (1978: 27), and Kerry Segrave suggests that the American share increased before the First World War and that 'U.S. screen presence amounted to 50 to 60 per cent of the British releases in the 1910 to 1914 period (1997: 4).

The cartelization of the major American companies, their effective domination of the domestic film supply and the strict control of foreign competition meant that the industry could turn its attention to the export of films to the developing global market. Britain was to prove important to this process in two ways. Firstly, it was an important and potentially lucrative foreign market in which cinema-going had developed into a key dimension of popular entertainment, creating the kind of demand for films comparable to that in America itself. Secondly, for a range of reasons, Britain became an important strategic base from which the American industry was to market its films to a range of foreign territories. Indeed, as film historians have noted, with 'its large domestic exhibition market, the world's most developed shipping and sales network, a system of dependent colonial and commonwealth trading partners, and until 1915 tariff-free imports, Britain served as the heart of pre-war international export' (Urrichio, 1996: 65). However, this concentration upon distribution on behalf of American firms, together with a reliance on American films by British exhibitors, meant a difficult time for the production sector and paved the way for its future subordination to the American film industry. As Kristin Thompson has suggested:

> This strategy may have been profitable in the short run, but it helped create problems that were to plague the British film industry for years. By downplaying production in favour of distribution and exhibition, the British firms left the field open for foreign films; with so little screen time being devoted to native production, it became increasingly difficult to interest investors in making British films. (1985: 30)

The British industry had acquired a particular shape during this period, exhibition thriving, though on the basis of imported films, distribution developing as a service to the American industry, production lagging behind despite the export successes of the very early years. The war accentuated the exhibitors' dependence on American films as British production fell to about 9 per cent of the British market (Thompson, 1985: 67); other sources, the French and Italian industries, were also in decline and the fast-growing American production industry was in a good position to fill the gaps left by previous suppliers. It was also during the war that the distribution arrangements changed with the American industry abandoning Britain as the centre of their export trade and relocating it in New York.

By the 1920s, the American film industry had established a substantial place in the international market for films taking advantage of the disruption to the production industries of its pre-war competitors such as France and Italy and, to an extent, Britain. The decade was marked by a substantial expansion in cinema building, the formation of the large vertically integrated companies which were to dominate the cinema during its 'golden years', from the advent of sound to the early 1960s, and a consolidation of the style of picture – the long feature narrative with stars – which became definitive of cinema for audiences around the world. The transition from the industry in the early years characterized by a medley of small companies to a big business dominated by conglomerates was facilitated by the increasing involvement of orthodox financial institutions. The advantages of a large domestic market, which enabled American film companies to market their films abroad at highly competitive prices, converted into a domination of many foreign markets and evoked protectionist responses in many countries. The British and American industries interacted in various ways during this period. American films continued to dominate the British screen and, although there were some attempts to set up production bases in Britain, the bulk of the films were made in Hollywood. There were also a few attempts to establish an American presence in the exhibition sector of the industry but cinema ownership tended to remain British controlled. The American industry, however, did establish a number of firms to distribute and market its films in Britain and its domination of the British screen was secured through its network of distribution agencies.

American companies in Britain in the 1920s

By the early 1920s a powerful configuration of American distribution companies was settled as an important and influential dimension of the British film industry. By 1926, Paramount, Fox, Warner Bros., and MGM, four of the 'big five' firms that were to dominate Hollywood during the 'golden years', had established distribution companies in Britain and, together with a string of smaller companies handling other American films, they distributed most of the films screened in Britain during the 1920s. The post-war period also saw Hollywood companies turning their attention to other sectors of the industry – production in particular. A report in *The Bioscope* in May 1919 claimed that 'all of the big (American) firms are thinking of sending companies to Europe, and especially to England, which is regarded as an especially good field for producing'. One reason offered for considering Europe, and Britain in particular, as a production centre was economic; it was noted that transporting a company from New York to Britain was less expensive than transporting them to the West Coast of America (*The Bioscope*, 1 May 1919). Although during the course of the 1920s, the West Coast was to become the effective centre of American film production, in the immediate post-war period, New York was still important. The administrative and financial headquarters of the major companies were there but, also, important firms including Vitagraph, Goldwyn and, Metro increased the volume of their East Coast production during this period, and new studios were opened in the New York area by D. W. Griffith, Famous Players-Lasky and Fox (Koszarski, 1990: 102). Other reasons for considering alternative production venues offered included the need for new locations for filming as 'California has been photographed to death'; also, interesting in the context of the many comments on the inferiority of Britain in terms of film talent, it was pointed out that 'more than 50 per cent of the actors and producers who have made big reputations in America are British-born'. There was no reason why 'equal reputations should not be made by actors and producers in England as soon as they realise that it is well worth while to make the attempt' (*The Bioscope*, 15 May 1919: 8).

There was some caution expressed in the context of uncertain economic conditions in post-war Europe; for example, Winfield Sheehan of the Fox company was reported as saying that the idea of European production 'has not been permanently dismissed, and when conditions have become more normal in Europe generally we shall undoubtedly see some move in this direction' (*Kinematograph Weekly*, 4 March 1920: 103). However, a number of American companies expressed firmer plans, or were reported as having them in place. Vitagraph, one of the key pioneer companies in America, had established a distribution branch in Britain in 1906 and, in 1919, *Kinematograph Weekly* carried a story headlined 'Vitagraph to produce in Great Britain' (18 September 1919: 81). J. Stuart Blackton, a key figure in the company's pioneer days, actually did come to Britain in 1921 and made three films, including *The Glorious Adventure*, which was shot in Prizmacolor – an American colour system developed from the British Kinemacolor process (Low, 1971: 126). *Kinematograph Weekly* also carried stories about Lewis Selznick's intentions 'to organize a big British company' incorporating both production and distribution, although by May of the following year the press was reporting the failure of the plans and arrangements for the distribution of Selznick pictures in Britain to be handled by a British company, Walturdaw (*Kinematograph Weekly*, 2 October 1919; 6 May 1920). There was even a story about one of the leading American stars of the day, Rudolph Valentino, coming to the country to make a series of pictures (*The Bioscope*, 26 July 1923: 23).

In 1920, the trade press announced the arrival of one of the most prominent of the American movie moguls – Sam Goldwyn:

> Samuel Goldwyn, President of the Goldwyn Pictures Corporation, who is on his way to England, is coming especially to create a permanent organization for the production of Goldwyn Pictures in the United Kingdom. Plans for film production in England by the Goldwyn Corporation have been under way for some time and extensive studios will be established in or near London as soon as the requisite factors for production can be brought together. (*The Bioscope*, 1 April 1920: 16)

Goldwyn, who was to become one of America's small number of independent 'quality' producers in the 1930s and 1940s, was quoted in the article on his reasons for the move and these included the familiar 'possibilities of setting and landscape, variety of atmosphere, freshness of artistic quality, both in acting talent as well as in the general elements of production'; he also spoke of his intention to base the production programme on the works of British writers continuing a trend – the 'Eminent Authors' project – that he had established in America using novelists and short story writers to 'inject literary values into the studio's output' (Koszarski, 1990: 244). One company which did establish a base in Britain and produce a number of films in the early 1920s was Famous Players–Lasky (Paramount), the leading American company of the 1910s. The company's origins, and the origin of its eventual name as one of Hollywood's most powerful companies, was in the early 1910s with a merger between film-making companies – Adolph Zukor's Famous Players and the Jesse Lasky Feature Play Company – and Paramount Pictures, a company which specialized in the nationwide distribution of feature films. By the late 1910s, the company had 'become the world's most impressive producing concern, as the *Film Daily* put it, "the United States Steel Corp. of the motion picture industry"' (Koszarski, 1990: 69). By 1919, the British distribution arm of the company was established as the leading firm supplying British exhibitors with many of the most popular titles of the day, and Famous Players announced plans to move into exhibition and to set up a cinema circuit. Although the finance was to be raised almost entirely in Britain, the plan was fiercely resisted by the exhibitors trade body – the Cinematograph Exhibitors' Association (CEA) – fearing that access to the American films of the company would be threatened by such a move, that the parent company would favour their own circuit.

During the 1910s, under Zukor's stewardship, Famous Players' films were made by leading directors such as D. W. Griffith and Cecil B. DeMille and, more importantly as far as the public were concerned, they featured the most popular stars of the day including Mary Pickford, Douglas Fairbanks, Gloria Swanson and Western star, W. S. Hart. By 1919, when the company was planning its British forays, the situation was changing with some of the leading stars and directors setting up their own organization – United Artists – and distancing themselves from the powerful integrated companies which were developing in the American industry. Nevertheless, the company remained a substantial force and, particularly with its business practices of block and blind booking, exercised considerable influence in Britain. There was talk of boycotting the Famous Players' films but the exhibition sector was not really organized well enough for such a move. In fact, Famous Players soon abandoned their British exhibition plans, perhaps in the context of their attention turning to building cinema circuits in the United States itself. Exhibition interests were not to prove important for American companies in Britain although most of them owned a small number of large cinemas in key cities for pre-release purposes. It was the distribution base that was crucial and the powerful hold of American films on the British public could be maintained through that sector. As Rachael Low has noted, the 'big American firms had pre-release cinemas in London by the end of the twenties, and there was little reason for American producers or renters to seek further participation in ordinary British exhibition, which was already completely dominated by their films' (1971: 84). In fact, the one exception was Paramount itself, which during the course of the 1920s and 1930s acquired a small London suburban chain as well as building a number of cinemas in large cities such as Birmingham, Glasgow and Manchester (Eyles, 1997: 219).

A move into production, however, seemed more of a proposition in the early 1920s for a range of reasons, including the increasing importance of the British market and the economic and cultural advantages which would derive from British-based production. As with Goldwyn and Lewis Selznick, the trade press announced the Famous Players' plans with a fanfare, as in the following report in the middle of 1919:

> When the "Aquitania" leaves New York Harbour on June 28 she will have on board her several of the best-known studio experts in the United States, bound for Great Britain in the interests of the new Famous Players British Producers Ltd. Actors and actresses will follow shortly after, to take part in pictures "shot" on spots of historical interest, which are now familiar to thousands of American soldiers and countless others, and the work of our greatest novelists and writers will be perpetuated by kinematography amid the actual scenes described. (*Kinematograph Weekly*, 12 June 1919: 55)

The company – Famous Players–Lasky British Producers Ltd. – had been registered earlier in the year in April, with capital of £600,000. The scale and ambition of the project was significant and compare quite dramatically with the scale and ambition of the indigenous industry. For example, the registered capital of one of the most prominent British companies of the time – Hepworth Picture Plays – was £100,000 (*The Bioscope*, 17 April 1919: 42). The majority of its directors were British, although the key role of managing director went to an American – J. C. Graham – and the new company was hailed by the trade press as a 'great enterprise . . . which cannot fail to play an important part in the future of British film production' (*The Bioscope*, 24 April 1919: 5). Premises were acquired at Islington, North London, in the form of a disused power station which was extensively converted into a modern studio with two stages, one of which incorporated a sunken water tank, an expensive and sophisticated interior studio lighting system and a range of ancillary accommodation (*Kinematograph Weekly*, 6 May 1920: 121). Low (1971: 220) described the studio as large by British standards and a trade journal studio survey from the time claimed that 'it represents probably the most completely and perfectly equipped producing studios in this country, and is possessed of certain technical resources not to be found elsewhere in the United Kingdom' (*The Bioscope*, 1 July 1920: supplement, xix). Producer/director, Victor Saville, who worked at Islington in the early 1920s with Michael Balcon, referred in his memoirs to 'a studio with the best American lighting, cameras and workshops' and facilities for producing films of a higher technical quality than those reliant on British studio facilities: 'In the ordinary way, air pollution would have made photography very second-rate, but they had equipped this old building with an air-washing and filter plant, something quite unique in a factory in the twenties' (1974: 28).

Indeed, one of the motives for establishing a production outpost in Britain was to raise the standard of British production to that of Hollywood; the equipping of a modern studio was seen to be a key element in this strategy which 'emphasized key technical and creative personnel and some physical plant with little or no direct capital investment for production purposes' (Walsh, 1997: 15). There was no intention to use American personnel extensively but rather to establish a basis from which British personnel could develop under American tutelage. Milton Hoffman, the general manager of the new company who had occupied a senior position in the Lasky studio, intended to return to the United States when the 'native producer reached the stage of being able to make pictures which were marketable in America' (*Kinematograph Weekly*, 20 October 1919: 96). In fact, Hoffman returned to the United States in October 1920, handing the reins over to the assistant manager, Major Charles H. Bell (*The Bioscope*, 28 October, 1920: 56). Key American experience was to be utilized particularly to begin with, but the intention was to groom native talent rather than to replace it. Director Hugh Ford suggested that although American audiences were interested in British subject-matter, American film-makers were failing in their attempts to render the relevant indigenous detail convincingly. *Kinematograph Weekly* reported his opinion as follows:

> He says that American audiences are becoming hypercritical, and will no longer accept the American attempts to imitate British and foreign atmosphere and settings. One of the reasons for this attitude is, of course, to be found in the fact that many thousands of Americans have been to this country and France during the latter days of the war and have a real knowledge of local colour, customs, habits and traditions, and cannot be put off with imitations especially when those imitations contain inaccuracies. (6 May 1920: 109)

While the point about Americans requiring representational verisimilitude in the light of their personal wartime experiences may well be *Kinematograph Weekly's* fanciful speculation, the desire for a kind of 'realism' deriving from local actuality filming is present in a number of comments by other Americans, including Zukor himself and Milton Hoffman, which were reported in *Kinematograph Weekly* (25 March 1920: 103; 20 October 1919: 96). Another explanation of this concern is the growing importance of foreign markets to the Hollywood companies and the concomitant requirement for sensitivity to local culture and customs. The British market was the most important of foreign territories and pictures which reflected the realities of its life and culture may have been politic for the company in a context in which Hollywood was becoming increasingly aware of the problems posed by the adverse representation of foreign cultures in their films (Vasey, 1997: 18-20). Advance comments on the company's strategy by senior American executives also stressed the intention to exploit indigenous writing talent and, in particular, writers. Jesse Lasky, writing in *The Bioscope*, mentioned Arnold Bennett, J. M. Barrie and H. G. Wells as examples of writers which the studio proposed to employ to write original work for the screen (15 July 1920: 10).

During a period of around two years, from the middle of 1920 to the middle of

1922, some eleven films were actually made using a mixture of American and British personnel, and utilizing the well-equipped Islington studio together with a variety of locations in Britain and Europe. Output was not on the scale of large British companies such as Stoll and Ideal but more on a par with a concern such as Welsh–Pearson with its four or five productions per year in the early 1920s. This was roughly in line with Milton Hoffman's advance comments about production to *Kinematograph Weekly* in 1919, when he stated that if 'he could produce six pictures a year and all of them were good pictures, he would have accomplished a definite purpose' (20 November 1919: 96). The five directors used – Hugh Ford, Paul Powell, Donald Crisp, George Fitzmaurice and John Stuart Robertson – were either American or American trained. Three of them – Crisp, Fitzmaurice and Robertson – were, or were to become, prominent figures in the American industry, as indicated in their mention in a confidential studio memorandum listing 'the most important directors' of the day in the American film industry, prepared for Carl Laemmle, head of Universal Pictures (Koszarski, 1990: 212-13). American screenwriting expertise, including Eve Unsell, Margaret Turnbull and Ouida Bergere, was also utilized rather than the galaxy of indigenous writing talent referred to in the company's advance plans. Most of the films were released in America as well as Britain.

One or two of the films overtly displayed the American origins of the company and played with what was to become a familiar element of 'Anglo-US' films – the inclusion of an American character in a British setting – which might be called the 'Yank at Oxford' theme. *The Princess of New York* (1921) tells the story of an American heiress who comes to England and becomes romantically entangled with both an Oxford undergraduate and an upper-class crook; in *Three Live Ghosts* (1922) – a comic tale of escapees from a German prison camp who arrive in London on Armistice night – one of the leading characters is an American soldier (Norman Kerry) with an 'American sweetheart'. However, most of the titles did not angle themselves in this way, although some of them used another strategy which subsequently became a common ploy for British films aimed at an international and particularly American market. Jesse Lasky, in the course of discussing Famous–Lasky's British production approach, had stated that 'it is a matter of policy to develop British talent in the matter of screen stars, and not to import ready made stars, whether of American or any other nationality' (*The Bioscope*, 15 July 1921: 10). Yet, the 'American sweetheart' in *Three Live Ghosts* was played by Anna Q. Nilsson imported from Hollywood. Another American star – Evelyn Brent already in Britain working for Ideal – was brought in for the final Famous Players–Lasky British film, *Spanish Jade* (1922), although her role was that of a Spanish peasant woman. In other ways some of the films produced did correspond to the various statements about British production made by company executives. Some of them exploited the English scenery in ways promised by the advance publicity. According to *Kinematograph Weekly*, the best thing about *The Call of Youth* (1920) – one of the first films released by the company – was 'its background which represents well-selected Devon beauty shots'(2 December 1920: 66). However, when the same Devon scenery was pressed into service as Scottish landscape for *Beside the Bonnie Brier Bush* (1921), *The Bioscope* commented that the film was 'no more convincing as a picture of North British life than if it had been produced in America' (1 December 1921: 57). *Variety*, though disappointed with *Appearances* (1921), a film 'lacking in the essential dramatic element', did enthuse about its exteriors stating that the 'settings are splendid. The out of doors backgrounds show scenes in some fine English country estate and there are none finer in the world' (24 June 1921*). The Princess of New York* offered, according to *The Bioscope*, 'many pleasant glimpses of English scenery, and some good Oxford exteriors', though it was judged to be 'in spirit as in technique, an American production' (30 June 1921: 50-1). Some of the films featured continental locations, with scenes for *The Man from Home* (1922) shot in Italy, and *Spanish Jade* made in Spain.

The trade press reviews of the Famous Players–Lasky British output were mixed. Some of the advance comment on the project stressed the need to bring British production, which had been disrupted by the war, up to American standards. However, one of the first films to come from Islington – *The Great Day* (1920) – was judged by the trade press to have failed on that count. Both *Kinematograph Weekly* and *Variety* started their reviews in almost identical fashion: 'If this is the best Famous–Lasky British Producers can do, British film-makers can heave a sigh of relief' (*Kinematograph Weekly*, 2 December 1920: 67); 'If this is the best the Famous producing firm can do, British producers can breathe freely once more' (*Variety*, 17 December 1920: 42). Improvements were noted in some subsequent films, however. *Variety*, for example, thought that *The Princess of New York* brought 'the British studios of the American firm several steps nearer to their goal'(22 July 1921); with *Perpetua* (1922), *The Bioscope* suggested that 'Famous Players–Lasky studio have indeed produced a masterpiece (25 February 1922: 36); yet, the studio's final film –*Spanish Jade* – was judged to be 'rather pointless, slow-moving and productive of only moderate entertainment' (*Kinematograph Weekly*, 10 August 1922: 26). Production ceased sometime in 1922, though the press announcement of the company's dissolution was not until February 1924, when J. C. Graham in a trade paper interview admitted that the production experiment in Britain had not been a success and that the company proposed to wind up its British operation. Although, Graham suggested, the company had 'done a certain amount of pioneer work in that direction . . . in the opinion of the American company the productions had failed to reach a quality comparable with those made in the States, hence the determination not to proceed here (*The Bioscope*, 7 February 1924: 29). Their departure was ominous and, indeed, British film-making was moving towards the dark days of the mid-1920s when production dwindled dramatically. As Low commented 'it would seem that financial backing, adequate studios and equipment and distribution arrangements were not the only obstacles to British production, and that the climate and the scarcity of first-class talent, particularly writers, were of decisive importance' (1971: 143-4). In other words, a company with much going for it found production standards difficult to raise to the American level; in such a context what hope was there for the under-capitalized British companies of the day?

The Paramount company was wound up after two years of production but the studios at Islington remained to become significant venue for many subsequent British films. Other producers were using the studio on a tenant basis in the early 1920s. *Flames of Passion* (1922) and *Paddy-the-Next-Best-Thing* (1923), the first films of the Graham–Wilcox company formed in the early 1920s by Herbert Wilcox and Jack Graham Cutts, were made there, as were John Stuart Blackton's Prizmacolor films. Perhaps the most important British tenant was the Balcon–Freedman–Saville syndicate. Their first film – *Woman to Woman* (1923), directed by Cutts and featuring an American star, Betty Compson – was a success both in Britain and in the United States. The Islington studios thereby played host to some of the very few important films made in Britain in the early 1920s, films whose significance may be related partly to the superior technical infrastructure which the studio provided compared with other British studios of the time. Balcon registered a new company – Gainsborough Pictures – in 1924, acquired the Islington premises at a knock-down price and went on to become one of the most important producers in the British cinema. In addition to the studio, Balcon was also to inherit a handful of technical staff from the Famous Players company, including studio manager Harold Boxall, cinematographer Bernard Knowles and, the most valuable, a young man called Alfred Hitchcock who had joined the American firm as a title designer in 1920.

The Paramount experiment had bequeathed a modern studio to the industry, and another significant development on the studio front was to be piloted, initially at any rate, by an American, J. D. Williams, working in Britain during the 1920s. Williams had moved to Britain 'to create either a big company or a big combination of companies to secure the competitive advantages of large-scale operation for British production' in the context of the anticipated quota legislation which would create a guaranteed indigenous market for British films (Low, 1971: 176). As co-founder and manager of the powerful American company, First National, Williams had supervised a substantial response to the growing power of the Paramount company by mobilizing the power of first-run exhibitors; he was used to operating on an ambitious scale, although the First National challenge to Paramount was in the process of failure. With some British backing, he set up a company, British National Films, combined forces with the producer/director Herbert Wilcox and secured financial backing for production from Paramount. The company also planned to build a large-scale studio complex on American lines, and a site was acquired at Borehamwood for such purposes. Williams had fallen out with his First National colleagues and had left the company in 1922, and his experience at British National was not dissimilar. By 1927, the company and the studio were controlled by British International Pictures; the Borehamwood site became the Elstree Studios complex – 'the British Hollywood' – with Williams relegated to a catalyst role in the development of a more modern vertically integrated industry in Britain. Nevertheless, another American had followed Charles Urban, Milton Hoffman and J. C. Graham of the Famous Players–Lasky company in nudging the industry towards the modern forms of organization and equipment required in the face of the American example. Although, in some respects, such figures contributed much to the development of the British film industry, the presence of the American cinema was beginning to evoke substantial concerns both in the film industry and in the wider world of politics and culture.

Protection of an industry – the American invasion

When expressions such as 'the American invasion' began to appear in the trade press after the First World War, the reference was to 'the predominance of American material in our kinemas, theatres and magazines' rather than to companies such as Famous Players–Lasky and their British production ambitions or to figures such as Williams (*Kinematograph Weekly*, 31 July 1919: 75). The huge volume of American films imported for screening in British cinemas created a problem for British companies, which struggled firstly to raise finance for production and then to secure exhibition outlets for the films that were actually made. The significant American presence in the British cinema was located in the London-based distribution arms of the major companies which, by 1920, included Famous–Lasky, Fox, Vitagraph, Film Booking Offices and Goldwyn together with a number of British concerns handling American pictures. These acted as the primary supplier of films to British exhibitors with even prominent British firms such as Jury's Imperial, Walturdaw, Butchers and Stoll handling more American than British films. The statistics are well known, especially the notorious 1926 figures which indicated that foreign, mainly American, films so dominated the British screen that 'the proportion of British films shown over the country as a whole appears to be not more than 5 per cent' (PEP, 1952: 41). Other countries also found that their film market was similarly dominated by American films and many introduced protective measures to limit the number of foreign films on the domestic screen. Even Germany, relatively strong in relation to Hollywood, had introduced such measures in 1925, obliging distributors to release a foreign film only when they financed and distributed a German one.

In Britain, the strength of the American industry and popularity of American films posed a considerable threat to the very existence of an indigenous cinema. In the period just after the First World War, Britain's film production industry, though not especially large, was producing over 100 feature films annually, comparable in scale with French production, though smaller than the German. By the middle of the decade, however, production had dwindled to the level of just over 30 features per year. Various strategies were employed by British producers both to establish a viable domestic industry and to make British films with international, particularly American, appeal. Stars such as Dorothy Gish, Mae Marsh and Betty Compson were brought from Hollywood in the hope that their presence in British films would provide an established appeal factor for American audiences and make them easier to sell in the American market.

Another strategy discussed in the trade press was the establishment of a distribution consortium for British films in America (*Kinematograph Weekly*, 5 July 1923: Supplement, xiii). There were also proposals to strengthen British production by the pooling of domestic production resources and there were suggestions that this could best be achieved through the creation of a national film studio (*Kinematograph Weekly*, 25 July 1925: 61). There was even a plan to produce films in Britain 'from plans and data provided by American producing and distributing organizations'. The 'Ridgewell plan', as it was known, argued that it would be cheaper to produce films in Britain that, if precisely tailored to American tastes, would be marketable in America (*Kinematograph Weekly*, 15 January 1925: 38). The British film industry was also caught up during the 1920s in the various pan-European attempts at challenging the hegemonic position of Hollywood now referred to as 'Film Europe'. The term embraced a number of things:

> At one level, Film Europe meant the development of international co-productions, the use of international production teams and casts for otherwise nationally based productions and the exploitation of international settings, themes and storylines in such films. At another level, it meant reciprocal distribution agreements between renters in different nation-states, and other efforts to rationalise distribution on a pan-European basis, in order to secure long-term collective market share by establishing all Europe as their domestic market. It even involved attempts to create exhibition syndicates which paid no heed to national borders. (Higson and Maltby, 1999: 3)

Early in the decade, Herbert Wilcox and Michael Balcon had organized international co-production deals with the major German firm of the time, U.F.A, and films such as *Chu Chin Chow* (1924), *The Blackguard* (1925) and Hitchcock's early features were made in Germany under such arrangements. Subsequently, British International Pictures embarked upon a programme of international films, and arranged distribution deals with continental European firms in the spirit of the 'Film Europe' project. Central to BIP's strategy were the films of the German director, E. A. Dupont, using European stars and technical personnel and, in the words of one historian, exhibiting a 'spectacular cosmopolitanism'(Ibid.: 281). Films such as *Moulin Rouge* (1928) and *Piccadilly* (1928), though technically British in terms of the quota legislation, reflected the creative endeavour of their pan-European production teams but, as Andrew Higson has suggested, their international quality 'was not simply a question of personnel but was embodied too in the spectacular scale and the self-conscious exoticism of the films' (1999: 280-1).

BIP's participation in 'Film Europe' can be seen in the context of the stabilization of the British industry, with the passage of quota legislation which encouraged the formation of vertically integrated companies with the resources to mount spectacular and stylish 'quality' production and to attract top European and American talent to the 'British Hollywood' at Elstree for this purpose. The introduction of quotas, the establishment of a protected market for indigenous production, was in line with the arrangements made in a number of European countries at the time to deal with the problems of American competition. Germany, for example, though strong in relation to the American industry, introduced quota arrangements in 1925 which obliged distributors to finance and distribute one German film for each foreign film imported. Yet, the British industry as a whole was not unified on the matter of quotas and, while the weak production sector might welcome protection, the interests of the powerful American- dominated distributors and exhibitors would not necessarily be served by the introduction of legislation. Distributors and exhibitors were often in conflict over trade practices – block and blind booking, clearance arrangements, pre-release runs – but they were united in their dependence upon American films. Indeed, as Ian Jarvie has suggested, 'exhibitors, distributors and the unions were happy about the availability of American films and the production of some of them in Britain' (1992: 275). Quota arrangements designed to create a space for the production sector would run counter to the interests of the American distribution branches, and could jeopardize the profitability of the exhibitor sector with its success based upon the well-established public taste for the popular American films of the day.

The existence of a production industry, however, was seen in somewhat broader terms than those relating to its economic and financial significance and its impact on employment. Its disappearance would have had some impact but it is probable that, for example, the job losses involved would have been absorbed in the new and developing light engineering and consumer industries located in the same part of the country as the film industry. It was the significance of the industry as part of the social and cultural fabric of the nation that generated a powerful and vocal argument for the protection and preservation of an indigenous cultural practice perceived to be important for political, ideological and artistic reasons. Despite the free-trade ideology held by the government of the time, intervention in the market-place was felt to be necessary on a range of grounds, with the cultural arguments presented vigorously in the elevated columns of the broadsheet newspapers and prosecuted by a cross-section of the political and cultural intelligentsia of the time. Part of the argument was couched in terms of national prestige, and a national film industry, like a national literature, was considered crucial in such terms. As *Kinematograph Weekly*, commenting on the almost absolute domination of British cinemas by American films, put it: 'Supposing 95 per cent of our school books were written and published for us in the United States of America, Germany and France. What would be the nature of the outcry raised? And yet the position is not dissimilar' (9 July 1925: 69). A number of commentators had noted that American films effectively presented perspectives on the American way of life, its manners and customs, its characteristics and qualities, and that this had economic consequences for American manufacturing industries. Benjamin Hampton, one of the first historians of the film industry, argued that the rise of the American cinema was linked to the successful penetration of European markets by American consumer goods. For American industry, Hollywood provided global advertising even before the First World War:

English and German traders noted that American merchandise was beginning to supersede theirs in markets formerly under their control. Investigation proved that American films were responsible for the change in conditions. They began to complain to their governments that audiences saw American sewing-machines, typewriters, furniture, clothing, shoes, steam shovels, saddles, automobiles, and all sorts of things in cinema shows, and soon began wanting these things and insist on buying them in preference to similar articles made in England, Germany, France or elsewhere. (Hampton, 1970: 351)

The impact of American cinema and its ethos on the collective consciousness was not confined to its influence on consumer tastes and preferences. There was concern about the general tenor of the commercial and popular culture coming from America which 'posed a challenge in its apparent classlessness' to the hierarchical societies in Europe (de Grazia, 189: 54). In 1925 a letter to the *Morning Post* signed by a cross-section of politicians, businessmen and artists drew attention to the propaganda implications of film and to the 'non-British atmosphere' of the 'bulk of the films shown in this country' which were, of course, American (Jarvie, 1992: 106). The overall ideology presented in the American cinema could be argued as 'non-British' in terms of its broad egalitarianism and lampooning of authority, as Ian Jarvie suggests in the following characterization of American film genres:

Slapstick comedy ridiculed authority figures, from policemen to the clergy; business and political elites were frequently portrayed as unscrupulous and corrupt; and atmosphere of egalitarianism and opportunity for all was pervasive; and narratives often achieved closure only by the efforts of an individual hero, acting in the spirit but not the letter of the law. There was no place for deference and respect to those set over us; no natural social station where ordinary people would find unambitious contentment. (1992: 108)

The cultural arguments for promoting British films had as much to do with resisting Americanization as they had to do with supporting a distinctive cultural dimension of British life, or the preservation of a small sector of the economy. In high art the plurality of forms available is usually considered an important enriching dimension of the culture which benefits from the international circulation of music, painting and literature. Cinema, and popular culture in general, was seen differently partly because it addressed a mass audience, and partly because its primary source was America.

The 1927 Cinematograph Films Act was the legislative response to the problems of British film production in the context of the 'American invasion' and its creation of a protected space for British films was to stimulate production over the ten years of its life. An exhibitors' quota reserved a portion of screen time for British films which was designed to rise to 20 per cent by the mid-1930s. In fact, the percentage achieved by British films exceeded this. Whether the Act succeeded in mounting an effective resistance to the cultural impact of American films is another matter. The distributors' quota required the big Hollywood companies either to make films in Britain or to commission them from British firms, and the varied responses of the American companies to the quota arrangements were to have consequences for the British film industry of the 1930s, as production increased from the 'near extinction' position of the mid-1920s to the statistically buoyant figure of 200-plus features in 1936. The next chapter will survey the response of the American companies confronted by the new legislative framework, which dictated that they participated in domestic production in order to guarantee the continuing success of their films in the British market.

3 American Companies in Britain after Sound

The late 1920s was marked in both the American and British film industries by adaptation to the sound picture, an event which had significant technological, economic and artistic consequences for cinema throughout the world. It was also marked in both countries by a pattern of mergers between existing interests in the various branches of the industry, leading to a relative stabilization of the structures of ownership and control and to orthodox financial interests playing a much greater role in the industries than hitherto. In the case of the United States the patterns of vertical integration, established in the 1910s and early 1920s with the formation of the Paramount corporation, continued through the decade and settled towards its end with the establishment of what historians often refer to as the 'mature oligopoly'. The 'mature oligopoly' – the constellation of five large companies, Paramount, Metro–Goldwyn–Mayer, RKO, Warner Bros. and Fox – acted co-operatively to dominate the industry during its most successful decades (Balio, 1985: 253). The five powerful companies were supplemented by a number of other firms of varying size and significance, including the important minor companies Columbia, Universal and United Artists, independent producers such as Goldwyn, Disney and David Selznick, and the host of small companies producing B-pictures, newsreels and other kinds of films which made up the cinema programmes of the day. In the smaller British industry, the passage of the 1927 Cinematograph Films Act with its guaranteed exhibition space for British films encouraged the formation of two large combines – British International Pictures (later the Associated British Picture Corporation), and the Gaumont British Picture Corporation – which drew together the existing strengths of established distribution concerns, strong cinema circuits (especially in the case of Gaumont British) and a potential for production, embodied in ventures such as the studio complex at Elstree owned by BIP. As in the American industry, there was a medley of other firms of varying sizes including smaller but significant companies such as Korda's London Films, Associated Talking Pictures, British and Dominions, and a variety of small-scale enterprises producing films for the American distributors' quota requirements.

A number of the leading American companies became more closely involved with British firms in the period following the 'quota act'. Whereas in the 1920s, the dominating position of American films was achieved through the London-based distribution subsidiaries of the major companies, through effective commercial practices such as block and blind booking and through the quality and evident popularity of the films with British audiences, the conditions after the quota legislation prompted a wider range of involvement. American companies became further involved with the British industry through investment in, and part-ownership of, British companies; through the commissioning of films from British production firms, both to meet the quota requirements of their British distributing subsidiaries and, in the case of United Artists, for American release as well; through the establishment of film production units in Britain for quota production, both in the 'quickie' phase of the early 1930s and the 'quality' phase later in the decade; and, in less direct ways, through the concerted lobbying of the British government about the terms of the 'quota act' which, under the terms of the original legislation, was due to be reviewed in the late 1930s.

 The most immediate kind of involvement from the late 1920s was prompted by the introduction of the sound picture, when the American firms, Western Electric , a subsidiary of the American Telephone and Telegraph Company, and the Radio Corporation of America, the power behind the RKO company, eventually established a dominant position in the British market for the supply of equipment, both for production and exhibition. Initially there was some competition from British firms, including British Acoustic, British Talking Pictures and British Phototone, and from the most important European company, Tobis–Klangfilm. However, the British companies could not compete in terms of quality and reliability, and agreements between the Americans and Tobis–Klangfilm led to a sharing of the British market weighted in favour of the American firms (Murphy, 1984: 146-50). The 1927 legislation – the 'quota act' – affected the American industry's relationships with the British market in a range of ways in addition to the possibilities opened up by the development of the new technology of sound. Hollywood films had thrived in the British market during the silent era, providing the American industry with its most substantial single source of foreign earnings without significant direct investment in either production or exhibition. Even after the quota arrangements had been put in place, American films continued to dominate the protected market, returning substantial revenues to their producers. As Ruth Vasey has noted, despite 'its relatively stringent quota restrictions, Britain provided 30 percent of the American industry's foreign gross and was indispensable to every producer' (1997: 144-5). Yet, under the terms of the Act, the American distribution firms were obliged to offer a certain number of films for rental alongside the American pictures which had been their main source of profits and their *raison d'être*. The legislation also had other significant implications for the major American firms which might have affected the ways in which they conducted operations in Britain. As the PEP report put it:

> Not only were they encouraged to undertake the production of films in this country, but there was also the possibility that distribution power might not be enough and that it would be necessary to have an advantage over their competitors, either by owning, or by having an important interest in, a British cinema circuit. (1952: 51)

During the 1920s when the American films had unrestricted access to British screens, American ownership of cinemas was less important, although some firms had established first-run flagship cinemas in London and other big cities.

In 1919, the involvement of Famous Players–Lasky in the formation of Picture Playhouses, an exhibition circuit, led to a violent outcry from British exhibitors. Famous Players–Lasky films provided some of the most popular films featuring the biggest stars of the day and it was feared that the new exhibition company would have exclusive access to them. The plan was shelved as the company concentrated upon establishing its British production base and expanding its exhibition holdings in America itself (Low, 1971: 84). However, the provisions of the 'quota act' prompted a rethink, and in the course of the 1930s and 1940s, the major American companies such as the Fox Corporation (Twentieth Century-Fox), Universal, United Artists and Warner Bros. resumed plans to diversify their involvement with the British industry. Although the American industry had moved down the road of vertical integration in the late 1910s when Paramount started to add exhibition to its production and distribution interests, the 'mature oligopoly' was still in the process of formation in 1928. A new vertically integrated company, Radio-Keith-Orpheum (RKO), had just been formed out of a number of existing firms, organized by the Radio Corporation of America in order to exploit its sound patents. At the same time, the market leaders such as Warner Bros. were expanding and mergers between some of them were planned. The most notorious involved the Fox Corporation, which was engaged in an ambitious attempt to become the leading American film company through the acquisition of the theatre chain Loew's Incorporated and its producing subsidiary Metro-Goldwyn-Mayer, which was fast becoming the leading studio in Hollywood.

The major American companies were also looking at Britain and other European countries and, in particular, were being prompted by the US government to invest in exhibition overseas. *Kinematograph Weekly* carried a report of an interview with the American Trade Commissioner in Europe in which he stated that 'potentiality in Europe is great, but the American film industry should try to strengthen demand for films by assisting in the construction of suitable theatres in the key cities of Europe' (19 December 1929: 17). The Fox Corporation had already moved down such a path by acquiring an interest in the Gaumont British combine. The motivations for the move into the British industry were mixed, involving both the position of Fox's films in the British market and the supply of sound equipment to the British company. Britain's first talking pictures were not made until 1929 and much was still to be done in the way of equipping studios and cinemas for sound. By February, 1929 the Gaumont combine had increased its cinema holdings through the acquisition of the largest of the existing independent exhibition companies, Provincial Cinematograph Theatres, and Fox's interest in the company and its expanding theatre holdings was based partly on a perception that the company was not returning sufficiently on Fox's films and that earnings would be substantially increased through such an investment (Sinclair, 1933: 78). Fox was already involved with the American Telephone and Telegraph

Company in the financing of the Loew's deal, and the company lent their support to the Gaumont British bid in order to facilitate the sale of Western Electric equipment to the British exhibition industry (Sinclair, 1933: 76-9). In fact, the plans for the merger with Loew's/MGM failed for various reasons, including an anti-trust suit brought against the company by the Justice department, serious financial problems in the wake of the stock market crash of 1929 and, possibly, political machinations at the highest level involving the production head of MGM, Louis B. Mayer, who was on friendly terms with President Herbert Hoover (Sklar, 1976: 166-7). In addition, Fox himself was severely injured in a car crash in the summer of 1929. The plans with Gaumont British, however, did proceed although many of the trade-paper reports during 1929 carried conflicting reports of ownership and much comment on the danger of the company passing into American control. Despite such warnings, early in 1930 *Kinematograph Weekly* reported that Fox had acquired a substantial stake in a holding company – the Metropolis and Bradford Trust Company – set up to control the various companies which constituted the Gaumont combine. Fox's holding – just under half of the ordinary shares – did not secure control as the company's regulations specified that non-British shareholders could not have voting rights. The controlling interest remained with the Ostrer family, the city financiers who had organized the merger of companies that formed the Gaumont British combine in 1927.

In 1936, the same companies were involved in further negotiations. Initially, the trade press carried reports of an American take-over, with Twentieth Century-Fox acquiring the remaining shares in the holding company (*Variety*, 6 May 1936: 5). However, these soon gave way to stories about a more ambitious attempt to build an Anglo-American film consortium based upon the existing link between Twentieth Century-Fox and Gaumont British, but also involving MGM buying a share of the British company. *Variety* presented the plan in terms of international co-operation:

> Parties to the current Ostrer–Schenck negotiations on Gaumont-British shares are striving for reciprocal trade objectives of an unprecedented kind for the British and the American film industries. Broad and cooperative interchange of manpower, talent, production and distribution facilities are planned between the British and American companies. Thus, a strong link for international amity may be forged also. (22 July 1936: 5)

Under the terms of the deal, Gaumont British would act as British distributor for the two American firms which, in turn, would distribute Gaumont British films in the USA on favourable terms; the British firm would also provide Twentieth Century-Fox and MGM with British films to meet their quota requirements. Control would remain in the hands of the Ostrers under the original company stipulations and the British company would benefit from a cash injection, and from the distribution arrangements which would make it easier to sell Gaumont British films in America. The deal foundered for a number of reasons, although MGM did acquire a 14 per cent share in the company, which remained subject to this dual American influence though it fell somewhat short of control (Higham, 1994: 257; Segrave, 1997: 127). Other British companies were drawn into what can be seen as a battle in the struggle for control of the British film industry. Previously, John Maxwell's Associated British Picture Corporation had made attempts to take over Gaumont British in 1934, and, towards the end of 1936, with the Anglo-American negotiations faltering, another unsuccessful bid for control was made. Eventually the Gaumont British combine was to be absorbed into the developing film empire known as the Rank Organization which, by the early 1940s, had acquired control of the company's various production and exhibition interests.

It was not just large Hollywood firms such as Twentieth Century-Fox and MGM that were interested in establishing British connections. Smaller companies such as United Artists and Universal were also involved in buying into British firms and positioning themselves as significant forces in the British film industry. United Artists, the specialist distribution company formed in 1919 by the leading stars of the day, was unique among the prominent American companies in so far as it concentrated upon the distribution of quality films. Although it did have its own production facilities, it relied upon a small number of independent production companies for films, and its theatre holdings were small. Its strength derived partly from the reputations and popularity of its founder members – Charles Chaplin, Mary Pickford, Douglas Fairbanks, D. W. Griffith; but the company also benefited from the particular structure of the American industry which evolved during the 1920s. Although the major companies were engaged in the volume production of films, with the development of double-feature programmes and frequent programme changes, they could not provide sufficient films to meet the needs of their theatre chains. The major companies depended upon each other to provide a supply of films which met the exhibition demands, and there was also some space for a limited number of other companies if they could supply an attractive product.

In the interdependency that was the American film industry during its golden decades of the 1930s and 1940s, United Artists was able to occupy a niche position as supplier of quality films to the majors (Balio, 1976: 65-6). Britain was important to the company during the 1930s in two ways. Firstly, the company from early in its existence had difficulties in sustaining an adequate supply of films from its founder members. Indeed, during the 1930s, apart from Chaplin their careers were more or less at an end. Chaplin's suspicion of sound pictures and his meagre output meant that United Artists required other sources for their films and various independent producers of the time became linked with the company including Samuel Goldwyn, Walt Disney, Howard Hughes and David Selznick. The quota legislation meant that the company had to get involved in British-based production in order to distribute its American films in Britain. In 1932, after a period of relying on 'quickie' production, United Artists signed contracts with Herbert Wilcox's company – British and Dominions – for the production of quality quota pictures which would also be marketable in the USA. The company also became involved in financing Alexander Korda's *The Private Life of Henry VIII* (1933)   and, with the spectacular success of the film, developing a longer-term relationship with the Hungarian-born British producer/director. Korda, whose standing in the British film industry was extremely high in the wake of *The Private Life of Henry VIII*, signed a sixteen-picture contract and subsequently became a partner in the company. He was also involved in a number of attempts to buy the company from its founder-owners (Balio, 1976: 134-5). Plans were laid with independent producer, David Selznick, and leading director, Frank Capra, and with fellow member–owner, Samuel Goldwyn, UA's major source of films in the 1930s. The plan with Goldwyn which would have turned United Artists into a British-financed company failed to materialize amidst the general crisis in the British cinema in the late 1930s (Kulik, 1990: 199-202). In addition to links with producers such as Korda and Wilcox, United Artists' interests in Britain extended into theatre ownership as well. The British market was a major source of revenue for the American industry as a whole but, as Tino Balio has noted, it was particularly important for United Artists:

> The British market accounted for nearly 80 per cent of the company's profits. UA barely broke even in the United States, the result of high overhead costs. Its earnings came from abroad and the largest overseas market for United Artists as well as the other American film companies, was Great Britain. (1976: 128)

In 1934 the company bought a first-run theatre in London – the London Pavilion – and proceeded to expand its British cinema interests by buying into existing circuits, notably Oscar Deutsch's rapidly expanding Odeon group. As with the Fox company some years earlier, the release of films through partly owned cinema circuits was likely to be more lucrative than releasing on regular commercial terms through the large chains. The Odeon group was amenable to such a move because, although large, it did not have the buying power of the big combines; the UA deal provided it with a the guaranteed source of quality pictures required to maintain and enhance its status as a significant cinema chain. United Artists bought a half-share in the Odeon group, although control remained in British hands with Oscar Deutsch.

Another American 'minor major', Universal, became caught up in the various manoeuvres that were to culminate in the formation of the Rank Organization in the early 1940s. In 1936 a new grouping appeared in the industry which drew together C. M. Woolf, late of Gaumont British, and J. Arthur Rank, in a consortium – the General Cinema Finance Corporation. This had been formed by Rank and various associates to act as a holding company for existing and potential interests and, effectively, it formed the basis of the Rank Organization, the company that was to become the leading force in the British cinema in the 1940s and 1950s. Unlike the other companies in the industry which were dominated by individuals from various branches of the film business, the incipient Rank grouping included a number of figures from the wider world of finance and commerce. Rank, of course, was from the flour-milling industry and other interested parties included city financier, Lord Portal, chairman of the Bovril Company, Lord Luke and representatives of a banking firm – Japhets.

Lord Portal, 'a trouble shooter for the Conservative party' and a member of a long-established and influential banking company, played a behind-the-scenes role in the formation of the grouping. According to one American business magazine, the Board of Trade, concerned about the precarious state of the film industry, sought City help in the formation of a sound company which would bring a degree of stability to the industry (*Fortune*, October 1945: 150). Portal, with his close links with both government and the City, in conjunction with the banking firm – Japhets – envisaged a company built upon distribution and exhibition with production based upon the profits from those enterprises. The General Cinema Finance Corporation, formed in 1936, drew together C. M. Woolf's distribution firm, General Film Distributors, and production interests, including the recently opened Pinewood Studios and the British and Dominions company. The Rank grouping took some years to evolve into the powerful Rank Organization but an important factor in its early success was the link with the American company, Universal.

Universal occupied a minor though important position in the American film industry as a producer of 'modest genre pictures, programmers and serials' (Schatz, 1989: 228). In the early 1930s, the studio made the classic horror films, *Dracula* (1930) and *Frankenstein* (1931), together with a handful of 'prestige' pictures directed by John Stahl and an ambitious musical – *Showboat* (1936) – directed by the British-film maker, James Whale, better known for his horror films. Towards the end of the decade the studio's fortunes were based on the success of teenage star, Deanna Durbin, and her cycle of musical comedies. Like many of the big Hollywood firms, it struggled in the 1930s and went into receivership in 1933; unlike the powerful firms such as MGM and Paramount it lacked a significant theatre chain that may have stabilized it in the years of depression. The company had borrowed heavily from a New York banking firm in a deal which granted the bank an option on purchasing a majority interest in the company. The bank 'exercised the option in March 1936 and took over operating control of Universal Pictures' (Balio, 1993: 17). The Rank group was involved in the take-over. According to *Fortune*, the American group 'needed someone who would buy a 25 per cent interest for $2 million' in order to complete the deal (October 1945: 151). Unlike the previous examples of American firms buying into British firms, this was an example of a British firm buying into Hollywood, albeit in a minority interest collaboration with an American company. Hailed in the trade press as the 'biggest deal in British film history', it was a move of singular importance which gave the Rank interests distribution rights to Universal's films in Britain. This was, as *Kinematograph Weekly* observed, 'the first occasion on record that the output of a major Hollywood company has been available in its entirety for distribution by a British renting house' (26 March 1936: 5).

The British cinema of the 1930s

There is no doubt that the quota provision in the 1927 legislation acted as a stimulus to the ailing British production industry. Several indices can be used to establish this. The two large companies formed in the late 1920s incorporated some of the ambitious production firms of the previous decade, including Gainsborough and British International Pictures, and underpinned their activities with the formation of cinema chains which guaranteed their films a domestic screening. The capital funds flowing into production increased dramatically in the course of the decade to the extent that 'the value of production in 1937 was just over £7 million as against about £500,000 in 1928' (PEP, 1952: 67). Studio building had begun on a large scale in the 1920s with the major developments at Elstree, and 'the British Hollywood' was augmented in the 1930s with new studios at Ealing, Pinewood, Shepperton and Denham, together with the extensive refurbishing of existing studios such as those at Lime Grove. The ten-year life of the Act saw a dramatic increase in the number of British films, with some 1,600 films produced and Britain becoming the most prolific of the producing countries in Europe. During the years following the Act the industry moved from the annual figure of 34 British produced films in 1926 to over 200 a year by 1936 – an annual output of about 40 per cent of the American industry. American companies played a significant role in this expansion, prompted by the distributors' quota requirements of the 1927 Act. Some established subsidiary production companies in Britain while others relied on the commissioning of films from existing British production companies. Large firms such as British International Pictures and London Films made pictures which were used for quota by the Hollywood companies, but the abiding image from the period is of small concerns such as Julius Hagen's Twickenham Studios turning out quota pictures at low cost and of minimal critical value, according to both contemporary and subsequent critical and historical comment. Although production did expand significantly in statistical terms, Rachael Low has suggested that 'approximately half the enormous number of films turned out by British studios up to 1937 were produced at minimum cost simply to exploit the protected market or, at worst, to comply with the law' (1985: 115). Much of the increase consisted of films made on minimal budgets, sometimes outside Britain as films made within the British Commonwealth, in Australia, Canada and India for example, counted as 'British' for quota purposes. 'Quota quickies' – as such films were called – were often designed simply to fulfil the distribution and exhibition quotas as they increased during the course of the decade and sometimes remained unscreened on the distributors shelves.

However, the very existence of these low-budget pictures gave the British cinema a poor reputation with both critics and the general cinema-going public and, in retrospect, the absence of a 'quality provision' in the legislation was seen as a flaw which produced the alleged degradation of British production during the 1930s. More pictures were undoubtedly made but the quality of many of them was in doubt. The quota legislation came into force in 1928 and the trade press soon noted the deleterious effects that the Act was having on production. By early 1929, P. L. Mannock was referring to 'the quickie scandal' and lamenting the Act's impact on production values:

Unfortunately there is . . . a definite outlet for British films of a quality which reflect little or no credit on those who make them. Four or five years ago such pictures would be hawked round the trade with little success. Today there is a demand for them, apart from their merit. . . . It is a scandal that slapdash films should have any artificial premium. (14 February 1929: 44)

The American industry had conquered the British market in the 1920s and was supplying a range of films efficiently produced in the Hollywood film factories and highly popular with the British public. Their effective amortization in the home market meant that they were a highly profitable export commodity and the quota legislation in effect was imposing a kind of levy on their success. Meeting the quota obligations posed the American companies with a choice between commissioning films from indigenous companies in an industry rapidly expanding from the bleak position of the mid-1920s; or, establishing their own production subsidiaries in Britain. Although some did opt for the latter course, the precedents such as Paramount's failure in the early 1920s were not encouraging, and the efficient production machines in Hollywood were far better equipped to produce films than the still-evolving facilities in Britain. The other alternative – commissioning films from British firms – was also fraught with difficulty. The production arms of the large combines, together with Korda's London Films, envisaged a competitive rather than a complementary role in the industry. Although British International Pictures abandoned their international ambitions in the early 1930s settling for the production of modest programme pictures for their theatre chain, Gaumont British continued to pursue competitive policies until the production crisis of 1937. In such a context, it is suggested that the Hollywood majors acted cynically, commissioned, sponsored or acquired 'shoddy pictures' simply to adhere to the letter of the law, often losing money in the process with films remaining unscreened on the distributors' shelves. P. L. Mannock presented a more nuanced view, suggesting that the impoverished quota films provided by the British industry of the time, and by a somewhat opportunist low-budget sector, presented American companies with a dilemma. They could accept the low-quality material and treat it as a kind of tax on their profitable activity – distributing Hollywood films – or they had to establish their own production units in Britain with the financing required to produce films of quality:

The American must realise the inevitable. If he is being stung into buying bad films, why not make good ones himself in this country, and put them on the world market.

If, for example, William Fox and Carl Laemmle grumble at the compulsory foisting of 'dud' British films on them, they have the obvious remedy – let them produce here themselves on a decent scale, and have their own world markets to play with.

At present, it seems they prefer to lose money on British 'quickies.' Yet, surely they must grow tired of this? If they seriously made films to comply with the Act, it would be a better thing for everybody in our studios, and, in my opinion, the object of the Act would be achieved – *more and better British films for the world market*. (*Kinematograph Weekly*, 30 January 1930: 6 emphasis in original)

Mannock's contemporary observations and Low's subsequent historical judgements constitute the orthodox view of American-sponsored quota production. Such films, it was felt, were a major impediment to the building of a satisfactory indigenous industry; the 'quota quickie' brought the British cinema as a whole into disrepute. As a corollary, it has often been suggested that exhibitors treated British films with a cynicism matching that of the distributors. The 1927 legislation required exhibitors to screen a percentage of British films alongside their Hollywood pictures, but there are a number of anecdotal accounts which suggest that all sorts of strategies were used to hide such films away from the regular custom. For example, Michael Balcon claimed that 'certain American-controlled cinemas in the West End of London used to project the "quota quickies" to a non-audience in the early hours of the day, or for the exclusive benefit of the theatre cleaners' (1969: 93); and, in 1936, *Variety* carried a report of a London cinema cramming in an additional screening of a British picture at the end of the day's programming in order to maximize the footage qualifying for the exhibitor quota (7 October 1936: 12).

However, the picture of American villainy ruining a potentially vibrant British film production industry has been challenged in recent years from a range of perspectives. A number of writers have argued that the quality of quota production was not uniformly dire and that raking around in this undergrowth of the British cinema of the time reveals a richer picture of achievement than is implied by some of the personal reminiscences from the time (Napper, 1997; Richards, 1998; Wood, 1997). It is also necessary to distinguish 'quota quickies', with their built-in negative definition of 'films made solely to fulfil quota requirements', from quota production generally, which covered a range of films. American interests were involved in films as diverse in their qualities and ambitions as Korda's lavish *The Private Life of Henry VIII*, which had backing from United Artists; John Baxter's essay in underclass 'realism', *Doss House* (1933), which was distributed by MGM; Gracie Fields's film debut, *Sally in Our Alley* (1931), made by Basil Dean's company for RKO distribution; a number of Michael Powell's early films; and MGM's prestige pictures – *A Yank at Oxford* (1938) and *The Citadel* (1938) – made in the late 1930s and featuring major stars such as Robert Taylor, Robert Donat and Rosalind Russell. Even in the 'quickie' category, the numerous crime films produced because they were cheap to make compared with, for example, musicals and costume films, nevertheless constituted a distinctive indigenous genre; effective quota pictures such as *The Ghost Camera* (1933) and *They Drive By Night* (1939) contributed to a bedrock of activity significant as a context for more distinguished instances of the genre by leading directors such as Alfred Hitchcock and Walter Forde. A similar case could be made for the other preponderant genre – the comedy film – with its exploitation of music hall traditions and its distinctive balance of narrative and spectacle, focused upon the talents of leading performers such as Gracie Fields and George Formby. Also, as Linda Wood has argued, quota production and low-budget production in general was beneficial to the British cinema and played an important role in the building of the production industry of the time, by providing a 'training school' function for British film-makers:

> Among the directors who got their initial directing experience through working on films commissioned for quota purposes were Anthony Asquith, Michael Powell and Walter Forde. Other directors who first learnt about film-making from working as technicians on low-budget productions included Michael Relph, Thorold Dickinson, Guy Green, David Macdonald, Ronald Neame and Leslie Norman. (1997: 55)

Quota production and the Hollywood firms

The Famous–Players Lasky (Paramount) production experiment of the early 1920s apart, it was not until after the introduction of the quota legislation that Hollywood companies began making films in Britain on any scale. Initially, the main companies commissioned their quota requirements from various British firms. These included British International Pictures, which made a number of films for Warner Bros. and First National in 1929 and 1930, a few smaller companies from the 1920s, such as Welsh–Pearson–Elder, supplying Paramount, and British Instructional Films which made a handful of films for the Fox company and the Producers Distributing Corporation. The 'quota Act' prompted a 'mushrooming' of small production companies and a number of obscure company names appear in the American distribution firms' offerings, particularly in the early years of the quota. In 1929, for example, some 16 firms produced 33 quota films, while in 1930 around 25 firms produced 38 films (statistics based on Gifford's *The British Film Catalogue*). Many of these companies were short-lived concerns and by the middle of the decade there had been a settlement of sorts with quota pictures supplied by British-based American subsidiary companies, smaller British firms specializing in quota production, such as those based at Twickenham and Shepperton, and companies such as London Films and British and Dominions supplying 'quality' quota films to United Artists and Paramount respectively. As a statistical comparison, in 1935 around 23 companies produced some 90 quota films, with American-owned but British-based firms such as Fox-British making 13 pictures and the Twickenham studio making 11 such films.

In the early 1930s, the American companies, responding to the adverse accounts of their quota films, began to review their strategies. From around 1934 the trade press began to carry reports about the upgrading of American production in Britain from 'quickies' to something more ambitious. In August of that year, *Variety* reported Fox's (Fox-British) intentions to improve their productions through the leasing of the Wembley Studios, which they eventually bought, and by allocating budgets for the films of $30,000–50,000 which at the top end of that scale was around 40-50 per cent higher than the standard quota picture budget. These plans, it was suggested, 'look to give native-made British pictures by American firms increasing impetus. It is known that Fox has been desirous of finding suitable means whereby its quota product could be improved' (21 August 1934: 14). The following year, *Variety* indicated that Warner-British 'will completely give up production of quota pictures and devote itself to regulation features'(1 May 1935: 4). There were also accounts of the upgrading of the Teddington Studios and an expansion of the production programme. In addition to upgrading studio facilities and investing more in the films produced, the American firms intended to incorporate American stars in their production plans. Another *Variety* piece mentioned a Hollywood trip by Irving Asher – head of the British concern:

> Asher goes to Hollywood to confer with the Warner execs on the matter of stellar exchange with his own studios. He has been promised a cut on Warner stock talent for some time . . . Deal was on for Cagney to come over, when the actor had his break with the studio, and walked out. (3 June 1936: 12)

Paramount, however, took a different line, after their unsuccessful British production experiments. The company decided to commission rather than produce and to work with companies such as British and Dominions. Company head, Adolph Zukor, was reported as thinking that 'English producers are doing as good as Hollywood invaders could' and that 'the progress that is being made in native production' meant that co-operation with British producers was a better strategy (*Variety,* 20 October 1937: 3).

The Moyne Committee set up to investigate the workings of the 1927 'quota' Act reported in 1936, recommending a number of revisions, including a continuation of the feature film quota to reach 50 per cent ultimately – a much higher level than hitherto; a new short film quota; a quality test to eliminate the abuses of 'quickie production; the establishment of bodies to administer the quota and to assist in the financing of indigenous production; and a plea to the government to 'keep a close watch on transfers of interests in British producing, renting and exhibiting units with a view to taking such steps as may be practicable to prevent control passing abroad' (*Report of the Committee on Cinematograph Films*, 1936: 37). The latter injunction, of course, was highly relevant in the context of the various attempts by American companies to buy into the industry in the middle of the decade, and, in particular, the Twentieth Century-Fox/MGM attempt to take over Gaumont British. As in the period before the 1927 legislation, the various interests involved – British film-makers, London-based US distribution companies, exhibitors, cultural lobbies and the government – presented a range of views on the way ahead. While the 1927 Act can be seen as having successfully stimulated the growth and development of the production sector, at least in terms of the volume of films produced, its renewal was due at a time when studios were living through the consequences of the mid-1930s production boom, which though producing a massive increase in films, did not bring a matching increase in earnings. Twickenham Studios went into receivership early in 1937 following their heavy borrowing to finance quality production, London Films announced pay cuts and Isidore Ostrer spoke of Gaumont British abandoning production altogether and closed the Shepherd's Bush studio. Some 228 feature films were released in 1938, reflecting the mid-decade boom production years, but the figure for 1939 reflecting the 'crash' was down to 103 films (PEP, 1952: 70). Although it had been hoped that the previous legislation would enable the production industry to establish itself in a protected market, this had not happened, and it was generally agreed that continuing quota arrangements were necessary for the survival of the national cinema. As the PEP report on the industry noted, the 'test of the previous ten years had shown that official support was not to be a temporary expedient but that henceforward, if production was to survive, then it could only do so as a protected industry' (1952: 78). Raymond Moley, offering an American perspective, wrote later about the situation and argued more bluntly that protection had failed:

> . . . the effects of the 1927 law had been highly unsatisfactory. In spite of the protection it afforded, in spite of the huge investments made in some of the most magnificent studios the world had yet seen, the artificially fed British industry produced fewer commercial successes than could be counted on the fingers of two hands. (1945: 178)

Many in Britain blamed the situation on the cynical exploitation of the 'quota' provisions and the sponsorship of the inferior 'quickie', which had brought the British cinema into disrepute. The American view, however, was that for the Hollywood companies, the artificially high quota (20 per cent) 'precluded the production of quality pictures and forced them into destructive competition for studio space and artists with British producers to the detriment of the latter' (Moley, 1945: 178-9). The Moyne proposal for a quota increasing to 50 per cent ran counter to the American view that the quota should be reduced to enable the production of quality films for quota purposes, and American interests, through their representative body, the Hays Office, began lobbying in Britain to secure more favourable conditions of operation. The Hays Office, which had been established in 1922 to represent the American film industry's interests both in the USA and abroad, had evolved a series of strategies to ensure the success that American films enjoyed in Europe from the First World War onwards continued in the face of the various attempts throughout the world to restrict the circulation of American films. One of these was working through diplomatic channels in close co-operation with 'the foreign managers of the Hays Office member companies, with their representatives abroad, with officials in the Departments of State and Commerce and with key officials of foreign governments in the United States and abroad' (Moley, 1945: 171). Various attempts were made in a range of countries to counter the dominant position of the Hollywood film, including import duties, censorship taxes, 'dubbing' taxes following the introduction of the sound picture and the subsidization of domestic industries, as well as the more straightforward exhibitor and renter quota requirements. However, the American film had remained strong during the 1930s, surviving the initial impact of sound which posed language problems for American films in non-English speaking territories. The situation in the late 1930s was changing, especially in respect of the importance of the British market. It was, as has been noted, Hollywood's most important foreign market and was to become even more crucial to the American industry's export activity during the period in the context of growing international tension in Europe and the eventual war which enveloped and affected a number of Hollywood's markets. By the end of the decade the powerful German film industry was more or less government owned and the market effectively closed to American films, while the Italian government policy towards imported films had led to a major withdrawal of Hollywood pictures from that market. The diplomatic efforts of the Hays Office were stepped up in the aftermath of the Moyne Committee's report, and the ensuing legislation, while retaining protection, did contain some provisions which benefited the American companies, notably those which allowed multiple-credit counting for films which reached certain financial thresholds. This provision meant that American companies could make fewer but more expensive films to satisfy their quota requirements. From the British side, it has been argued that such provisions were supported by the Board of Trade 'to encourage American capital and expertise to rejuvenate the ailing British film industry by producing expensive films in Britain' (Street, 1985: 52). One American company in particular responded to the new provisions and embarked upon an ambitious production programme based in Britain and involving large budgets, top stars and seasoned Hollywood film-makers.

MGM-British

The impact of the revised quota provisions and, in particular, the incentive to produce 'quality' films is highlighted in the production record of MGM 's British production subsidiary towards the end of the decade. MGM -British made three films – *A Yank at Oxford*, *The Citadel* and *Goodbye Mr. Chips* (1939) – which contrast greatly with the 'quota' pictures made by the US companies in Britain, or by the British firms supplying commissioned quota product, in the scale of their ambition both in terms of production values and in terms of subject-matter and theme. Through the 1930s, the company effectively moved from low-budget 'quota quickies' to big-budget 'prestige pictures'. Rachael Low has suggested that MGM were the worst offenders among the US companies for abusing the quota system with their reliance on cheaply made pictures, alleging that they 'dredged the industry for the worst hack shorts and short features' and used imported material from the Commonwealth (which counted as quota) for their quota requirements (1985: 195). Yet, accounts of their British production intentions in the trade press suggest a more ambitious approach was envisaged some years before the appearance of the bigger budget pictures made by MGM -British. In 1934, *Variety* reported that:

Metro is practically set to break into British production. Company has made up its mind to turn out a few films there. Just how soon or who will be in charge of production is not certain yet, but David O. Selznick will fly over in the fall to make three or four pictures splitting his time between production in London and Hollywood'. (7 August 1934: 5)

Selznick was not only the son-in-law of Louis B. Mayer, the powerful production boss of MGM, but was one of the leading 'creative producers' in Hollywood. Producers of the status of Selznick were not involved with low-budget pictures but rather with the prestige film, as defined by Tino Balio in terms of big budget pictures with long running times and special exhibition arrangements (road showing), usually based on pre-sold properties – classic literature, best-selling novels, hit plays, biographical and historical material – and utilizing the studios' top stars. According to Balio (1993: 180), budgets averaged $1 million but were sometimes higher, reaching $2.3 million for *Marie Antoinette* (1938) and $4.1 million for *Gone with the Wind* (1939). Furthermore, 'prestige pictures' could define studio image and standing in the film industry and traded to an extent on less tangible qualities summed up by the tag 'prestige' itself. The films were 'serious', 'elevated' and 'respectable' and they addressed a middlebrow culture not satisfied with the glossy entertainment represented by the musical and romantic pictures, or by the various action genres of the time. Richard Maltby has related the rise of the 'prestige picture' to pressure from the Hays Office on producers to make films 'aimed at convincing middle-class America of the bourgeois respectability of the cinema'. He has also drawn attention to the ways in which such films were marketed with an eye on the school audience (Balio, 1993: 63).

MGM, as the most successful, the most financially secure film company of 1930s Hollywood, the one with the biggest roster of stars, was closely identified with such a production trend. Indeed, as the decade went on, the trade press carried stories about MGM's East Coast executives (the business end of the operation) arguing for the elimination of low-grade/low-budget picture production entirely from the MGM schedules. This culminated in the company announcing its withdrawal from B-picture production for its 1938/39 season and its intention to concentrate its energies on 'product . . . designed for first run class 'A' theatres' (*Variety*, 16 March 1938: 5). Selznick did not, in fact, become involved with the British production project, but the reports indicate a policy turnaround, in terms of MGM's British quota production; one which lines up more closely with its American profile as a producer of top-quality, high budget, middlebrow entertainment. In budget terms the company was proposing to move from around $25,000 for the quota film to $1 million for the prestige picture, but cautiously and with a secure grip on pre-production from the Hollywood base at Culver City and with experienced Americans in key production roles. As *Variety* commented: 'Metro expects to plan the entire thing carefully from this side, sending over script, stars, producers and technicians for making of the pictures. Local British talent will be used, however, for the secondary acting parts' (7 August 1934: 5). This can be interpreted as a vote of no-confidence in British production, and/or understandable business caution in terms of 'quality control'. The other Hollywood companies producing in Britain leased and bought studios and, initially at any rate, MGM considered establishing their own studio base. *Variety* ran stories of the company proposing to set up a studio in Bayswater (18 March 1936: 3), and of plans to build a studio complex at Bushey Park (24 April 1936: 1). By 1937, however, it was decided that the company would rent studio space rather than build their own facilities, and the three films were eventually made at Denham Studios. From 1936, the trade press carried reports of the prospective production schedule, with titles such as *The Wind and the Rain, Rage in Heaven, Silas Marner, Soldiers Three, And So Victorious, Finishing School* and *Shadow of the Wing* (*Variety*, 3 February 1937: 11, 21 April 1937: 21). Some of these titles were subsequently made in Hollywood while others came to nothing. The reports sometimes included two of the titles eventually made, *Goodbye Mr Chips*, an Irving Thalberg project, and *A Yank at Oxford*. There were also references to a number of top MGM stars heading for Britain, including Luise Rainer, Clark Gable, Robert Taylor, Spencer Tracy, James Stewart and even Garbo. Although Robert Taylor was the only one of those mentioned to feature in an MGM-British film, players eventually appearing did include Lionel Barrymore, Robert Donat and Rosalind Russell – from MGM's top star roster, as well as Maureen O'Sullivan and the up-and-coming Greer Garson, from the studio's featured player lists. The trade press reports promised more than was actually carried out and it took almost four years from the first indications of a policy change to the arrival of a 'quality' film from MGM. This may be put down partly to the vicissitudes of film-making, film-making at a distance in particular, and partly to the exaggerations of studio publicity. Yet, given the eventual outcome – three top-quality films – the invariable hyperbole of the studio press interview did not entirely misrepresent the studio's intentions, even if they took some time to be implemented.

By the summer of 1937, *A Yank at Oxford* had been scheduled as the company's opening production. The American, Ben Goetz, had been appointed as managing director, with the experienced British producer Michael Balcon as head of production. The trade press saw the appointment of Balcon as further evidence of MGM's large-scale ambitions for their British production. As *Variety* put it:

> Statements and news items which have emerged from Metro over here [i.e. London] indicate that the company is not going to work in any niggardly fashion. It has made a good beginning by capturing Michael Balcon, who, perhaps with the exception of Korda, is the outstanding producer in the British ranks. (6.January 1937: 7)

A Yank at Oxford, an existing MGM project, was, in some ways, an obvious inaugural film, with its familiar stranger/foreign culture clash theme placing a brash American student in an Oxford college. The quota regulations allowed MGM to use the American stars Robert Taylor and Lionel Barrymore together with a featured player, Irish-born Maureen O'Sullivan, who would be familiar to audiences, British and American, from her role as Jane in the *Tarzan* pictures. The film also had an American director – the experienced MGM house director, Jack Conway – and the scriptwriting credits included a number of Americans, along with the British writer Sidney Gilliat. The film reflected the American origins of the company rather more than its two successors, obviously through its theme, but also in some aspects of its production. Indeed, Lionel Barrymore (*Variety*, 20 October 1937: 17) claimed that much of the film was shot in Hollywood and suspicions of 'over-American-ness' are flagged in a *Variety* report which suggested that 'Metro is scared it won't get quota registration for 'Yank at Oxford' . . . picture is heavily weighted with aliens and it is believed the Board of Trade is stalling on this account' (5 January 1938: 54). In addition to the American personnel already mentioned, top MGM production staff, including the cinematographer Harold Rosson and the supervising editor, Margaret Booth, were also involved in its production. The film's identity was clearly a problem at various levels.

In the middle of 1938, Michael Balcon was replaced as head of production by Victor Saville who had joined MGM-British in the previous year. He had sold the rights to the A. J. Cronin novel, *The Citadel*, to MGM and it became the second film in the British list. Unlike *A Yank at Oxford*, *The Citadel* had no Anglo-US thematic dimension; it was a medical story about an idealistic doctor who starts working in a Welsh mining community but loses his idealism and eventually takes a job in Harley Street treating the wealthy. The American presence, however, was registered in the production team with the director, King Vidor, a screenplay credit for Frank Wead, and MGM star Rosalind Russell in a key role as the doctor's wife. The star of the film – Robert Donat – a British actor – had been signed up by MGM on a six-picture deal and was being promoted as a top MGM star. Indeed, his biographer suggests that one of the reasons for MGM coming to produce in Britain was to secure his services (Barrow, 1985: 100). The final film in the 'cycle', also under the supervision of Saville – *Goodbye Mr. Chips* – was an adaptation of the James Hilton novella about a public schoolmaster and his life of devotion to the profession. The American connection was confined to director, Sam Wood – like Conway, an MGM house director – although Greer Garson, later to become a big Hollywood star partly through the success of the film, was featured as Donat's wife. The film reran the 'heritage' elements of *A Yank at Oxford* with its somewhat romanticized images of an august British institution, combining them with a bittersweet romantic dimension – a young woman falling for a shy, middle-aged bachelor, their subsequent marriage and her tragic death during childbirth.

All three films were successful in box-office terms both in Britain and in America; and both *The Citadel* and *Goodbye Mr. Chips* figured prominently in Hollywood's premier ranking system – the Academy Awards. In 1938, *The Citadel* was nominated in four categories – best picture, best director, best actor and best screenplay – and although it failed to win anything, it did secure the New York Critics' award for best motion picture of the year. In the following year, *Goodbye Mr Chips* secured nominations in five categories – like *The Citadel* – for best picture, best director, best actor and best screenplay, but, in addition, Greer Garson was nominated in the best actress category despite the fact that her appearance in the film was relatively brief. Donat actually won the 'best actor' award – a not inconsiderable feat as the film was in competition with *Gone With the Wind* which won the awards for most of the other major categories. *The Citadel* was one of the *Film Daily*'s 'Ten Best Films' of 1938 and in *Kinematograph Weekly*'s top three box-office successes; *Goodbye Mr. Chips* topped *Film Daily*'s 1939 poll and was listed among *Variety*'s top-grossing films for that year as well.

The films, then, appeared to vindicate MGM's foreign production policy in the context of the 1938 legislation matching British themes with American expertise to produce pictures with appeal on both sides of the Atlantic. Indeed, *Variety*'s review of *The Citadel* confirmed that the film 'compares favorably with the production quality of pictures made on the Culver City lot' (26 October 1938). MGM's move to more ambitious production in Britain can be seen in a number of ways. It was widely anticipated that the 1938 legislation renewing the quota would incorporate some provisions related to quality, some tightening of the regulations to eliminate the 'quota quickie'. In the event, a minimum cost provision was introduced, with double and triple quota credit for productions exceeding minimum cost, as an incentive for producers make more expensive films. The budget for *A Yank at Oxford* was reported as $900,000, which though around the low end of the prestige category in Balio's terms, was in line with the budget for a top 1930s MGM film, and considerably more expensive than the quota pictures of earlier in the decade (*Variety*, 13 April 1938: 2).

MGM's new approach meant also that the films were treated in America as equals with their Hollywood films, and, as such, incorporated in their advertising. For example, in a 1938 advertisement, along with the trumpeting of the lavishly budgeted Norma Shearer picture, *Marie Antoinette*, James Stewart in *The Shopworn Angel* and the latest 'Andy Hardy' film, the display stated that 'Reports from the filming of "THE CITADEL" are exciting. . . . Looks like the MEF (Metro Expeditionary Forces) will bring back an attraction bigger than "Yank at Oxford" ' (*Variety*, 13 July 1938: 20). Earlier in the 1930s, Gaumont-British had embarked on a policy of large-scale production (by British standards), importing American stars and directors with a view to making films that would have transatlantic appeal but, as Balcon acknowledged in his autobiography, the venture failed. In contrast to this, MGM-British appeared to succeed in their not too dissimilar venture. The films were made using American stars and directors, working with British supporting casts and technical staff, and their subject-matter was predominantly or wholly British. The films were popular on both sides of the Atlantic, and although the success in America may be explained by their access to the MGM distribution facilities and the company's theatre network, it was achieved without tailoring the films unduly to American subject-matter. Indeed, it looks as if the films became more British as the series progressed. *A Yank at Oxford* had the most explicit address to a US audience, while *The Citadel* and *Goodbye Mr. Chips* were firmly rooted in British subject-matter. In addition, the American performing influences became less prominent after Robert Taylor's central role in *A Yank at Oxford*.

Robert Donat, though included in MGM's star roster in their American publicity, was a British-born actor and his presence dominates *The Citadel* and *Goodbye Mr. Chips*. Rosalind Russell did play Donat's wife in *The Citadel* but without any real foregrounding of her American-ness. *Goodbye Mr. Chips* did include Greer Garson, being groomed for stardom at Culver City, but she was in fact Irish, and had been taken to Hollywood after Louis B Mayer had seen her on the London stage while he was in Britain on MGM-British business.

As a final comment on the identity of the films, it is worth noting that officialdom regarded *Goodbye Mr. Chips* as a thoroughly British film despite its American connections. The film was promoted as model propaganda in a government memorandum – 'Programme for Film Propaganda' – circulated early in the war. The document, which described it as an example of a British film which embodied the qualities of national character – 'independence, toughness of fibre, sympathy with the underdog' – suggested that it be emulated by other feature film-makers during the wartime propaganda drive. A British film, then, in respect of its 'national–cultural' character, its US connections notwithstanding. (Christie, 1978: 121; Richards, 1997: 85). The MGM-British episode demonstrated that despite the earlier experiences of American production companies it was possible to make satisfactory pictures in Britain, pictures which both incorporated indigenous subject-matter but which also had considerable appeal for an American audience. It has been argued that the ambitious MGM-British production schedule was not simply a response to the 1938 legislation but was, in fact, motivated by the need to compete more aggressively with the British cinema:

> British film-makers and stars had achieved success and notoriety, and enjoyed a growing following. This was not in Hollywood's interests. A successful and independent British film industry could only diminish Hollywood's foreign earnings even further. The logical reaction, therefore, was to move into British production and to place Britain's own film-makers and stars under contract. The purpose of MGM-British was not 'window-dressing', but to colonise the British film industry. (Glancy, 1999: 66)

British films, contrary to much received opinion, had increased in popularity during the 1930s (Aldgate, 1983; Sedgwick, 1998). Faced with diminishing markets in other European countries such as Italy and Germany, the American cinema could not afford to lose its grip on the British market. Although the MGM pictures were greeted with scepticism in some quarters, the venture was a deliberate strategy to protect Hollywood in the context of a perceived threat to its interests in the overseas market. As Glancy has suggested, the enhanced production ambitions of the company need to be seen in the context of the radically altered prospects for British film-makers towards the end of the 1930s.

4 American Interests in Britain from the 1940s

The 1938 Act appeared to set the parameters of US involvement with British production for another ten years and, as in the case of MGM -British, encouraged a more expansive approach to production in Britain on behalf of the American majors than was the case earlier in the decade. The success of the MGM -British films in America as well as Britain despite, or maybe because of, their British subject-matter, shifted the perspectives of American companies making films in Britain. However, the war intervened and 'the results of the 1938 Cinematograph Films Act were to be fundamentally distorted and defeated by the depredations of World War II' (Jarvie, 1992: 179). British production declined in quantity from the already diminished production schedules following the slump of the late 1930s. Many studios, including major ones such as Pinewood and Elstree, were requisitioned for war usage, for storing munitions or emergency food supplies, for use as military bases and for a more predictable use – the production of government propaganda films. There were shortages of materials, including film stock, and of staff as a consequence of the war itself; the annual rate of production fell from the late 1930s figure of around 100 films per year to an average of around 60 for the war years (PEP, 1952: 83). Cinemas were ordered to close in the early days of the war but it was not long before the value of entertainment to civilian morale and to the propagation of war necessitated their reopening. Some wartime closure was inevitable because of staff conscription and bomb damage to buildings, but the PEP report estimated that 'the maximum numbers closed at any one stage of the war was probably never more than 10 per cent of the total' (ibid.: 80-1). Such was the importance attached to film exhibition that projection was declared a 'reserved occupation' with exemption from conscription. Films constituted a propaganda weapon capable of informing the public about war activities and of instilling in them the will to suffer the hardships and shortages of wartime conditions; also, regardless of specific content and, indeed, of national origins, they provided relaxation and recreation for a hard-pressed civilian population.

The government, accordingly, was engaged in a dual task in relation to the film industry covering, on the one hand, the supervision of film content and, on the other, the supply of films to cinemas in adequate numbers. Film content had to be controlled effectively enough to ensure that some films, at least, reflected wartime aims and provided 'a channel of war information, . . . news of the fighting, and . . . government instructions, information and propaganda' (Jarvie, 1992: 183). State information and propaganda material was made for the government by the Crown Film Unit, the armed services produced their own propaganda and training films, and, in addition, there was some state sponsorship of films made by private companies. There was also the matter of overseeing the content of British feature films to ensure harmony with the war effort, a task undertaken by the Ministry of Information, using a range of formal and informal methods, and by the British Board of Film Censors. It was necessary to ensure that sufficient films – British and American – were in circulation to keep the cinema screens filled and to sustain its presence in British life as a key source of entertainment for the mass of the population. The business of filling cinema screens depended on two sources of supply. Firstly, a domestic industry which was still in the aftermath of the 1937 production crash, and with the most powerful and stable element – the Rank grouping – still in the development process and yet to register an impact in production terms. Secondly, the American film industry, which was also suffering a decline in production volume from the 1930s levels and was subject to the various restrictions of the recent legislation. The key response to the 1938 Act by majors such as MGM was to concentrate upon better quality production which would qualify for multiple-quota status, thus further diminishing the volume of films available to cinemas. The government was also concerned about currency exchange and sought to restrict the level of remittances that the American majors could return to the USA. A balancing act was involved here as it was necessary to maintain imports of American pictures at a high level while at the same time preventing the Hollywood companies from deriving the full benefits of their income. While it was hoped that some of the blocked earnings would be used for the production of films in Britain, it was acknowledged by the Board of Trade that domestic production capacity could not absorb 'all the blocked American earnings unless U.K. costs were unacceptably inflated above U.S. averages' (Jarvie, 1992: 188). The position was complicated. Britain needed American films to service an entertainment industry that was increasing its audience during the wartime period; the American film industry, which had lost many of its previous European and Far Eastern markets, needed the British market to maintain its profit levels. In the context of war, this was not a simple trade dispute, and particularly after America's entry into the war, Anglo-American co-operation was subject to ideological as well as economic imperatives.

A film renaissance?

The British cinema which appeared in the wake of the 1927 quota arrangements – the thrillers and comedies, the imperial epics, the musicals – was frequently dismissed as failing to add up to something distinctively 'national'. As film critic Dilys Powell suggested, despite the dramatic expansion in studio space, equipment, production finance and the guaranteed exhibition space for British pictures, the increased production during the 1930s produced 'no tradition of British films as there was a tradition of French ironic drama or a tradition of American fast comedy. The national characteristics of the British, whether good or bad, had not been infused into a national cinema' (Powell, 1948: 65). 1930s British cinema was dismissed as trivial and escapist, unduly dependent on the West End theatre, oblivious to social realities, defined by cheaply made quota pictures, or, where more money was spent, by inferior imitations of the successful genre pictures from Hollywood. The cinema of the 1940s, by contrast, was presented in terms of a cinema maturing into a distinctive component of the national culture, one which was less dependent upon Hollywood styles and themes, a period of 'new excellence of British films', in the words of journalist Cyril Ray, an excellence which he and many writers related to the particular conditions of the war. Writing in the American magazine *Harpers* in 1947, Ray suggested that 'most critics agree not only that the war was the occasion for our renaissance but that it was the direct cause' (1947: 516). The war with its restrictions forced British film-makers into more disciplined forms of working compared with the years of excessive and wasteful financing in the mid-1930s; it also drew together the separate strands of documentary and fiction film-making into a relationship producing distinctive forms of drama-documentary, which came to be regarded as a hallmark of 'quality' British cinema; and it capitalized on an inherently compelling subject-matter for British audiences – the war itself. The post-war period then began on a high note for British films. Although the war had seen a diminution in production volume, many of the films themselves attracted very favourable critical judgement. The particular blend of documentary and fiction, in films such as *In Which We Serve* (1942), *Millions Like Us* (1943) and *Fires Were Started* (1943), appeared to suggest a pathway for British cinema which would distinguish it from the still-popular Hollywood films. As John Ellis has written: 'British films suddenly seemed to have acquired a positive cultural identity of their own. No longer were they patently inferior to Hollywood' (1996: 66).

Part of the explanation for 'the golden age of British cinema' lies in the major reconfiguration of the industry early in the war. American interests in the industry were increased when John Maxwell, head of the Associated British Picture Corporation, died in 1941 and Warner Bros. acquired a significant interest in the company through its British subsidiary, an interest which was to be increased through further share purchases just after the war. However, the key events of the period concern the ways in which the Rank group moved into a position of power acquiring the Gaumont British and Odeon firms to become the largest company in the industry and a vertically integrated combine with assets comparable to those of an American major. The development of the Rank group stabilized the industry and created conditions for the cinematic renaissance. The crises of the late 1930s had enabled the Rank group to take control of the massive Gaumont British interests, including production facilities and the important exhibition chain, and together with the group's acquisition of the Odeon cinema chain in 1941, the combined facilities constituted the biggest concentration of power in the three sectors of the industry. 'Stability', however, though considered important in the industry as a bulwark against American domination, was construed in some circles as 'monopoly'. In 1943 the government commissioned a report on the situation in the industry and the result, the Palache report (Board of Trade, 1944), advocated a number of interventionist measures, including a film finance corporation, and the direction of production resources into 'medium cost feature pictures, rather than . . . highly speculative luxury products which may or may not prove acceptable overseas'. It also made recommendations to address the various problems deriving from the relationship between the British and American film industries, including the US distribution of British films and the exchange problems created by the import of American films. Although the government did not act immediately on the report, some of the issues touched upon in the committee's deliberations, especially in relation to America, were to become highly urgent later in the decade and were then to prompt state action of the kind envisaged by the Report.

For some writers the renaissance in British cinema was in spite of the growing power of Rank; for others – some film-makers included – the specific structure of production adopted by the Rank Organization provided an explanation for the success. In 1947, one of Rank's most prominent directors, David Lean, wrote:

> J. Arthur Rank is often spoken of as an all-embracing monopolist who must be watched lest he crush the creative talents of the British film industry. Let the facts speak for themselves, and I doubt if any other group of film-makers anywhere in the world can claim as much freedom. We of Independent Producers can make any subject we wish, with as much money as we think that subject should have spent on it. We can cast whatever actors we choose, and we have no interference at all in the way the film is made. . . .
>
> Such is the enviable position of British film-makers today, and such are the conditions which have at last given our films a style and nationality of their own. (1947: 34-5)

The 'Independent Producers' mentioned by Lean was one of a number of groups which provided the Rank Organization with films. It was 'a loose affiliation of producer/director teams' (Macnab, 1993: 93) financed by Rank in an arrangement which, initially at any rate, conceded a high degree of control to the creative personnel on which each team was based with the minimum of interference from any central Rank body. The group included the Cineguild team of which Lean was a part, along with Ronald Neame and Anthony Havelock-Allan, Powell and Pressburger's Archer Films, the Launder and Gilliat team and Ian Dalrymple's Wessex Films. Rank's other sources of films were Fillipo Del Guidice's Two Cities, with its 'prestige' orientation and its eyes on the American market, and the Gainsborough company, with its contrasting tradition of modestly budgeted genre film-making. Not all in the industry shared Lean's view of Rank and, indeed, numerous attacks on him and his organization were mounted by independent producers, such as Michael Balcon, by the ACT, the film union, and by the Labour and Communist parties. Yet the structures established by the Rank group did produce the bulk of the films cited when the glories of 1940s British cinema are being celebrated. It was also this infrastructure, tightened somewhat to provide a greater degree of central control of the film production process, that was to form the basis of Rank's attempts to break into the American market and to fill the gaps in the exhibitor schedules in 1947 left by the American boycott of the British market.

Early in the post-war period, the British government was involved in managing a foreign exchange crisis and, although film imports from America represented 'only about 4 per cent of dollar expenditure' (Dickinson and Street, 1985: 179), they were to figure in the government's attempts to deal with the problem. The British people were presented with a choice by the government, a choice summed up in a series of catchphrases from the Parliamentary debates on the situation, such as 'Bacon before Bogart' (the best known), 'Food before Flicks' and 'Grub before Gable' (Jarvie, 1992: 227). The severity of the balance of payments problem meant that control of imports, particularly those defined as non-essential, was necessary for the government to steer the country through its economic problems; for the cinema, the mechanism to achieve this, decided after much debate, was a swingeing import duty to be imposed upon American films at their point of entry into the country. The *ad valorem* tax, as it was known, was set at 75 per cent and based upon the estimated earnings of a film. Despite American protestations that such a move contravened the terms of inter-governmental loan agreements, and despite opposition to the move in Britain, particularly from exhibitors who feared the threat to the ready supply of the popular American films on which their business was based, the tax was introduced in August 1947. Hollywood's response was swift and dramatic, a ban on the export of films to Britain; the British people could have their 'bacon', but the price of this was no 'Bogart'.

In one sense, the boycott extended the logic of the quota system and made the entire domestic film market available to British producers, although not immediately, for when the embargo started the Hollywood companies had a number of unreleased films already in Britain. These were to offset the effects of the embargo for a few months but if the situation continued then the British production industry would have to step up production to make up the substantial shortfall in supply. As an indication of the scale of the shortfall, in 1946, the year prior to the embargo, 83 British films were registered with the Board of Trade, yet the total number of films registered for the year was almost 450 (PEP 1952: 82). Alternative strategies to boosting production – extending film runs, single instead of double feature programmes, reissues – could have been tried, but such moves could only delay the full impact of the US embargo and would not have been popular with an audience already in decline from the high attendances of the wartime period. In terms of the response from British producers, the Associated British combine was short of studio space, with one working studio, Welwyn, the smallest of the three owned by the company, available for use. The other two, at Elstree and Teddington, were still in the process of reconstruction after wartime requisition and, in the case of Teddington, its destruction by bombing. Rank, as the primary British producer with more studio space available, stepped into the breach and embarked upon an ambitious production programme costing more than £9 million, although the diversion of finances from the reliable exhibition part of the Rank operation to the risky sphere of production did not go down well with Odeon shareholders, in particular. In many respects, the 'boycott' war was 'phoney'. The American distributors had enough films in the country at the time of the embargo to enable them to continue supplying cinemas for a number of months. The dispute itself was settled early in 1948, leading to a resumption of imported American films and a return to the *status quo ante* – a quota-protected space for British production in the context of a market dominated by the American film.

The resolution of the dispute attacked the problem of dollar expenditure by placing limits on the amount of earnings that the US majors could take out of the country, reviving moves made at the beginning of the war in similar conditions of currency crisis. Some of the blocked earnings could be released if American companies exhibited British films in America, but it was envisaged that the bulk of the revenue remaining in Britain would be invested in, among other enterprises, the British production industry. From no new American films, the situation had certainly moved on. The backlog of films from Hollywood meant further difficulties for the British production industry; Rank's ambitious programme of films had eaten up the organization's resources at an alarming rate, eventually leaving the company with a staggering £16 million bank overdraft (Macnab, 1993: 187). American opinion was divided on the merits of the Anglo-American agreement, with some seeing it as a devious British plot to use American money to build up the British industry and to strengthen the competitive threat posed by Rank and Korda; others had a less cynical attitude and took the view that the agreement, with its potential release of more than 60 per cent or more of the majors' British income on the most optimistic estimates, together with the range of ways in which the frozen earnings could be used, represented the best that could be achieved in the situation (*Variety*, 17 March 1948: 9).

Government intervention

The Anglo-American dispute was only one of the ways in which the government was involved with the cinema and the end of the decade saw a flurry of government activity in relation to the industry, including further commissioned reports on distribution and exhibition (the Plant report) and production costs (the Gater report), new arrangements for film financing and alterations to the taxation arrangements for the industry. The 1938 legislation was due for review and renewal in 1948, the end of its ten-year life, and the 'boycott' episode can be seen as a distraction from the abiding realities of the industry; an interlude prior to the industry returning to its 'regular' problems, the quest for production survival in the context of the powerful and popular American cinema. It may be, however, that the episode prompted the flurry of government activity and subsequent action. The 1938 act had acknowledged both the persistence of the problems originally identified in the late 1920s and the necessity for continuing some form of protection for the production industry. According to critical opinion, British films had improved during the wartime period, and the special conditions of the time had enabled Sidney Bernstein, acting on behalf of the government, to arrange regular distribution in the United States for a small number of British films. However, the new-found confidence among critics and producers did not guarantee that British films could either dislodge American films from their position in British cinemas, or penetrate the broad American market with any degree of consistency. British films were beginning to enjoy some success among the minority 'art' cinema audiences in America but access to the regular American circuits was as far away as ever. The 1948 legislation addressed the problems of stability in the production industry through a renewal of quota which was to continue as an instrument of protection but with one significant difference. Henceforth quotas were to apply only to exhibitors and not to distributors, following international agreement on this matter at the GATT meetings in 1948. The quota for feature films was to be set annually by the Board of Trade after consultation with the Films Council so that the quota levels could be related realistically to production capacity in the industry. However, the initial quota of 45 per cent for feature films was clearly unrealistic in the context of the production crisis which hit the industry in the late 1940s.

The government also introduced measures to help the industry to deal with other problems. The high level of Entertainments Tax had been long regarded as a substantial drain on the exhibition sector. It was first levied during the First World War and by 1950 the industry was paying 35.4 per cent of its gross box-office revenues in tax (PEP, 1952: 125). The Plant report on film distribution and exhibition suggested that the tax prevented exhibitors from paying 'British producers a sufficient return on the films they produce', so for once both exhibitors and producers were united in a lobby designed to bring about a reduction in the tax. The government secured a voluntary arrangement with exhibitors in which the tax was reduced in exchange for a ticket levy which exhibitors paid into a fund established to help producers. The revenues raised from the tax were to be partially diverted into the vulnerable production sector. The Eady Levy, named after the civil servant who devised its detailed working, returned money from exhibitors' earnings according to their success at the box-office; although initially a voluntary agreement with the industry, it was made statutory in 1957.

The government also tackled the problem of production funding which impacted particularly on independent producers. It established another source of funding for film-makers, the National Film Finance Corporation – a film bank. Such a move was originally suggested in the 1920s and subsequently appeared as a recommendation in the Moyne Committee report of 1936 and the Palache report of 1944. By the late 1940s, it was regarded by many as necessary to protect the independent producers working outside of the integrated combine structures – the Rank Organization and the Associated British Picture Corporation – whose access to production funding was difficult and unpredictable. The very future of 'independent' production was seen to depend upon state support, at least as a temporary source of finance until the orthodox financial institutions showed more confidence in the industry. Early in the post-war period, some government money had been provided for Alexander Korda's British Lion company; the new corporation can be seen as an extension of this *ad hoc* response to a specific problem and its transformation into a policy for independent production as such. Korda had resurrected London Films just after the war, acquiring British Lion and setting up an American distribution arrangement with Twentieth Century-Fox to replace his United Artists distribution facility. In addition, Shepperton Studios was acquired to replace Denham. Korda was in the early stages of rebuilding the film combine which had collapsed in the production crises of the late 1930s (Kulik, 1990: 308-9). In 1947 the government had set up the National Film Production Council as part of its general enquiry into the state of the industry and its deliberations led to the inescapable conclusion that some form of state financing for production was essential. The immediate beneficiary was Korda's British Lion, the leading independent distributor which was on the brink of collapse. In order to prevent this, the government authorized a loan of £3 million on an emergency basis.

The National Film Finance Corporation was set up in 1949, the year after the Korda loan, to manage the further allocation of state funding for production. It was given a revolving fund of £5 million, later to be increased to £6 million, and became a major source of high-risk capital providing 'end money' for film producers in subsequent decades. Orthodox finance was still expected to provide the bulk of a film's budget, underwritten by a distribution guarantee, but government money was to be available for the final proportion of the budget (30 per cent) to be repaid out of the film's profits and after the distributor had been paid. Given the precarious nature of the production industry, the 'end money' was difficult to arrange through orthodox financing concerns and was frequently lost in the project. Although the impetus for the establishment of the corporation was the protection of independent production, it did establish financing arrangements with the large combines – Rank and ABPC – through the group production project. Like the quota provisions in the late 1920s, the corporation was given a limited lifespan of five years, presumably on the assumption that orthodox finance would take over its role once the production industry had been stabilized. However, it was to survive as an essential bolster for the industry until the mid-1980s and was especially important in sustaining British Lion as an independent force in the industry. It was replaced eventually by the British Screen Finance Corporation, set up by the Conservative government and designed to operate on a completely privatized basis.

The 1940s ended with greater government intervention than hitherto, with state funding of production, the diversion of tax receipts to film-makers, as well as the quota systems that had guaranteed a market share for indigenous films since the late 1920s. This is not surprising as the Labour government of the day was intervening in many other areas of public life, of industry and welfare provision. Yet, intervention on behalf of the film production industry was not as radical as in other European countries, and was, to an extent, market led. As Margaret Dickinson has noted, the forms of assistance 'rewarded whatever the market rewarded and could not encourage developments of a kind the trade was unlikely to foster' (1983: 91). In that context, it is also unsurprising that the Conservative government which replaced Labour in 1951 left the various arrangements intact. The framework for the development of the British cinema in the 1950s was formed by an enlarged and flexible quota fixed according to indigenous production capacity, by newly established sources of production finance from the NFFC and the British Film Production Fund. In addition, out of the Anglo-US agreement which ended the US screen boycott, there was also a diversion of some of the revenues earned by American films in Britain into domestic production.

Hollywood abroad: 'runaway' production

The post-war period saw profound changes to the structure and operation of the American cinema, changes which were to impact significantly on the British film industry. Some of these derived from key legal decisions, the culmination of several years of government pursuit of Hollywood for breaches of the anti-trust legislation. The 'consent' decree of 1940 had placed restrictions on the block and blind booking of films, a trade practice originating in the late 1910s which was important to the efficient production of films in volume, and the 1948 'divorcement decrees' ordered the separation of the production and distribution activities from the exhibition business. Both decisions had crucial effects on the Hollywood system of production and played their part in moving the Hollywood majors away from mass production. Whereas during Hollywood's 'golden age' the large companies had a guaranteed exhibition outlet for their films, even those still in the planning stage, the new conditions of the post-war period threatened the 'classical' model of studio operation. The production of around fifty films per year and the maintenance of an army of employees to carry out this – production supervisors, directors, stars, bit-players, writers, designers, caterers, carpenters, electricians and so on – became less of an economic proposition in the changing industrial and social environment of the post-war period. The structural changes required by the court judgements deprived the production arms of the major companies of their guaranteed exhibition outlets, but there were other factors which radically altered the context in which the industry conducted its business.

Cultural and demographic changes in the post-war period, the growth of suburbanization, the baby boom, the development of new forms of entertainment such as television, contributed to a dramatic decline in cinema audiences so that by '1953, only half as many people in the US were going to the movies as had gone seven years earlier' (Maltby, 1995: 71). Commentary on this period has often adopted the vocabulary of 'decline' and 'collapse' (see, for example, chapter titles in Jowett, 1976: Ch. XIII; Sklar, 1976: Ch. 17). Yet, 'transition', the term used by another writer (MacCann, 1962), is perhaps a better indication of the changes in the post-war period, which signalled an adjustment to the new conditions by the major companies and ensured their survival, although in a different form. What undoubtedly did collapse was the 'factory production of films' on a volume basis by individual companies which had characterized film-making in the 1930s. The post-war period saw the growth of 'independent production' and the 'package-unit system of production' with production carried on in a film-by-film basis by companies organized for the purpose of making individual films, often in conjunction with one of the majors which could supply part of the finance, together with studio facilities and distribution expertise to sell the film to exhibitors both in America and overseas. This system of production 'differed from former systems on its industry-wide pooling of labor and materials, the disappearance of the self-contained studio, and the transitory combination of labor-force and means of production' (Bordwell, Staiger and Thompson, 1985: 332). The pooling of labour and materials was not confined to America but also drew upon facilities and personnel from all parts of the world. The post-war period saw the growth of what became known as 'runaway' production, in which US companies moved the production of films or parts of films to Europe and elsewhere from their traditional base on the West Coast of America. Over the next decade or so there was a significant internationalizing of the production base, with 'American' films made in a range of countries including Britain, France and Italy. It was a trend that was to continue and increase to a point in 'the late 1960s, when nearly half the features made by American companies were produced abroad' (Maltby, 1995: 70).

In Britain, as has been noted, American companies had set up production units in the early 1930s to meet their quota requirements and, after the 1938 Films Act, MGM in particular had produced a small number of high-quality films in Britain. MGM -British had resumed production in the mid-1940s but the subsequent decades saw a dramatic expansion of runaway production in Britain. This was, in part, a response to the 1948 Anglo-American agreement, as a way of investing some of their 'frozen coin', as *Variety* called it, but it can also be seen in the context of the structural changes brought about by the block booking and 'divorcement' decisions. There was also an economic logic at work, especially as the costs of Hollywood film-making had increased substantially. As Jim Hillier has noted, runaway 'productions tended to be cheaper than American-made movies; labour costs were lower, and ways were found to exploit foreign government subsidies' (1992: 8). Runaway production was, in part, a consequence of British government action in 1948 which kept American film revenues in Britain to help the sterling balance situation, but Hollywood companies also benefited from the various government systems of financial support for production. It also turned out to be a strategy which enabled Hollywood to produce films more economically in a period of declining domestic and overseas audiences and in the highly competitive environment of challenge for the 'entertainment dollar' from alternative leisure activities and especially from television. Indeed, overseas production was a strategy that preceded the 1948 settlement. MGM, for example, had laid plans to resume their quality quota production in Britain at the end of the war and had renovated its bomb-damaged Elstree studio complex for this purpose. The films which

MGM produced in Britain, such as *Edward My Son* (1949) and *Conspirator* (1949), were simply incorporated into release lists as part of the studio's normal production schedule, as indicated in their trade press advertising (*Variety*, 8 June 1948: 19).

Other companies were also planning such overseas production. *Variety* noted in a report on the consequences of the 1948 agreement: 'Most of the majors had large-scale plans for British production before last August, but were forced to shelve them when the 75% tax was first imposed' (17 March 1948: 71). There was also an aesthetic dimension to the strategy. Location shooting had become more common in post-war Hollywood and, as Dorothy Jones suggested:

> Documentary techniques, which had been developed during the war and which became generally prevalent in Hollywood during the late 1940's, required that a story laid in a foreign country be, in part at least, shot on location. More recently, it has been found that color and the new wide-screen techniques can be employed to best advantage by using the most fascinating sights of the world as a backdrop for Hollywood productions. (1951: 371)

There was also the related matter of securing period and geographical authenticity. Darryl Zanuck, head of production at Twentieth Century-Fox, was quoted in *Variety* as suggesting that 'his studio never makes pictures abroad merely for the sake of unblocking escrowed funds. Such projects, he said, are only undertaken when the story is suited for a foreign locale. Fitting in with this concept [is] "Mudlark" . . . whose natural backgrounds could only have been duplicated in Hollywood with difficulty' (10 January 1951: 20). *The Mudlark* (1950), made at the Denham studio, featured American star Irene Dunne as Queen Victoria, and was set in the period following the death of Prince Albert.

Initially, at any rate, Hollywood's overseas production plans were not without advantages for the British film industry and, indeed, British governments had been keen on Hollywood investing in British production since at least the late 1930s. One positive dimension was the employment opportunities for British film-workers, while another was the profiling of British films in the United States:

> While strident criticisms of the subsequent infiltration from Hollywood were raised, several positive factors had to be borne in mind. Most obviously British studios were in use, and British technicians were given work. Also, of course, the presence of Hollywood stars and directors gained valuable publicity in America for British films. But most important of all, films like *Night and the City*, *The Mudlark*, *The Miniver Story* and *Captain Horatio Hornblower, R. .N.* were recognized in the course of their wide release in America as British, thus conditioning audiences towards a more general acceptance of British films. (Perry, 1975: 143)

There were some expansive forecasts of the extent of US production overseas, with the studios' press handouts indicating up to 50 projected films with 25 of these scheduled for Britain (*Variety*, 5 May 1948: 15). However, initially there was a great deal of scepticism about production in Britain in particular and the advantages to the American industry were not apparent to all Hollywood executives. Barney Balaban, the Paramount chief, cautioned the industry, telling *Variety* that it was 'no answer to reach for a lot of British production and then come up with stringy pictures that won't pay off in the international market' (24 March 1948: 3). There was also the matter of facilities in Britain and in the other countries where 'runaway' production was contemplated. As *Variety* put it:

> Many a glib Yank producer is expected to do some swift backtracking when he sees the incomplete, inadequate and antique facilities which will be the only ones – if any – available to him, not only in England, but in Italy and Australia, where Hollywoodites are also talking of going. Whatever firstrate space is available is pretty well tied up already for a limited number of US pix. (5 May 1948: 15)

There was criticism of British technical expertise and the existence of general production practices which would impede efficient production. Top Hollywood cinematographer, Gregg Toland, thought that there were not enough British technicians, that 'an insufficient number of top technical people had been developed because of the irregularities of British filmmaking in the past' (*Variety*, 28 July 1948: 4). Indeed, part of the negotiations which led to the Anglo-American agreement concerned the numbers of Hollywood producers, directors and technicians to be granted work permits on British-based productions. MGM-British had showed similar caution in its 1930s British production schedule, which was carefully planned, with substantial American involvement and the films entrusted to seasoned Hollywood directors. A *Variety* report in 1949, after the first year of British 'runaway' production, was severely critical of the industry from a number of perspectives. 'Britain's film plant,' it reported, 'is still handicapped by lack of materials, inadequately sized lots and an unsuitable trade union structure' (4 May 1949: 15). Although, according to the report, British studios rarely got films completed on schedule, this was offset by the relatively low cost of British labour compared to Hollywood. There were understandable concerns about the impact of runaway production on Hollywood's own studio costs. Each film produced abroad meant one film fewer made in a Hollywood studio and this would have the effect of spreading the fixed studio overhead over a smaller number of films, making Hollywood production costs even higher. The prospect of filming abroad also brought with it a familiar fear – that the films produced in Britain and elsewhere would not have the requisite 'American qualities' and audience appeal. As *Variety* noted, 'another factor discouraging Yank production in England is the generally mediocre success in this country of pix made there, even if producer, writers, director and chief technicians are American. It is said that some of the British atmosphere is absorbed that makes the films unpalatable to Americans' (4 August 1948: 1). British pictures had not fared well in America during the 1947/48 season and although this was attributed by Rank and others to retaliation by American exhibitors over the *ad valorem* tax, a number of criticisms were levelled at British pictures, particularly about the unintelligibility of dialogue. Yet, despite such misgivings, Anglo-American productions – films registered as British with the Board of Trade but involving American finance and personnel – began appearing on British screens in the late 1940s. Many, though not all, of these projects were within the terms of the Anglo-American agreement and linked to the 'unfreezing' of blocked funds. According to *Variety*: 'More than $10,000,000 in frozen sterling was expended on film production and story acquisitions in England by five American majors during the two year period of the Anglo-US films agreement' (28 June 1950: 4). Although 'thawing currency' gave the majors a strong incentive to film abroad, Columbia, MGM, RKO, Twentieth Century-Fox and Warner Bros., the companies mentioned in the *Variety* report, did have substantial studios in the US and had to balance production overseas for 'currency unfreezing' purposes with the expenses of their film factories. By 1951, the major incentives for shooting abroad were with the independent producers. The trade press outlined the distinction in the following terms:

> Prime reason for the Indies' tendency to roll their films abroad, trade observers feel, are the obvious one: lower costs and an opportunity to capitalize upon natural backgrounds. Majors also effect similar budgetary savings in overseas shooting, but in contrast to the Indies, they have huge studios to maintain and a sufficient quantity of product must be made at home to keep down the domestic overhead. (*Variety*, 5 September 1951: 7)

The availability of the Eady money was to provide another incentive for the big US firms to continue foreign production but, by the early 1950s, independents such as Irving Allen, Albert Lewin, the Hecht–Lancaster team, Douglas Fairbanks Jr. and Orson Welles were turning out twice as many foreign productions as the majors. Indeed, a figure such as Sam Spiegel established a substantial reputation mainly on the basis of Anglo-US productions, including *The African Queen* (1952), *The Bridge on the River Kwai* (1957) and, in the 1960s, *Suddenly Last Summer* (1960) and *Lawrence of Arabia* (1962). Some of Hollywood's best-known stars were to work in Britain, including Humphrey Bogart and Katharine Hepburn in *The African Queen*, Spencer Tracy in *Edward My Son*, James Stewart and Marlene Dietrich in *No Highway* (1951), Greer Garson and Walter Pidgeon in *The Miniver Story* (1950), Gregory Peck in *Captain Horatio Hornblower R. N.* (1951) and *Moby Dick* (1956), Cary Grant and Ingrid Bergman in *Indiscreet* (1958), Clark Gable in *Never Let Me Go* (1953) and James Cagney in *Shake Hands with the Devil* (1959). In fact, the list could be extended considerably and others who came to Britain for one or more films include Robert Taylor, Joan Crawford, José Ferrer, Ray Milland, Dana Andrews, Joseph Cotton, George Raft, Tyrone Power, Glenn Ford, Alan Ladd, Burt Lancaster, Elizabeth Taylor, Ava Gardner, Errol Flynn, Richard Widmark, Victor Mature, Jayne Mansfield, Robert Mitchum and William Holden. The policy of featuring American stars in British productions to enhance a film's international appeal had been tried previously by Balcon and Wilcox in the 1920s and by Gaumont British in the 1930s; the influx of American stars in the 1950s was on a much greater scale and it did involve those at the very top of the Hollywood lists. Among the directors brought over from Hollywood to Britain were major figures such as John Ford, John Huston, George Cukor, and Alfred Hitchcock, although *Under Capricorn* (1949) was made outside the Anglo-American agreement (*Variety*, 7 September 1949: 4). The full list of 'visiting film-makers' was extensive and included numerous experienced Hollywood figures, such as Edward Dmytryk, Albert Lewin, Jean Negulesco, Vincent Sherman, Jules Dassin, Raoul Walsh, Jacques Tourneur, William Kieghly, Robert Siodmak, Henry Koster, Richard Thorpe, Byron Haskin, George Marshall, Tay Garnett, Sidney Franklin, Otto Preminger, Joseph Mankiewicz and Stanley Donen. However, the films were Anglo-American productions and many of them involved British directors and stars as well. Englishman Alfred Hitchcock may be regarded as an 'American import' of sorts but other British film-makers, such as Carol Reed, David Lean, Michael Powell and Emeric Pressburger, Alexander Korda, Victor Saville, Terence Young, and Ken Annakin, directed some of the runaway productions.

American involvement with the British cinema in the 1950s led to films of varying qualities, at various budget levels and with different ambitions. Many of the overseas films were routine genre pictures and, in Thomas Guback's words, 'of little merit, hardly more noteworthy than the grade B pictures made in this country. Their claims to fame, it seems, were in unmotivated pans of landscapes and towns, contrived scenes taking place in "native" cafes, and local actors in secondary roles saying a few words (but not too many) in their own languages to add color' (1969: 165). However, a number were more ambitious and achieved a higher profile, lodging themselves in certain critical pantheons – *The African Queen* as 'classic' film – and performing successfully in both critical and commercial terms. *Ivanhoe* (1952) and *The Bridge on the River Kwai* were top box-office performers in the USA, while *Treasure Island* (1950), *Captain Horatio Hornblower R. N.*, *The Mudlark*, *The African Queen*, *Indiscreet, Heaven Knows, Mr Allison* (1957) and *Moulin Rouge* (1953) were successful in Britain, registering assorted mentions in the fan and trade journal annual awards (Ray, 1985: 141; Thumim, 1991: 258-9). It is not easy to discern specific generic and artistic trends in this kind of production. The British domestic cinema of the period was dominated by comedies, Ealing, Norman Wisdom, the 'Doctor' series, the work of Launder and Gilliat and the Boultings; war films both celebratory and critical of the Second World War; 'colonial adventure' films, most of them set in Africa; and the 'social problem' and crime genres. Towards the end of the decade the comedy profile was supplemented by the advent of the 'Carry On' series, Hammer started the cycle of horror films and the social problem strand of British cinema continued with the 'new wave' films, such as *Room at the Top* (1959) and *Saturday Night and Sunday Morning* (1960). Some of these genres are reflected in the US-financed output. *The Cockleshell Heroes* (1955), *The Miniver Story* and *The Bridge on the River Kwai* relate to the films set during the war, and those which are set in the immediate post-war period; *The Long Haul* (1957), *Gideon's Day* (1958) and *Town on Trial* (1957) are crime films; while *The Naked Earth* (1958), *Safari* (1956) and *Harry Black and the Tiger* (1958) are 'colonial adventure' films. The number of films with American involvement of one sort or another – financing through blocked earnings, distribution, co-productions – increased during the decade from a dozen or so released in 1950 to almost 30 in 1960, reflecting the increasing influence on the industry by American interests. In some respects, the kinds of films made with US financing represented the 'international' dimension of British film production in the 1950s, with Rank, the Associated British Picture Corporation, the various smaller British producers and the National Film Finance Corporation concentrating upon moderately budgeted pictures. Rank, for example, had retrenched after the problems of the late 1940s and had achieved a degree of profitability in the mid-1950s based on the popularity of comedian Norman Wisdom, the 'Doctor' films and war pictures such as *Reach for the Sky* (1956) and *A Town Like Alice* (1956). Subsequently, the company did change policy and relaunched a bid to make films with international prospects but the failure of this move led to a diminution of Rank as a production force through the 1960s and 1970s (Porter, 1997: 126-30).

The 1950s saw one other form of Anglo-American involvement with films targeted at both the British and American markets. Prior to its identification with the horror genre, Hammer Film Productions had specialized in making low-budget supporting pictures based on popular radio material originally designed for release through the ABC cinema chain. In 1951 the company set up a deal with an American company, Robert Lippert Productions, to make low-budget films for American distribution as B-pictures. The majors were abandoning B-production at this time and independents such as Lippert were stepping up their supply of programmers. American stars were used as the selling point for US audiences, although these tended to fall into the 'minor' or 'second-rank' star category – Dane Clark in *The Gambler and the Lady* (1952), John Ireland in *The Glass Cage* (1955) – or the 'fading' star past his or her prime, such as George Brent in *The Last Page* (1952) or Paulette Goddard in *The Stranger Came Home* (1954). This approach echoed the earlier attempts by Balcon and Wilcox to enhance the American appeal of their films by using US personnel; it differed markedly, however, from the usual British approach to penetrating the American market through the production of big-budget prestige films (Porter, 1983: 193-5).

The 1960s – American investment in British cinema

The 1960s saw a massive increase in the American investment in British production. Robert Murphy has observed that by '1956 one third of the films made in Britain had some form of American involvement' (1992: 257), but in the 1960s this contribution began to escalate dramatically. As Thomas Guback has noted: 'the proportion of American-financed pictures increased steadily from 43 per cent in 1962 to 71 per cent in 1966. Concerning the magnitude of finance, American sources provided almost 75 percent of the production money for British films in 1965 and 1966. The NFFC predicted that the "corresponding proportions for 1967 and 1968 may exceed 90 percent" ' (1969: 171). He went on to suggest that by the middle of the decade, the 'British production industry, if one can argue that a substantial *national* one does exist today, is little more than a branch of Hollywood, dependent upon American companies for both finance and distribution' (1969: 172; emphasis in original). US majors such as MGM , already planning British-based production in the immediate post-war period, were given an incentive to continue this after the Anglo-American agreement of 1948, as a strategy to utilize blocked currency derived from their British exhibition earnings and to circumvent the restrictions on currency transfers to the US. The continuing and increasing presence of American finance for British production, however, through to the end of the 1960s was consequent upon other factors. The various measures introduced in the late 1940s to aid British production – the Eady levy, the National Film Finance Corporation – although designed as a support for the indigenous industry, actually helped American companies, both major and independent, reinforcing the runaway trend and leading to the establishment of a number of US subsidiary companies, including Paramount British Pictures, MGM British Studios and offshoots of Twentieth Century-Fox, Disney and Warner Bros., as well as the numerous independent companies set up by producers and directors such as Carl Foreman, Sam Spiegel, Stanley Kubrick and Martin Ritt (Guback, 1969: 167-8). As in 1927, the government legislation effectively defined British films and British film companies in such a way as to allow a certain amount of foreign participation; the leeway was sufficient to allow the American companies formed for the runaway productions, access to the principal form of subsidy, the British Film Production Fund (the Eady Levy). By 1965, it was estimated that 'American subsidiaries in Great Britain now receive as much as 80 per cent of the payments from the British Production Fund' (Guback, 1967: 17).

Although American companies operated in other European countries which provided forms of subsidy as well, the British context offered the highest rate of subsidy, and the government tacitly ignored the potential contradictions of a state subsidy for a foreign interest. Indeed, as several bodies, including the Federation of British Film Makers, acknowledged, the British production industry benefited greatly from US investment. It was that which kept the studios working and gave employment to directors, actors and technical staff, together with the armies of support staff required for the operation of the film production process. For the British cinema, as Guback has pointed out, the 'choice has been between American money ensuring relative economic health, on the one hand, and no American money and probable economic sickness on the other' (1969: 175). Other factors cited as reinforcing the runaway trend in the 1960s include the dramatic ways in which the production costs of Hollywood-based film-making had escalated during the post-war period. According to Garth Jowett, 'costs of production had risen steadily since 1945, and the decade between 1960 and 1970 saw a further 50 per cent increase', with the Hollywood craft unions unwilling to scale down their wage demands in the new context of overseas competition (1976: 431-2). In addition, William Fadiman has argued that a principal reason for the continuation of runaways was the attitude of a small number of influential stars:

> The major consideration, and in many instances the absolute necessity, for American sponsored films being produced outside of our 50 states, lies in the attitude of some dozen or so American stars who have now become residents of Europe. Added to these is a smaller group of European performers who have attained international fame and prefer to live and work in their homelands. (1962: 40)

Whatever the reasons, US involvement in the British cinema of the 1960s was considerable and, indeed, sought after by British film-makers for various reasons, itemized by Terence Kelly as follows:

> The advantages offered by an American company to British film men have usually included 100 per cent finance for the independent production company (compared with 70 per cent or so offered by British distributors), little interference in working, a well connected god-father to look after the sale of the finished product in world markets, reputedly easier access to a British circuit booking if the film is marginal, and some 50 per cent of the profits. (1966: 88)

Although the National Film Finance Corporation was often a reliable source of 'end money' to supplement the 70 per cent of the budget available from a British distributor, the guarantee of comprehensive financing from the American majors, together with the other advantages, encouraged British film-makers into alliances with their Hollywood counterparts. As ever the fear of cultural domination was expressed, although it is possible to argue that the US financing of British film in the 1960s was somewhat different from that of the previous decade and, indeed, that the such involvement was central to the construction of a distinctive British cinema of the time. The profile of the British cinema of the 1950s outlined previously included comedies, war pictures, crime and social problem films, the majority of which emerged from Rank, Ealing, British Lion or other small British companies. The runaways do not seem to lodge comfortably in such a profile. The historical costume films, *The African Queen, Captain Horatio Hornblower R. N., The Bridge on the River Kwai*, although 'British' in some cultural respects, bear the hallmarks of their Hollywood genesis in terms of grandeur, scale and the presence of figures such as Humphrey Bogart, Katharine Hepburn, Gregory Peck and William Holden. They match more closely the Hollywood versions of British history, literature and culture made in Hollywood in the 1930s. Some of the 1960s runaways – *The Guns of Navarone* (1961), *Lawrence of Arabia, Where Eagles Dare* (1968) – were similar in character and appeal to those of the 1950s. Yet, a profile of 1960s British cinema would undoubtedly include American-financed

titles such as *Tom Jones* (1963), *The Charge of the Light Brigade* (1968), *Women in Love* (1969), *Alfie* (1966), *If . . .* (1968), *Far From the Madding Crowd* (1967), *Sons and Lovers* (1960), *A Man for All Seasons* (1966), *The L-Shaped Room* (1962), *The Knack* (1965), *Funeral in Berlin* (1966), *The Spy Who Came in from the Cold* (1965), *Zulu* (1963) and *The Prime of Miss Jean Brodie* (1969). Also, series such as the Margaret Rutherford 'Miss Marple' films, the Beatles films, *A Hard Day's Night* (1964) and *Help!* (1965), the 'Swinging London' films, *Georgy Girl* (1966) and *Joanna* (1968), and the James Bond cycle, with its 'mid-Atlantic' qualities, would have to be included to make up a convincing profile of the national cinema in the mid-1960s. Of course, a complete picture would have to include films more reliant upon domestic financing, such as those produced by the Bryanston group and British Lion, but the US-financed films contributed in a significant way to the British cinema of the decade, unlike their predecessors in the 1950s. The principal film trends with little US involvement include the realist 'new wave', although a film such as *The L-Shaped Room*, financed by Columbia, shares many characteristics of the new realism; the *Carry On . . .* comedy series, which began in 1958 but which became a staple of British cinema in the following decade; and the horror film associated with Hammer and a medley of smaller companies, including Amicus, a British company with American management personnel. There was some US involvement with the horror genre, however, in the shape of Roger Corman's Edgar Allan Poe cycle, two of which – *The Tomb of Ligeia* (1964), *The Masque of the Red Death* (1964) – were made by American International Pictures in conjunction with the British company, Anglo-Amalgamated, and shot in England.

As in the 1950s a number of Hollywood directors, some prominent and prestigious, other less so, worked on 'British' films. The list includes Otto Preminger, Martin Ritt, André De Toth, Blake Edwards, Billy Wilder, Fred Zinnemann, Delmer Daves, Richard Fleischer, Stanley Donen and Sidney Lumet. In addition, a handful of American film-makers effectively made Britain their working base and contributed to the British cinema in a substantial way. Joseph Losey had arrived in Britain in the 1950s, a refugee from the Hollywood anti-communist purges. He began his British career with a number of low-budget thrillers, such as *The Sleeping Tiger* (1954) and *Blind Date* (1959), but was to carve out a distinctive niche in the 1960s with films such as *The Servant* (1963), *Accident* (1967), *Secret Ceremony* (1968) and *The Go-Between* (1970), which located his work in the world of the 'art' film. Stanley Kubrick had settled in Britain in the late 1950s, and had made *Lolita* (1962) and *Dr. Strangelove* (1963), while Richard Lester's Beatles films and *The Knack* made him a key figure in the mid-1960s.

Unlike the 1950s, however, where the main indigenous film-making talents – Hamer, Mackendrick, the Boultings, Launder and Gilliat – worked outside the American-financed sector, a number of important British directors were involved in the American-produced 'British' films of the 1960s. Well established film-makers such as Anthony Asquith, David Lean, Michael Powell, Charles Crichton, Carol Reed and J. Lee Thompson made films for US firms such as MGM, Twentieth Century-Fox and Columbia. The American companies, however, also showed considerable interest in the new and younger directors. Although Tony Richardson, John Schlesinger and Karel Reisz had established their reputations in the 'new wave' era with gritty working-class dramas, they were subsequently to make US-financed films such as *Tom Jones*, *Far From the Madding Crowd* and *Isadora* (1969), which were marked by larger budgets and more spectacular production values.

Indigenous finance and production

Outside of American finance, the British film industry struggled to maintain a production foothold. The Rank Organization had sustained a modest production profile in the 1950s of around 15 films a year out of its Pinewood studio base, and with a roster of stars such as Dirk Bogarde and Diana Dors on contract. For a short period in the early 1950s, in collaboration with the National Film Finance Corporation, the group had financed British Film Makers, a consortium of independent film-makers, and Rank also had a co-financing and distribution arrangement with Michael Balcon's Ealing company. After a failed attempt to revive internationally targeted production in the late 1950s, the group retrenched once more, planning a more diversified future in non-film enterprises such as photocopying, television, bingo and home entertainment (Porter, 1997). Although Rank was to remain a key force in the industry through its distribution network and cinema chain, its production profile was to diminish through the 1960s.

Throughout the 1950s the American majors had been withdrawing from direct large-scale production in favour of backing independent companies, renting studio space to them and distributing their films. This was a way forward for the British majors and in 1959 Rank agreed to provide a small financial contribution to the Allied Film Makers group, one of the many independent production groupings which were set up towards the end of the 1950s. In 1964 the group combined with the National Film Finance Corporation in a joint-financing deal which would enable British independent producers to obtain 100 per cent financing from a single source. The American companies offered this, and one way of reviving British-financed films was to offer similar terms. As previously, this was a short-lived arrangement with disappointing results and was terminated a few years later. Some money was invested in large-scale productions such as *The Fall of the Roman Empire* (1963) through distribution deals with independent producers, and the group took over the *Carry On* series in 1967; it continued to invest modestly in production in the 1970s and, indeed, announced another ambitious but unsuccessful attempt to re-establish itself as a production force towards the end of the decade. In 1980, however, Rank announced its withdrawal from film production. ABC, the other major British company, followed a similar path in the 1960s, a very small amount of direct production activity together with investment in the work of independent producers. The company also had financial interests in companies such as

Anglo Amalgamated, which backed the *Carry On* series before Rank, and the Grade Organization's film concern, Elstree Distributors. Its subsequent fortunes were to include a change of ownership – in 1969 the company was acquired by EMI – and an ambitious international film production programme in the 1970s.

In many respects the major companies yielded to the Americans in terms of production. Their interests, as ever, were served by the screening of both Hollywood films and US-financed British films on their theatre circuits, and ABC itself was still part-owned by Warner Bros. . Thus each company had specific and exclusive links with the American majors, with Rank getting films from United Artists, Twentieth Century-Fox, Columbia and Disney, and with ABC getting films from its part-owner, Warner Bros., as well as from Paramount and MGM (Kelly, 1966: 50). The incentives for indigenous production lay with the small independent companies which were in competition with an external force, the American film industry and its films, and an internal force, the British majors, whose tight control of the primary exhibition venues made it difficult for independently produced films to reach British cinemas, even if their changing policies on production meant an encouragement for independent producers. Some of the independents were closely linked to the US majors, while others – notably Hammer and Anglo Amalgamated – had found genre niches which gave them a degree of viability. A number of other small British concerns did attempt to establish themselves in this context. Allied Film Makers drew together actors Richard Attenborough, Jack Hawkins and Bryan Forbes, and the Michael Relph/Basil Dearden production team, while Bryanston, set up in 1959 under the guidance of Michael Balcon, grouped together some of the leading independents including the Tony Richardson/John Osborne company, Woodfall Films, which made a number of the 'new wave' films. British Lion, the principal independent distributor and owner of Shepperton Studios, had been 'nationalized' by default in the 1950s through its indebtedness to the National Film Finance Corporation, but had re-established itself financially on the basis of the films of the Boulting brothers and the Launder and Gilliat team, who became directors of the company. It was relaunched as a private company in 1963, with Michael Balcon leading 'an uneasy coalition of the old management team, the vanguard of the New Wave (Tony Richardson, John Osborne, John Schlesinger and Joseph Janni), Brian Epstein, and the American art cinema distributor Walter Reade' (Murphy, 1992: 111). The independents made a limited impression on the British cinema of the time, which was dominated by US-financed films until the end of the 1960s when the lavish American financing of the middle years of the decade began to diminish.

The situation altered once again in the 1970s and 1980s with renewed attempts to establish Britain as a force in the international film industry, as will be noted in the next chapter. American films remained at the centre of British film culture, however, and the American influence also made itself felt in two further ways. Although in an earlier period, the quality of the technical provision in British studios was criticized, the 1960s saw the beginnings of the establishment of British studios as a base for the production of expensive films dependent in part upon the special effects industry. According to David Puttnam, it was their work on Stanley Kubrick's *2001: A Space Odyssey* (1968) and the James Bond films that enabled British technicians to develop 'an international reputation for their skills with physical and mechanical effects' (1997: 306). The subsequent shooting of *The Empire Strikes Back* (1980), the *Indiana Jones* cycle, the *Superman* and *Batman* films and *Alien* (1979) at studios such as Elstree, Pinewood and Shepperton was testimony to the high regard in which British special effects expertise was held. The second sphere of influence was in the exhibition sector. Although the post-war period saw a substantial decline in the cinema audience, from 1,640 million attendances in 1946 to below 100 million attendances in the mid-1980s, the 1990s has seen a revival of cinema-going based upon the multiplex cinema frequently situated in a leisure complex or shopping centre (Docherty *et al.*, 1987: 2-4). The multiplex was an American innovation and it was one of the companies closely involved in its development in the USA, American Multi-Cinema, which opened the first of a chain of multiplexes in Britain in 1985, the Point at Milton Keynes. Other American companies, the Cannon/MGM group, National Amusements and Warner Bros., emulated AMC and set up chains, establishing a new style of cinema attendance, often outside city centres in shopping complexes; British companies followed in the 1990s with the Odeon chain converting many of its cinemas to a multi-screen format and with the Virgin company acquiring the Cannon/MGM chain as well as building new multiplexes (Eyles, 1997: 224-5).

From the very earliest days of cinema, American companies have operated in Britain and American individuals have lent their expertise to the organization of the domestic industry. Although the principal focus of activity has been the distribution and marketing of films made in Hollywood, there have been periodic forays into the other areas of the industry, into production and exhibition. Such forays have often derived from the changing circumstances of the international film industry, and from the shifting policies of the British government, which have often been designed to protect British film production, the sector of the industry most adversely affected by the activities of Hollywood. The next chapter will examine the ways in which British companies have attempted to intervene in the American market, principally trying to compete with the American companies for their own indigenous audience in their own cinemas.

5 British Companies and America

Constructing a history of the American film industry's activities in Britain is relatively straightforward, as previous chapters have indicated. From the very earliest days of the cinema, America has provided a substantial flow of finance for various film industry enterprises in Britain, establishing distribution companies, setting up production companies, investing in British films, using British production facilities for its own films, buying cinemas and starting the multiplex boom; also, a number of Americans – producers, directors, actors – have worked in the British cinema from the earliest days. All this is in addition to the major effect of America providing British audiences with the bulk of its film entertainment. Constructing a 'reciprocal' history of the influence of the British cinema in America is more difficult, though not impossible. Many British films have had a significant impact on US audiences from the 'primitive' period to the present. The titles include *The Private Life of Henry VIII* (1933) in the 1930s, *Henry V* (1945) and *The Red Shoes* (1948) in the 1940s, *Tom Jones* (1963) and *Darling* (1965) in the 1960s, *Chariots of Fire* (1981) in the 1980s, and the recent successes of *Four Weddings and a Funeral* (1994), *The Full Monty* (1997) and *Shakespeare in Love* (1999). Such films have succeeded in attracting American audiences and performing well at the box-office; they have also earned wide critical respect, some have secured nominations for various Oscars at the annual Academy Awards ceremony and some have won them. They have served to boost the confidence of an industry which has, for most of its history, grappled with the apparent superiority of American films, Hollywood film techniques and the secure grip on the American domestic market held by the major American companies. At various times, their success has been treated as a green light for targeting the US market, but almost invariably, the production booms which have followed success have ended in crisis.

In addition to films, there is also a substantial history of British producers, directors, writers and actors making the transatlantic journey. Some went on a temporary basis to secure personnel or services which were then used in the production of British films. In the 1920s, for example, Victor Saville went to secure American stars for his British-made films in order to provide them with transatlantic appeal; Saville also went later in the decade to take advantage of the technical facilities not available in Britain in the early sound period. He re-shot the final reels of his silent film *Kitty* in the RCA Studios in New York in order to be able to release it as a part-talkie late in 1929. Others, however, including Saville himself in the late 1930s, made more permanent moves in order to work in Hollywood and many of them subsequently contributed in no small part to the development of the American cinema. Indeed, this history would include some of the most distinguished names in the cinema itself. In a pointed rebuff to those many commentators who saw 'a certain incompatibility between the terms "cinema" and "Britain" ', to quote Truffaut's notorious formulation, Charles Barr simply cited the examples of Chaplin and Hitchcock, two British film-makers with unchallengeable cinematic credentials by most criteria. As Barr has noted, the two 'above all others have attained worldwide recognition to the extent of becoming, at different periods, virtually synonymous with the notion of popular cinema' (1986: 9). Chaplin, of course, made his film name entirely in America, while Hitchcock went to Hollywood after a successful film career in Britain. Barr also mentions James Whale, director of Universal's *Frankenstein* in the early 1930s and a significant contributor to popular Hollywood cinema, as a further indication that the gloomy view of the British capacity for excellence in film is not based on an examination of fact. This chapter will chart the many attempts to market British films in America together with some of the contributions made by the British to the development of the world's most influential popular cinema.

Early excursions

The arrival of the motion picture at the end of the nineteenth century has generated many myths. Credit for its invention has been claimed on behalf of many photographers, inventors and entrepreneurs working in a number of countries, including America and Britain, but also including France and Germany. Perhaps the primary myth is that it was 'invented' at all. David Robinson has suggested that:

> The motion picture as we know it was never in the strict sense 'invented'. Nor was its development even a normal process of evolution. Rather it was like the assembling of a puzzle, the pieces of which were only vouchsafed intermittently, over a very long period of time. (1996: 3)

Robinson's history of the development of the medium reaches back to the fifteenth century and to the magic lantern, but the usual discussions of responsibility for its development tend to begin around the middle of the nineteenth century. In the late 1880s, Britain had a candidate in William Friese-Greene, although his contribution is not now regarded as significant nor is much of it regarded as his own work, despite its rendition in mythical form in the British film *The Magic Box* (1951). Friese-Greene worked in conjunction with many others and, as one writer has put it 'his technical accomplishments were largely the work of others' (Rossell, 1998: 108). He was, however, an enthusiastic publicist for the idea of moving pictures and, it has been suggested that his 'overoptimistic claims to have solved the problems of photographing and projecting moving pictures may at least have served to stimulate others' (Robinson, 1996: 16). In fact, more significant contributions to the development of early cinema came from émigré Britons working in America. Eadweard Muybridge's famous experiments in multiple serial photography constituted an important step on the road to motion pictures and his demonstrations and lecture tours reporting these played an important role in the development of cinematography and made a significant impression on Thomas Edison. In 1888, following one such demonstration of his zoopraxiscope, a machine which projected circular slides in conjunction with a magic lantern, Muybridge met the famous inventor at his New Jersey headquarters and 'helped to stimulate Thomas Edison into thinking about a new motion-picture system' (Musser, 1990: 51).

Over the next few years, Edison's team was to work towards the major breakthrough, 'the most significant single step toward cinematography as we know it today' (Robinson, 1996: 19), the invention of the Kinetoscope and Kinetograph machines. The former was a coin-operated 'peep-show' machine which played very brief films recorded by the Kinetograph. Edison's first demonstrated moving pictures in 1893 and the commercial exploitation of the equipment began in the following year when Kinetoscope Parlors were established in many American towns. One important figure in the development of the equipment was William Laurie Kennedy Dickson, a photographer and inventor who had joined the Edison company in 1883 after emigrating from Britain. Dickson was the senior figure working on motion picture research at the Edison company, and although, as in many innovatory situations, it is not possible to isolate a single individual as responsible, it seems clear that his contribution to the development of the equipment was significant. Two Britons then played important roles in the collective, and international endeavour, that culminated in motion pictures. A third – R. W. Paul – made a different kind of contribution in these early years. The Kinetoscope 'peep show' was soon replaced by a projection machine – the Vitascope. As has been noted previously, the first public exhibition using Edison's newly developed projection equipment in 1896 included a British film, *Rough Sea at Dover*, produced by Paul's company and photographed by Birt Acres. The film was isolated for specific praise in the press comment on the programme and attracted considerable audience approval, going on to 'become one of the most popular of early films' (Thompson and Bordwell, 1994: 10).

Further British films circulated in America during the early years of cinema and, indeed, as Charles Musser has argued, films such as *A Daring Daylight Burglary* (Sheffield Photo Company), *Trailed by Bloodhounds* (Paul) and *A Desperate Poaching Affray* (Walter Haggar), all made in 1903, provided important innovatory models for other film-makers. These were, Musser suggested, key films which offered new directions for the development of the narrative cinema, offering

> two important innovations. First, and in sharp contrast to the earlier fairy-tale films, they were films of violent crime. In A DARING DAYLIGHT

BURGLARY, for example, a burglar looting a house is discovered by the police, makes his escape, and is finally captured after a prolonged chase, while in DESPERATE POACHING AFFRAY, two poachers are chased by game wardens, with resulting shootings and hand-to-hand fights. Second, these films used the chase as a central narrative element. As a result, the British conveyed a sensationalistic energy that American and French producers soon emulated. (1990: 365)

This is a further indication of the capacity of British film-makers to produce work that compared well on the international stage, offering narrative and stylistic exemplars and influencing the course of cinema at this early stage in its development. It is also interesting in its characterization of British films in terms of 'sensationalist energy', as it is often the converse of such qualities – restraint, understatement – that are mentioned in conjunction with British cinema. Noël Burch has suggested that the embryonic British cinema at the turn of the century contained a strong 'populist' strand, incorporating 'anarchistic morals' and 'crude violence' and addressed to a working-class audience (1990: 99-103). In contrast, in the course of an article about the kind of cinema that had evolved in Britain by the 1950s, Lindsay Anderson was to use terms such as 'emotionally inhibited' (1957: 139). Although the early interventions by Haggar and Frank Mottershaw of the Sheffield Photo Company pointed to a cinema of vigour and energy, the subsequent history of British film, or the history of 'culturally approved' British film, moved in a different direction. Burch also draws attention to the innovatory dimension of the films in terms of the development of narrative form, suggesting that Haggar's '*Robbery of the Mail Coach* (1903) . . . seems to have been the model for Porter's *The Great Train Robbery*' (1990: 104).

This was a brief successful period for British film-makers and the demise of the British film is usually located from around 1906 onwards. Part of the explanation lies in the internal development of the industry and the shift of energy into distribution which led to London becoming an important centre for the international circulation of American films. However, Musser does point to problems with the marketing infrastructure for the films and the failure of British producers to establish a foothold in the American market. As he comments, in these crucial early years of cinema, 'not a single British company opened an American agency, but rather sold films through American sales agents' (1990: 365). In addition to the film-makers mentioned above, other British companies including Urban-Eclipse, James Williamson, Cecil Hepworth, Cricks and Martin, and the Walturdaw company had films circulating in the USA through established American agencies, including the most prominent importer of foreign films, George Kleine (Bowser, 1990: 28, 73). By contrast, the American firm, Maguire and Baucus, a company with European sales rights for Edison equipment and films, had established a base in London almost ten years before; subsequently numerous offices representing American companies were opened in London and other European cities in the period before the First World War. The Charles Urban company was involved

in the promotion of an early colour film technique – Kinemacolor – which was
to play a role in the development of the American film. The process had been
patented in 1906 by Urban and G. A. Smith, a pioneer inventor and film-maker
who had joined Urban in 1900 while he was still at the Warwick Trading
Company. Kinemacolor enjoyed some success in Britain and Urban soon
looked to its international exploitation. In America, as with the film-makers
who sold their films through agencies, Urban decided to sell the American
rights, rather than establish a US-based company himself. This may have been a
realistic assessment of the market situation in which the Motion Picture Patents
Company had established a fragile and temporary control over the industry.
Initially the powerful members of the Motion Picture Patents Company were
not interested in the process and this has been cited as one of the reasons for the
ultimate failure of the process regarded by many historians as 'the first
successful photographic color-motion-picture process' (Kindem, 1982: 136).
The rights were acquired outright by Kinemacolor of America, which began
exploiting the process in 1912 using some of Urban's British films featuring
royal pageantry and military displays. A number of Kinemacolor films were
made in America in the period 1912-13 and the company eventually became
licensed by the Motion Picture Patents Company. Kinemacolor of America and
Urban's company, the British Natural Kinematograph Company, collaborated
initially, but the relationship was terminated in 1914, and the process fell into
disuse in both countries. However, Kinemacolor, a British invention, did have
some impact upon picture making in the United States at least to the extent of
indicating the 'potential world market for photographic color motion pictures'
(Kindem, 1982: 145). Although one of many colour processes in the early
period of cinema, it was the most successful and can be regarded as having
paved the way for later developments, particularly the various Technicolor
processes used in the American cinema from the mid-1920s onwards.

British films and the transatlantic audience

British films circulated in the international market, including America, with a
degree of ease in the early years of the cinema, in a fluid market situation. A
number of the principal early British film producers, including Hepworth and
the Sheffield Photo Company, were also in the photographic and lantern trade,
and contacts with America had been established in these kindred enterprises.
Indeed, English and French suppliers had enjoyed a significant share of the
American market for magic lantern slides (Musser, 1990: 36). Other substantial
firms such as Warwick and British Mutoscope and Biograph were run by
Americans and had close links with the developing US industry. The latter
company, in fact, was an overseas supplier of films for the American Biograph
Company, an early example of 'runaway' production. The lines of exchange
were open and the films of a number of countries including Britain circulated
widely. As Kerry Segrave has noted, 'international film exhibition was not
dominated by American product. Motion pictures came and went from country

to country with few or no restrictions' (1997: 1). However, while many European films found their way into the US market through orthodox trading arrangements, many were simply copied by American manufacturers for screening in the nickelodeons (Musser, 1990: 364). The process of cartelization which began in the American film industry with the formation of the Motion Picture Patents Company in 1908 made it much more difficult for foreign films to get access to the American market. The disruption of the European industries during the First World War, together with the rapid transformation of the American film industry during this period, the rise of the large integrated corporations and the innovations of the star system and the long narrative created a radically different climate for the exchange of films in the 1920s. The European industries' attempts to restore their pre-war positions took place in changed circumstances; circumstances which required them to come to terms with the American industry's increasing economic and artistic power.

The attempts to re-introduce British films to the United States in the 1920s, and the many subsequent efforts to establish a foothold in American market, have generated much discussion centred upon the kind of films which the British industry should make to secure such a goal. Such discussions had, indeed have, an economic face and a cultural face; they have been especially evident during those times – 1927, 1938, the Second World War, 1948 – when state intervention in the industry was under scrutiny. In economic terms the American industry was characterized by an industrial mode of production geared to the volume production of films for international distribution, with graded expenditure levels from the very expensive 'quality' films to the low-budget programme picture. In cultural terms, the American industry had evolved a set of narrative and stylistic norms and a pattern of genres – comedies, Westerns, gangster films, musicals – which appeared to transcend cultural boundaries even after the advent of the dialogue picture and the cultural specificity which speech brought to individual national cinemas. Such conditions set the terms for the international circulation of the films, at times guiding indigenous non-American production into the niche markets of 'art' cinema, but, at other times and in some countries, provoking a competitive response in which film-makers sought to contend with American films on their own terms – high budgets, the adoption of genre models from Hollywood – and in their own domestic market.

Rachael Low's account of film production in Britain in the 1920s divides the industry into those producers whose presuppositions were still stuck in the pre-war days, when short films were made in great numbers on small budgets in cramped studio conditions or, more economically, on adjacent locations, and those with more ambition. The established companies were being left behind:

> The trouble with the older companies was that, faced with difficulties in getting capital or a wide market, they allowed themselves to think that films financed cheaply on a pre-war scale could survive in the post-war world. The higher cost of films coming over from America meant, in fact, a completely different style of production. (Low, 1971: 108)

Producers such as Herbert Wilcox, Michael Balcon and Victor Saville, new to the industry in the early 1920s, were more attentive to the changed conditions and had a greater awareness of the ways in which the rise of the American cinema, with its lavishly budgeted feature films and highly paid stars, was to dictate new patterns of film production, requiring a greater investment than hitherto. All had started their careers in distribution, selling American films in the regions, dealing with cinema owners and, possibly, developing a more precise knowledge of audience tastes than the pre-war pioneers. When Herbert Wilcox started his film-making career, he drew upon his knowledge of American films:

> We had distributed, amongst other films, a magnificent epic called *Intolerance*. It was produced and directed by D. W. Griffith, without doubt the greatest pioneer of film technique of all time. I would study *Intolerance*, see it several times and chart on paper the method Griffith used. (1967: 50)

But Wilcox knew that more than copying technique was required if the British produced films were to match up with the films coming in from Hollywood, and after positive critical comment on his first film – *The Wonderful Story* (1922) – he managed to raise finance for a more ambitious production programme. In order to secure access to the American market, Wilcox imported one of Griffith's stars – Mae Marsh – for his second film, *Flames of Passion* (1922), which became, in his own words, 'the first British film to be sold in the U. S. A. after the First World War' (1967: 53). Balcon and Victor Saville, who had set up a production company together, adopted the same strategy for their film debut – *Woman to Woman* (1923) – with Saville going to America to hire Betty Compson for the leading role. As with *Flames of Passion*, the film was a success both in Britain and abroad, and was particularly well received in the United States. Leading American director Rex Ingram praised it as 'one of the best and most sincere films I ever saw in my life', and it was screened at 'the largest theatre in Hollywood', at a venue normally reserved for the big Famous Players–Lasky features and not usually available to independent British or American films (*The Bioscope*, 1.February 1924: 9).

The idea of using American stars appeared to be paying off, and it was a strategy that Balcon carried into his Gainsborough production schedule. Gainsborough Pictures was formed in 1924 after Balcon had acquired the Islington Studios set up by the Famous Players–Lasky company at the beginning of the 1920s. A number of its early pictures, including some of the Anglo-German titles, featured Americans in leading roles. *The Blackguard* (1925) and *The Rat* (1925) starred Jane Novak and Mae Marsh respectively, while Hitchcock's first film – *The Pleasure Garden* (1925) – had Virginia Valli and Carmelita Geraghty in leading roles. Balcon did use British stars as well – Betty Balfour in *Sea Urchin* (1926) and Ivor Novello in *The Rat* – but the strategy of using American players to enhance the appeal of films to international and particularly American audiences was fast becoming an important dimension of British production in the 1920s. Wilcox's career progress was also bound up with the use of American stars. In 1926 he released *Nell Gwynne*, which starred Dorothy Gish, and went into business with J. D. Williams, the American co-founder of First National, who was 'trying to create either a big company or a big combination of companies to secure the advantages of large-scale operation for British production' (Low, 1971: 176). Further Gish titles were planned for British National with financial backing coming from Paramount, and the company also laid plans to build a 'British Hollywood' in the form of a studio complex at Elstree. Eventually, Wilcox set up his own company – British and Dominions – which supplied quota pictures to both United Artists and Paramount during the 1930s.

The business of making films for an international market required the large-scale operation sought by Williams rather than the piece-meal production operations mounted by Balcon and Wilcox in the early 1920s. The evolving hegemony of the American film dictated a need for high production values, lavish settings and large casts, as well as the use of familiar stars to provide access to American audiences. The reorganization of the British film industry in the late 1920s and the formation of the large vertically integrated companies appeared to answer this need and to provide the organizational and financial structures required for the production of quality films. Such structures, it was hoped, would enable the international ambitions displayed by forward-thinking producers such as Balcon and Wilcox to be satisfied, and would extricate them from the precarious picture to picture basis of their earlier endeavours. Both the large combines which were formed at the time – British International Pictures and Gaumont British – incorporated the American as well as the wider world market into their production thinking. There were other factors at work as well, reflecting the complex and sometimes contradictory patterns of response generated by the conditions of the international film industry. The 'art' cinemas of Europe in the period – German Expressionism, the French avant-garde and the Soviet montage school in particular – provided a fresh set of aesthetic influences to set aside the evolving Hollywood narrative, and could be promoted as offering an alternative or set of alternatives to the Hollywood model. British producers were caught up in the debates about 'cinema Europe' and the notion of an international cinema based upon a European distinctiveness. The 'British' film then found itself operating in the context of models from Hollywood which had a powerful influence on indigenous audiences, models from Europe which impressed intellectuals and taste-makers, yet the notion of a 'British' film defended by the quota legislation involved some conception of its relationship and its importance to British culture, ostensibly threatened by the possible absorption of British cinema by foreign models. 'Internationalizing' film production by the late 1920s involved a negotiation of this complex of factors.

British International Pictures, which grew out of the British National company, announced its ambitions both in its name and in the company trademark displayed at the beginning of a BIP film – Britannia seated in front of a revolving globe. Its international aspirations were reflected in the number of directors and stars recruited from various countries, a policy that Hollywood itself had followed in the 1920s, and in its brief experiment with films produced in multiple-language versions. Many of the imported talents came from America, including directors, Harry Lachman and Tim Whelan, and stars, Maria Corda, Syd Chaplin, Tallulah Bankhead, Lionel Barrymore and Anna May Wong, and BIP also set up of an American distribution base – World Wide Pictures. However, a number of BIP recruits came from continental Europe, notably directors such as E. A. Dupont and Arthur Robison from Germany, and stars such as Carl Brisson from Sweden, Anny Ondra from Czechoslovakia and the Russian star, Olga Tschechowa.

In addition to recruiting experienced American and European directors and stars, the company signed up some of the most significant British film personnel of the day. Director, Alfred Hitchcock, had already been recruited by Williams for British National Pictures, and he was followed by Victor Saville and Thomas Bentley; the company also signed Betty Balfour, one of the leading stars of the British cinema of the time. The BIP films emerged from this cosmopolitan array of personnel which embodied the range of constraints – international and domestic – which framed film production as it moved into the sound period. Sound, of course, brought speech and the further constraint of language which, in many respects, moved the British cinema away from Europe and cemented its close relationship with the American cinema. BIP's early schedules contain a range of films reflecting the complex of influences. Hitchcock's *The Ring* (1927) featured Swedish actor, Carl Brisson, although the setting and theme – an English fairground, romantic intrigue and the sport of boxing – rendered it accessible to a transatlantic audience. Dupont's *Moulin Rouge* (1928), by contrast, signalled its European character through its Parisian setting announced in the opening shots, and through its risqué theme of a man in love with both a mother and her daughter. Thomas Bentley's *The American Prisoner* (1929), as the title implies, addressed an American audience more explicitly although the lead character was played by Carl Brisson. However, the company's initial international ambitions soon faded.

The films, some of them made at high cost, failed to break into the American market and the company scaled down its production expenditure. Its characteristic films of the 1930s were low-budget programme pictures, many of them comedies with music hall origins, for the growing chain of ABC cinemas on which the organization depended for its profits; there was a brief flurry of more ambitious production in the middle of the decade but the international ambitions of the late 1920s had disappeared. The studio's trajectory was mirrored in the career of its premier British director. The studio's first release in 1927, Hitchcock's *The Ring*, although not particularly successful at the box-office, was hailed in the press as 'the greatest production ever made in this country' and 'a triumph for the British film industry (*The Bioscope*, 6 October 1927: 14). By 1932, however, Hitchcock was being assigned to low-budget pictures such as the thriller, *Number Seventeen* (1932), and *Lord Camber's Ladies* (1932), a quota picture which he produced. By 1934 Hitchcock had moved on to work with Michael Balcon at Gaumont British.

Gaumont British, which merged the production output of the Gaumont company and Balcon's Gainsborough Pictures, started a programme of internationally orientated production in 1932 after extensive refurbishing work on its Shepherd's Bush and Islington Studios. Like BIP in the late 1920s, the company imported a number of Americans and built a production roster which balanced the parochial – the comedies of Jack Hulbert and Cicely Courtneidge, Tom Walls's Aldwych farces – with more elaborate historical costume pictures aimed at the American market. Some American directors were used but the strategy for appealing to the American audience depended more on using stars well known in the USA, actors and actresses with established Hollywood reputations. Among Balcon's 'imports' were Sylvia Sidney, Edmund Lowe, Constance Bennett, Richard Dix, Constance Cummings, Esther Ralston, Robert Young, Noah Beery, Paul Robeson, Edward Everett Horton and Walter Huston. Also included were British names such as George Arliss, Boris Karloff, Herbert Marshall, and Madeleine Carroll, who had made their reputations in Hollywood pictures. The key requirement was that the players were known to an American audience; their actual nationality mattered less. It is often suggested that the success of Korda's *The Private Life of Henry VIII* in 1933 prompted British companies to aim their films at the American market. As Karol Kulik has suggested: 'The financial success of *The Private Life of Henry VIII* gave hope to the British film industry and marked Britain's final graduation into the international film world' (1990: 96). It is, however, important to note that Gaumont British had embarked on a production programme with the US audience in mind before Korda's success. A small number of films in their 1932 list used stars familiar to American audiences with *Rome Express* and *After the Ball* featuring Esther Ralston and *The Faithful Heart* and *The Calendar* starring Herbert Marshall; the following year's list included films with Madeleine Carroll, Edward Everett Horton and Boris Karloff. Although Korda's success undoubtedly encouraged other British companies, Gaumont British and, indeed, British International Pictures some years earlier, clearly had an international dimension in mind as an element of their production policies.

The Private Life of Henry VIII demonstrated, or appeared to demonstrate, that that British subject-matter – historical, literary - could appeal to American audiences. Charles Laughton, in the title role, had appeared in a small number of Hollywood films and was contracted to Paramount, so there was also an element of using an actor with some currency in America. The impact of the film derived also from its subject-matter – British history and royalty – and the next few years saw an increase in the use of British history and culture as explicit subject-matter for British films with international ambition, as well as constituting a source for a number of prestigious Hollywood productions of the period. Balcon, in his own categorization of the Gaumont British production schedule during the 1930s, included the '"epics" made with an eye on the American market' (1969: 63). Some of the epics – *The Iron Duke* (1935), *Rhodes of Africa* (1936), *King Solomon's Mines* (1937) – did use British history for their subject-matter, while other films falling into the 'epic' category had a range of subject-matter. *Jew Süss* (1934) was about eighteenth-century German history, *The Tunnel* (1935) had a futuristic theme – the building of a transatlantic tunnel – and *King of the Damned* (1936) was set in a Caribbean slave encampment. Balcon singles out the 'epics' as the films aimed at the American market but the stars with transatlantic appeal were also used in other kinds of films. Robert Young appeared in Hitchcock's *Secret Agent* (1936) and in a Jessie Matthews musical, *It's Love Again* (1936); Madeleine Carroll, in addition to playing with Young in *Secret Agent* (1936), also featured in Hitchcock's *The 39 Steps* (1935) and Victor Saville's *I Was a Spy* (1933), playing opposite Herbert Marshall. Many of the films produced did secure bookings in America through independent cinemas rather than those of the major companies. Although some Gaumont British titles enjoyed a degree of success in America, the project failed to establish Gaumont British in the American market and to prise sufficient booking dates out of the leading American cinema chains. In John Sedgwick's words, 'the Studio's output wasn't sufficiently attractive to the audiences of the leading American cities to persuade the "American majors to make room" '(1996: 345).

Korda's success with *The Private Life of Henry VIII* also led to a concerted attempt by his company, London Films, to secure consistent US distribution for British films through the course of the decade. Korda's studio was famously cosmopolitan, with directors and stars from Europe and America. His production was focused almost solely upon 'prestige' pictures, unlike his major British competitors, BIP and Gaumont British, studios which balanced quality production with more modest activities, although in quite different proportions. The films were also made with global as well as indigenous circulation in mind 'in a style which was international rather than parochial' (Sedgwick, 1997: 50), with their creative teams drawn from various countries. These included continental European directors such as René Clair, Paul Czinner, Jacques Feyder and Zoltan Korda, the cinematographer, Georges Périnal, together with American and British directors such as Allan Dwan, Tim Whelan, William Cameron Menzies, Victor Saville and Anthony Asquith. As with Gaumont British, London Films also used American stars and stars of other nationalities well known in America. Charles Laughton had appeared on the New York stage and in a few Hollywood films before *The Private Life of Henry VIII*, and subsequent films featured Douglas Fairbanks, Douglas Fairbanks Jr., Roland Young and Marlene Dietrich. However, Korda's films did not depend entirely upon using this particular export ploy and many of them featured young British players such as Laurence Olivier and Vivien Leigh, both later to achieve great success in Hollywood. Korda's strategy for placing his films in the American market depended rather more on their status as 'quality' products and on the substantial production values available to him in what, at the time of its opening in 1936, was the largest and best-equipped film studio in Britain (Warren, 1995: 30-1). Also important was the close link with United Artists, the Hollywood 'prestige' distributor, his eventual partnership in the company and UA's need for 'quality' films in the 1930s. The link appeared to give London Films something of an edge on other British companies, whose access to American markets depended upon the major integrated combines whose interests lay firstly in the promotion of their own films, and only secondarily in the distribution of the films of other American companies, let alone those of foreign competitors.

However, the key requirement for success was the quality of the films themselves and Korda's eventual failure to establish his films in the American market indicated that they failed to compare with the American 'quality' films of the time. The epics from Gaumont British and Korda's London Films, the Hitchcock thrillers, the musical comedy films of Gracie Fields and Jessie Matthews, though now regarded with some respect by film historians, did not prevent the crisis in the production industry in the late 1930s. With the exception of the Hitchcock thrillers, these films were not successful in America. The power of the 'mature oligopoly' which controlled the American industry made access to the market difficult and British firms which sought to establish distribution facilities in America were faced with considerable expense. In one respect, however, British films did succeed in Hollywood compared with other film-producing countries. The annual Academy Awards, Hollywood's prestigious and lavish ritual, began to include British films from the early 1930s. *The Private Life of Henry VIII* was nominated for the 'best picture' category in the 1932/33 ceremony, and Charles Laughton actually won the 'best actor' award for his performance in the film; *Pygmalion* (1938) won a screenwriting Oscar; the MGM-British pictures *The Citadel* (1938) and *Goodbye Mr Chips* (1939) earned various nominations, and Robert Donat won the 'best actor' award for his role as Mr Chips. Although British films did not win many awards, or indeed, earn many nominations during the period, their incorporation into this significant Hollywood institution suggests the 'special relationship' which existed between the two cinemas.

Wartime conditions: export and propaganda

The ambitions of the British film industry in the 1930s were not matched by the economic performance of the films produced, especially those which were aimed at the American market. However, the recovery during the decade from an industry previously 'well on the way to extinction' (PEP, 1952: 41) to one producing more than 200 films in 1936 did, at least, lay the foundations for the confident performance of the industry during the 1940s. Although the 1938 legislation had included a 'reciprocity' arrangement whereby the US companies could set British films distributed in America against their quota requirements, this had not led to a significant breakthrough. The war provided a specific opportunity for leaders of the British industry to press the claims of British films on grounds additional to the commercial, with ideological and cultural arguments now to be added in the special conditions of war. The desire to bring British films to American screens still had the same commercial rationale but there was now a need to use this means of communication in the service of the war effort. This meant inter-governmental negotiation of both the terms on which Hollywood films circulated in Britain and the conditions which would give British films easier access to American screens. It also meant a more detailed supervision of the content of British films for the American market to ensure that they conformed to the propaganda requirements of the day. The Ministry of Information considered Ealing's film *The Next of Kin* (1942) problematic in this latter respect, despite the relevance of its 'careless talk costs lives' theme for British audiences. According to David Selznick, whose advice was sought by the ministry, the film depicted 'English officers . . . as stupid, careless and derelict'; furthermore, his advice continued, the message to the American public, and especially to the mothers of US soldiers, was 'that the British are simply muddling along, and that their sons will die because of British incompetence'. Selznick concluded with the view that 'the film could be more profitably run in German for home consumption and for building German morale'. The film was distributed in America in a cut version with an introduction by J. Edgar Hoover, but the episode demonstrated the new complexities of Anglo-US film relationships brought about by the war (Aldgate and Richards, 1994: 112-13; Chapman, 1998: 191; Moorhead, 1984: 147-8).

British cinema was soon drawn into the war effort, with the government, through the Ministry of Information and the Board of Trade, exercising a degree of control over the industry. Films were seen as important for a number of reasons. Through the 1930s the cinema had embedded itself in the leisure life of the nation. Annual cinema admissions had risen from just over 900 million in 1936 to above 1,000 million in 1940 and the figure was to rise to above 1,500 million (Curran and Porter, 1983: 372). Although cinemas were closed at the outbreak of war as a precaution in the event of air raids, they were soon allowed to reopen and were recognized as an important source of domestic morale, a vital form of public relaxation in the stressful conditions of war. Films were also a key communication channel for information about the war and many documentaries and some fiction films fell into the category of war information films addressed to the civilian population and training films for the many varieties of service personnel. Films could also be used to propagandize effectively on behalf of the war effort, explaining the reasons for the conflict and the necessity of resistance, and focusing morale for both the civilian and the service population. In Britain, both the indigenous cinema and the American films which dominated the screen were implicated. As Ian Jarvie has noted: 'The war information function ensured that there was a role for continued British domestic production, both commercial and official, and both fictional and factual. The mass recreation function ensured that there was in addition a role for continued American imports' (1992: 183-4). British films may have to be formulated with the propaganda war in mind while Hollywood films could function in terms of general entertainment. The distinction, of course, was not absolute and many of the films of the time – British and American – blended propaganda and entertainment in a combination often presented as the basis for the rejuvenation of British cinema.

The problem of placing films in the American market still remained, together with a fresh set of constraints on the kinds of films which would be suitable for wartime export. America had moved away from the isolationism of the 1930s, which discouraged films with controversial political subject-matter, and the partisan content necessary in a propaganda film, which may have posed problems in the 1930s, was now acceptable. However, access to the American market was still a matter of complex negotiation with leverage, as previously, dependent partly upon the treatment of Hollywood films in the British market. The British government had imposed restrictions upon dollar remittances to the USA from the British distribution subsidiaries of the large American firms. It was hoped that the Americans would use some of the blocked funds to acquire American distribution rights to British films and thereby facilitate their access to the American market. In order to assist this process, the MOI had appointed Sidney Bernstein, the head of the Granada chain of cinemas, to the post of Films Adviser in the MOI, with a specific brief to liaise with the American industry over the distribution and promotion of British films in the USA. In such conditions the production of films which would have appeal for an American audience posed different problems from those of the 1930s. In many respects, British cinema was forced to address wartime subject-matter first and considerations about the exportability of the films had to be accommodated within those constraints. However, the revival of the British cinema during the war was based on its war pictures and some of these were successful in America. *49th Parallel* (1941) and *In Which We Serve* (1942) were nominated for an Academy Award in the 'best picture' category and awards were won by documentaries such as *Target for Tonight* (1941) and *Desert Victory* (1943).

Post-war British cinema and the American market

After the war, the ambition to penetrate the American market, to compete with Hollywood pictures on their own terms and on their own territory, was revived by the Rank Organization in the context of the growing confidence in the quality of British films. In some respects the way had been prepared by the wartime arrangements – 'the Rota System' - secured by Sidney Bernstein for the release of British films in the USA during the war. Each of the majors had agreed to distribute at least one British feature and some short films per year, ensuring that a small number of British films would achieve a wide circulation in the US (Griffith, 1949: 34). However, unlike wartime, during which the American public was predisposed towards matters British, the immediate post-war period was marked by considerable tension in Anglo-American film relationships. In many respects, it was an opportune time for British films to break into the American market. The Hollywood industry had been deprived of a good part of its European market during the war and the re-establishment of such markets depended upon the rebuilding of the economies in countries such as France, Germany and Italy; even the British market, which had held up during wartime, was vulnerable in the context of the post-war situation. Also, Hollywood was facing the outcome of the protracted anti-trust suit which had been in the legal arena since the late 1930s; demographic and cultural changes were having an effect on leisure habits; and television was lurking as a competitor for the 'entertainment dollar'. In addition to these factors, by the mid-1940s the Rank group itself had developed into a powerful corporation to match the big American firms, and its ownership of two of the three British cinema circuits, to which the Hollywood companies required access, provided a specific advantage in the bargaining with the American majors. As Geoffrey Macnab has noted, the 'newly robust state of the British cinema allied with a fear of recession in the American industry gave (Rank) a strong bargaining position' (1993: 75).

For Rank the American market, the overseas market generally, was essential to the establishment of a strong British production industry. In 1943, he told the union journal – *Cine-Technician* – that it 'is all very well to talk of being able to make good pictures here without bothering about America or world markets, but in all honesty the continued existence of British film production depends on overseas trade' (quoted in Macnab, 1993: 48). Rank's export drive, which began in the middle of the decade, like the previous attempts by Korda and Gaumont British in the 1930s, was unsuccessful despite the occasional success of certain films such as Olivier's Shakespeare films, *Henry V* (1945) and *Hamlet* (1948), and Powell and Pressburger's *The Red Shoes* (1948). The attempt was based partly on the new-found confidence of British film-makers, the critical acclaim won by many of the films of the time and the success of a small number of British films in America; it also required Rank's willingness to finance films on an lavish basis, the formation of distribution alliances with various American companies, and involved a programme of cinema acquisition overseas. However, the attempt was made at a time when Anglo-American film relations reached a new low, culminating in the boycott of the British market by the American majors. The trade press began to carry stories about Rank's plans late in 1943 and one such report promised:

> Up to fifteen feature films annually will be placed upon the American market. This will be accomplished either by a fixed deal or by securing an interest in one or more US companies: Universal, RKO-Radio, United Artists, Columbia or Monogram are the possibilities mentioned. (*Kinematograph Weekly*, 30 December 1943: 3)

Mention of that array of Hollywood companies was a reminder that, although the nature and quality of the films produced within the Rank orbit would be important in determining the success or failure of an export drive, such a drive depended crucially on adequate overseas, especially American, distribution. In the 1930s, Korda's links with United Artists had been important to the promotion of his films in the USA; Gaumont British had established an export organization in America, but Michael Balcon was subsequently to attribute the company's failure to penetrate the market to the lack of a 'sufficiently powerful and effective global selling organization' (1969: 95). Rank clearly wanted to establish a powerful and effective global-selling organization for his films and in February 1944 a new company – Eagle Lion Distributors Ltd. – was registered in London, with key staff recruited from United Artists, with whom Rank had also been discussing distribution plans. However, building a distribution network of offices and personnel in America was 'unrealistically ambitious' (Murphy, 1983: 167) and, although the company eventually established a network of offices in a handful of countries, Rank was obliged to find other partners for his American plans; partners such as Universal, United Artists and Twentieth Century-Fox with substantial experience of film distribution on a global scale and with existing networks of facilities and expertise .

United Artists had distributed British pictures in the USA during the 1930s for Korda and Wilcox The company also had a substantial holding in the Odeon Cinema group, which was part of the Rank empire, and an American distribution arrangement with them seemed an obvious move. At the time of Rank's interest, United Artists were engaged in a boardroom struggle about the position of Alexander Korda. Korda had been appointed to head MGM's British studio in 1943, causing a potential conflict of interest with his membership of the United Artists Board, and was looking to sell his shares. A Rank plan to buy them failed in circumstances which suggest a degree of incompetence on behalf of the American company. As Tino Balio suggested, 'UA's confused management bungled the Korda stock purchase and alienated J. Arthur Rank in the process' (1976: 241). Although Rank did arrive at some accommodation with United Artists over distribution, the company's treatment of films such as *The Life and Death of Colonel Blimp* (1943), *Blithe Spirit* (1945) and *The Way to the Stars* (1945) soon had Rank looking at alternatives. By 1945 he had struck a deal with Universal Pictures, the US company in which Rank was the largest single shareholder, for the future release of his quality pictures. Plans for an associated production company were abandoned but a further deal, between Eagle-Lion and the American distributor, the Producers Releasing Corporation, provided Rank with an additional distribution outlet for lower grade pictures. These moves, together with a projected deal with top independent producer, David Selznick, meant that Rank did make an impression in America. The Rank Organization, by the mid-1940s, was operating on a scale approaching that of a Hollywood major and, Geoffrey Macnab has suggested, Rank's attempt 'to carve British film a sizeable niche of the US market was more thorough, was better financed, and came closer to success than any attempts made on America by his predecessors or, indeed, successors' (1993: 50). Rank came closer but still not close enough. His travels through the USA, his wheeling and dealing with various American companies and his lofty proclamations on behalf of the British film led to a profile in *Life* magazine describing him as 'perhaps the world's biggest movie mogul, in point of capital and facilities under his control' (October 1945: 107). Yet, American commentary was still sceptical about the prospects of a successful British film invasion. *Fortune* suggested that 'Hollywood doubts profoundly that Rank *can* make pictures for the American market' and that 'the Americans are not worried because they think Rank's present power and prestige and hopes are all based on wartime profits' (October 1945: 226; emphasis in original). Certainly, the dramatic growth in the British audience during the war, in a context where Rank had acquired two of the three large exhibition circuits, did much to consolidate the wealth and power of the organization, with much of the profits poured into production on a scale which, at times, outstripped Hollywood. The Gabriel Pascal film, *Caesar and Cleopatra* (1946), in production during Rank's trip to America, was described as a 'prestige' film which required substantial overseas sales to recoup its costs, let alone move into profit. Indeed, it had a bigger budget than comparable Hollywood 'super specials'. Yet, as *Life* commented, the film 'is budgeted at an all-time high of $5,000,000, 20% more than the cost of *Gone with the Wind*, and thus it will be a minor miracle if Rank gets his money back' (October 1945: 121). In fact, in 1948, *Variety* was to report its disappointing returns from America despite a respectable performance in terms of bookings:

> 'Caesar and Cleopatra,' Rank's expensive opus which hit American theatres [*sic*] in mid-1946, was good for $2,000,000 in rentals but proved of minor help to dollar-starved Britain. It's estimated that only $500,000 from 'Caesar' reached England after Technicolor print costs, distribution fees and a whacking $500,000 and more for advertising expenses were deducted. 'Caesar' has copped top bookings to date, a total of 10,000 throughout the country. (17 March 1948: 4)

Nevertheless Rank's developing production and distribution links with America, together with the leverage he derived from his British exhibition interests, appeared to provide him with the kind of platform for an export drive not enjoyed by his predecessors. The general economic situation in post-war Britain, however, moved Anglo-American relationships to a level of crisis and, although Anglo-American film relationships were a small dimension of the general economic problems, Rank became embroiled in a situation where his control was limited. The 'dollar crisis' of 1947 prompted the government to devise measures to cut down on imports from America and to boost exports. Ironically, Rank's export ambitions suited government policy perfectly, although American scepticism about the prospects for British pictures in the USA appeared to be justified and 'British pictures were performing abysmally in the States' (Macnab, 1993: 163).

An 'original' British cinema

André Bazin saw British films made in the immediate post-war period as signalling 'the appearance of a British cinema that was original and free from the influences of Hollywood' (1968: 33). A. L. Vargas, writing in *The Penguin Film Review*, regarded films produced during the war, including *In Which We Serve*, *The Way Ahead* (1944) and *The Way to the Stars*, as evidence of 'the emergence of an artistically mature British cinema' (1949, 8: 71). Critical opinion in the pages of the broadsheet newspapers, intellectual journals such as the *New Statesman* and the *Spectator* and specialist publications such as *Sight and Sound* and *The Penguin Film Review* developed the notion of the 'quality' film characterized by a range of features including 'adult' and 'humanistic' themes, emotional restraint, attention to naturalistic detail, stylistic and narrative coherence, an ensemble of qualities converging on the somewhat elastic conceptions of 'realism' inherited from the wartime pictures. Exemplary films included *Brief Encounter* (1945) and *Odd Man Out* (1947), the literary adaptations, *Henry V* and *Great Expectations* (1946), together with other films emerging mainly from the various independent companies organized under the umbrella of the Rank group. Indeed, the 'quality film adventure' (Ellis, 1996), was very much bound up with the somewhat liberal production policies implemented by Rank in the mid-1940s. The putative 'renaissance' also coincided with the Rank attempt to penetrate the American market, but the performance of the Rank portfolio in the immediate post-war period indicated less of an impact on American audiences than that envisaged by those who saw the British industry engaging with Hollywood in head-to-head competitive terms. The scale and ambition of *Caesar and Cleopatra* has been noted as comparable with the Hollywood 'prestige' productions, yet its performance in the American market was not encouraging, despite being booked into theatres on a scale 'equal to that achieved by the average "A" picture from Hollywood' (Griffith, 1949: 34) and registering record grosses of $2 million for a British film (Balio, 1976: 220). The mass distribution of a film was a costly business which the major Hollywood companies could sustain because of the economies of scale involved in the mass production of films. The modest number of prestige productions coming from the Rank group were unlikely to succeed on such a basis.

However, the mass distribution appropriate for the Hollywood film was not the only way in which foreign films could insert themselves into the American market and impress themselves upon American audiences. Olivier's *Henry V* opened in specifically rented legitimate theatres, on a 'road show' basis', with its characteristic playing venue being the small art cinema in the big cities, rather than the traditional big city first-run opening and subsequent second and third run booking practice that was at the heart of the Hollywood system. Spearheaded by other foreign films, notably Rossellini's *Roma, città aperta* (US title: *Open City*; 1945) and *Paisà* (US title: *Paisan*; 1946), the art film became a minor but important feature of the American cinema experience, existing alongside the more traditional Hollywood diet of genres and blockbusters, and aiming at a more specialized audience drawn from the intelligentsia and the college communities; the pattern was repeated in many cities, indicating an alternative and maybe more appropriate way of presenting British films to American audiences. It was a strategy based upon a patient approach to building a public for a film, as opposed to the fanfare approach of the big city first run. The big city opening in a lavish Picture Palace was enormously expensive and was not a viable proposition for the British film. As Richard Griffith commented on *Henry V*:

> Had the film opened in any of the large Broadway houses, the vast overhead entailed would have forced its closing after a run of one or, at the most, two weeks. But the small theatres, with relatively high admission prices and relatively low operating costs could keep it going indefinitely, holding it through

temporary box-office slumps until its reputation had spread. Before it ended its run here, *Henry V* had become a New York institution. Its success was repeated throughout the country, wherever it was shown in small houses, at high prices, and for long runs. (1950: 39)

What British critics referred to as the 'quality' film tended to find a market in America as an 'art' film targeted quite specifically at a niche audience. For such films, the 'college audience' was of major importance and Prestige Pictures, the distribution offshoot of Universal set up to handle Rank's 'art' films, actively sought to sell such pictures through the university and college circuits as well as through art cinemas (*Variety*, 24 July 1946: 29). Using another approach indicative of the selective release of such pictures, *Henry V* was marketed using the subscription list of the Theatre Guild and presented 'under the banner: "The Theatre Guild presents Henry V" ' (*Variety*, 19 May 1948: 18; Griffith, 1950: 39). After its initial success during which the film earned a net profit of $700,000 after a limited number of road showings, the trade press reported that United Artists were 'planning also to continue the college town barnstorming, which has proved exceptionally popular' (*Variety*, 1 January 1947: 5). The focus upon audiences for a respectable and prestigious cultural form, the targeting of university towns, indicated a different set of cultural aspirations in respect of the target public and a move away from the 'mass audience' traditionally sought in the commercial cinema. As Arthur Knight suggested, the 'campaign for *Henry V* pre-shadowed a new form of film promotion designed to attract this non-habitual movie-goer, a special selling for special films' (1953: 192).

There was also an age dimension to the definition of the 'non-habitual movie-goer', with industry surveys indicating that the post-war film audience was beginning to be dominated by the under-30s. The film industry began to explore alternatives to the traditional Hollywood formulae as a method of attracting older people into cinemas. As *Variety* reported, some Hollywood executives 'feel that careful checking of foreign-lingo, semi-documentaries, "adult films" and other product deviating from the norm should be made to determine whether the same heavy proportion of youngsters is attracted to these. If not, Hollywood may swing further in that direction' (14 April 1948: 14). *Brief Encounter* also opened at a New York art house where it ran for eight months. Its status as an art film was endorsed by its success at the Cannes Film Festival in 1946 where it won the critics' prize; it also registered in more conventional commercial terms with David Lean's nomination in the Best Director category of the Academy Awards for the same year. In some respects, British films of this period, although marketed as art films, were also considered alongside the Hollywood mainstream, winning Academy Awards as well as prestigious European festival acclaim. *Hamlet* (1948), for example, won the Academy's Best Picture award in 1948 as well as the Venice Film Festival's International Grand Prize; in 1949 Carol Reed was nominated as best director for *The Third Man* (1949) which won the critics' prize at Cannes. The term 'art film' is, of course, multi-layered, and usually defined in terms which separate it out from the Hollywood mainstream film. The term connotes a set of narrative and stylistic protocols, meandering open-ended stories, thematic ambiguity, variants of 'realism', underwritten by a strong sense of the film director as author, of films which betray 'the urgency of individual expression, an independence of vision, the coherence of a single-minded statement', in the words of Arthur Knight (Mayer, 1965: vii). It also presupposes a different conception of audience as 'college-educated, middle-class cinéphiles looking for films consonant with contemporary ideas of modernism in art and literature' (Bordwell, 1985: 230), and is associated with a distinctive exhibition venue, the 'art house', physically distinct from the Picture Palaces in which Hollywood displayed its wares. 'Art houses' date back to the 1920s when they developed in Europe out of, and in relation to, the film society and cine-club movements. Some European films circulated in America during the period, and there were attempts to set up 'art cinemas' for this purpose. Key European films of the time such as *The Cabinet of Dr Caligari* (1919) and *October* (1928) were screened but the attempts to establish art cinemas were not successful. European films screened in their original language did find a home in 'foreign language theatres', established not to bring 'art' to the intellectual classes, but to meet the demands of specific ethnic communities in particular neighbourhoods (Gomery, 1992: Ch. 9). The rise of art cinema exhibition in America was a post-war phenomenon, with the 1950s witnessing a surge in the number of venues devoting themselves to this kind of film. As one history of cinema puts it:

> As of 1950, there were fewer than 100 art theatres in the entire country, but by the mid-1960s, there were over 600, most in cities and college towns. They were usually small, independent houses decorated in a modernist style calculated to appeal to an educated elite. (Thompson and Bordwell, 1994: 384)

Such a development can be related to a number of factors, including the structural changes in Hollywood brought about by divorcement, the changing conditions in the international film industry and to post-war cultural changes which affected the cinema audience. With no guaranteed theatre outlet for their product, the major companies reduced their production schedules, concentrating upon big budget pictures for first-run cinemas. The space for foreign, including British, films to get access to at least a small part of the American market was a fortuitous consequence of the shifting strategies of the major companies faced with the loss of their theatre chains. As Michael Mayer commented:

> Unwittingly, a great favor was done for foreign films. Numerous theatres in the 50's found themselves without pictures. Some took the easy way and were transformed into bowling alleys and supermarkets. But other, hardier exhibitors turned to the flood of foreign films available from around the world. (1965: 3)

Indeed, British films marketed as 'art' films had the added advantage of requiring no sub-titling. Other circumstances also played a role in the flow of films from outside the USA. Many countries, including Britain, had placed restrictions on the amount of money earned by Hollywood films overseas that could be remitted to the USA. The British arrangements allowed American companies to pay for British films to be imported to the USA out of their 'frozen coin', thus providing another reason for the growth of this market. The use of art films can also be seen as a minor aspect of the industry's attempts to differentiate their provision from that of television. The major companies were developing wide-screen processes, stereophonic sound and the blockbuster film to lure audiences away from the small screen, offering them the experience of spectacle; the art cinema offered a range of subject-matter, particularly in the realm of adult human experience, which the television could not broach. It was a cinema of significant content addressed to an educated audience and its success reflected the growing consciousness of European life and culture, in particular in the post-war period of growing American influence in global affairs.

How did the British film insert itself into such a market? As the art film developed in the 1950s, it became very much identified with Continental Europe, with France, Italy and Sweden, or with Japan, rather than Britain; with Godard, Fellini and Bergman, with Mizoguchi and Ozu, rather than David Lean or Carol Reed. The 1940s and early 1950s titles which circulated as art films included the Shakespeare adaptations, *Henry V* and *Hamlet*, *Brief Encounter*, Powell and Pressburger's *I Know Where I'm Going* (1945), the portmanteau film *Quartet* (1948), adapted from stories by Somerset Maugham, Carol Reed's *The Fallen Idol* (1948), *The Gay Lady* (British title: *Trottie True*; 1949), *The Hidden Room* (British title: *Obsession*; 1949.), *The Lavender Hill Mob* (1951) and *The Man in the White Suit* (1951). A range of films, adaptations of classic and modern authors, thrillers, historical costume pictures, Ealing comedies, locatable in the mainstream of British cinema but circulating in American film culture as specialized fare for the niche art house audience. The notion of an 'art cinema' was subsequently codified in terms – narrative, stylistic – drawn from a rather different set of films and based upon cinematic qualities approached only in a tangential fashion by some of the British pictures. The phenomenon of *The Lavender Hill Mob* as an art film, for example, is a reminder that cinematic categories can be based upon extra-textual factors, including exhibition networks through which a film circulates. The example of the foreign, including the British, art film of the 1940s and 1950s circulating in the US market suggests a process of 'cultural transformation'. The British material, including staples from Britain's domestic mainstream cinema, was transformed in some respects from routine commercial fare to a rung or so up on the cultural scale in its passage from Britain to the USA. The post-war period in American life was marked by a surge of cultural aspiration among many sections of the American public, fostered in part by the increasing access to higher education. Cultural ranking became an important feature of the American self-consciousness and this had repercussions on the cinema, the most widespread cultural and artistic experience of all. It has been argued that the foreign film, including the British, was a beneficiary of this for at 'a time when issues of taste became a major arbiter of status in society, foreign films offered a relatively accessible form of "high culture" and European art for middlebrow audiences' (Wilinsky, 1997: 22). This process was aided by the enthusiasm of American critics for foreign films and in 1947 many of the leading critics, such as Bosley Crowther, included a significant number of such films on their 'ten best' films for the year. *Henry V*, *Brief Encounter* and *Stairway to Heaven* (British title: *A Matter of Life and Death*; 1946) were among the British titles included, yet British films were not quite the same as their French and Italian counterparts; there were many differences between them and European titles such as Rossellini's *Roma, città aperta* and Pagnol's *La Fille du puisatier* (US title: *The Well-Digger's Daughter*; 1940.), which also figured on the lists. The leading British producer – Rank – was part-owner of an American major, Universal, and a prominent producer such as Alexander Korda had long-standing links with United Artists; access to the American market could be helped by these institutional links.

In addition, British films were more comprehensible to American audiences and could circulate more widely than their European counterparts. As Barbara Wilinsky has commented:

> Though foreign-language films played almost exclusively in art houses, British films, if only because they did not require subtitles for their U.S. audiences, had more opportunities for mainstream theatrical exhibition. On a very practical and basic level, British films used English dialogue, and although audiences complained about the lack of stars, the 'longhair themes' and the accents in British movies, these films did not require the subtitles or dubbed dialogue which made foreign-language films less appealing to U.S. audiences. (1997: 22-3)

The opportunities for mainstream theatrical exhibition were better for British films compared with those from Europe but even they were not perceived as entirely suitable for the mass audience. The language may have been a shared one but accents constituted a problem. As *Variety* reported:

> Primary point was that British films are still not intelligible enough for Yank audiences. Several company prexies declared that it took them 25-30 minutes of a British pic before they could understand what was being said. (5 May 1948: 5)

The art house audience was a different proposition. The Rank campaign to secure a foothold in the American market, like the Gaumont British campaign of the 1930s, was targeted at the mass American audience and attempted direct competition with the expensive Hollywood film. However, something of a successful foothold was gained by what the trade press termed 'lesser pix', mainly, though not exclusively, in the art house market aimed at the niche audience. The British film, though 'foreign' in some respects, was not too distant from American culture and, indeed, was a kindred culture in terms of history; it was, though, different enough to carry the kudos associated with a well-established traditional culture and, despite accent differences, the films did derive advantage from the commonalities of the shared language. However, the qualities which differentiated such films from Hollywood pictures and provided a specific appeal to certain sectors of the American public in the post-war period were just as likely to be available in moderately budgeted films as in spectaculars. In 1951, *Variety* ran a story titled 'British Films In U.S. Advance' which reflected upon the irony of the situation in which the Rank enterprise was more successful in America when producing lower budget pictures:

> British pix, which scarcely made a dent in the American market during the heavy postwar campaign of J. Arthur Rank to secure a U.S. beachhead, are being seen by more Yanks now than ever before. They've made a quiet but very steady advance in patronage over the past few years.
> . . . the British for the first time are really coining profits out of the American market. Four of five years ago, when Rank was making his big push, he was spending a tremendous amount of money for advertising, selling and maintenance of an organization in the U.S. Now he has nothing but a skeleton staff, and every pic in distribution represents a profit of some sort to the producer. (7 November 1951: 7, 25)

One further factor which affected the British film in America was the sale of films to television. The major Hollywood companies were initially reluctant to lease their films to television; as one writer has put it, 'the established Hollywood motion picture industry had sufficient economic and legal reasons not to release its vast film libraries to television' (Lafferty, 1990: 236). The majors were embroiled in negotiations with various film industry unions – the American Federation of Musicians, the Screen Actors Guild, the Screen Directors Guild, the Writers Guild of America – over their members' financial rights in respect of the television broadcast of films. Television screening of feature films appeared to threaten the interests of cinema exhibitors and there was a considerable lobby from that sector against the sale of films to television. Also, the economics of television release compared to theatrical re-release came down on the side of the latter, thus removing what might have been a prime incentive for the Hollywood majors to bargain their assets away to their small screen competitor. A final reason was the majors' own ambitions to establish themselves in the television industry, either through schemes such as theatre television or subscription television, or through the ownership and operation of television stations. The television industry itself was interested in feature films as part of their programming but, according to William Lafferty:

> Many within broadcasting believed that television's 'immediacy', anchored in live programming, was its aesthetic essence. As a result of this attitude, the networks and even individual stations focused their energies into developing formats and genres compatible with live-origination, particularly variety, sports, audience participation, and dramatic programming, both daytime 'soap operas' and evening 'serious' drama. (1990: 236)

Although this situation was to alter in the mid-1950s, the initial interest in feature-film programming for television was met from two very different sources – B-pictures from independent Hollywood companies, and foreign films. The foreign films situated in the cinema world as 'prestige' and 'art' pictures, brought those qualities to the world of television. The B-studios offered low-budget, low-brow entertainment exemplified by the Western genre, but the foreign picture, with its 'high' or at least 'middlebrow' cultural status, represented an attempt by television to provide programming on a higher cultural level. British films, for the reasons which made them more accessible to American cinema audiences, were of especial interest to television companies wishing to fill their schedules, and both Rank and Korda, the leading British producers, were involved with television negotiations for their films in the late 1940s.

In 1948, *Variety* carried a report of discussions between David Sarnoff, board chairman of RCA which owned the NBC television network, and J. Arthur Rank. As part of a proposed deal Sarnoff was reported as offering to play trailers on television for new Rank releases without charge. This, he claimed, would 'go a long way towards popularizing the Anglo imports with American audiences' (*Variety*, 28 April 1948: 3). In the same year, Korda sold the broadcast rights to films such as *The Private Life of Henry VIII* and *The Ghost Goes West* (1936) to a New York television station, WPIX. There were a number of reasons for British producers to sell their material to television. Both Rank and Korda had over-extended themselves on the production front in the context of the short-lived US embargo on film exports to Britain. When Hollywood resumed its film supply, the opportunities for both producers were, once again, limited. Also, although some British films were gradually getting established in the American market by way of the art cinema circuit, the major breakthrough to the mass US market was not happening. There were some big hits, such as *The Red Shoes* in 1948, but not the consistent penetration that the American industry had in Britain. Indeed, it has been suggested that the sales to television policy would be extended to embrace new releases as well as the archive collections as a bargaining counter to address the difficulties British producers encountered in getting their films on American screens. *Variety* quoted Korda as saying 'Rank and I will turn our films over to television if we cannot get theatre bookings. We'll see how the American picture industry likes that' (quoted in Wilinsky, 1997: 27). The threat, however, was never carried out. Foreign films, including those from Britain, made some inroads in the American market both through the art houses and by way of television. However, these were limited gains. The art houses were confined to New York and other large American cities and reached a relatively small and elite part of the US audience; the television screenings had a similar reach, with the earliest audiences for the medium coming from the upper-income brackets. The Rank and Korda films were initially presented as quality material, but the 'influx of British films both into theaters (as a result of the Anglo-U.S. trade agreement) and onto television seemed to decrease their status in the United States, changing their value for people searching for distinction' (Wilinsky, 1997: 27).

By the early 1950s, the British film industry was retrenching. The Rank group abandoned its international ambitions and was settling into a more modest pattern of production, including nostalgic war films and Norman Wisdom comedies, while the other large company, the Associated British Picture Corporation, concentrated on crime pictures and comedies but did include a small number of significant and successful war films such as *Angels One Five* (1952) and *The Dam Busters* (1955). Ealing had established a niche partly with its comedies but also with its dramas, including *The Blue Lamp* (1950) and *Mandy* (1952), and it continued to the middle of the decade with its modest annual output of around four or five films. The newly formed National Film Finance Corporation lent its assistance to the industry and became involved with a large number of films during the decade. As has been noted previously, 'runaway' productions – American films made in Britain and qualifying as 'British' for exhibitor quota registration – did establish a pattern of breaking into the US market. In a narrow technical sense, the international ambitions of Korda, Balcon and Rank were fulfilled by films such as *The African Queen* and *The Bridge on the River Kwai*. Another runaway, *Captain Horatio Hornblower R. N.,* based upon a C. S. Forrester novel, was one of the top US box-office performers for 1951. The film celebrated British naval prowess during the Napoleonic wars and although the cast did include a number of British actors, such as James Robertson Justice and Stanley Baker, the eponymous hero and the romantic lead were played by top American stars Gregory Peck and Virginia Mayo respectively, and the film was directed by the veteran American action specialist, Raoul Walsh. To call it a 'British' film is to acknowledge the cultural and historical character of the subject-matter, yet, rather than belonging to any specific strand in British cinema, the film is better regarded either as part of the genre of 'British' Hollywood traceable back to the 1930s, or to the evolving genre of 'international historical epics financed by the Hollywood majors' (Harper, 1994: 180).

The 1970s

The US withdrawal from the British production industry began towards the end of the 1960s and, although the impact had been felt earlier with the diminishing number of US-financed films in production, the single emblematic event was the closure of the MGM studios at Borehamwood in 1970. As with the other majors, the British-produced MGM films were not proving successful and sustaining studios in both Britain and America was considered an unnecessary drain for the company. MGM did agree to a co-financing deal with EMI, the new owners of the Associated British Picture Corporation, and, indeed, moved their modern equipment to the adjacent EMI–Elstree studio. Yet, the bulk of American financing had disappeared and, as Alexander Walker commented, the decade 'ended on a jittery note, much hanging on Elstree's film production programme, on non-major American companies, and on the self-help efforts of few remaining British independent producers or groups' (1974: 478). The British cinema moved into the new decade without the US backing which had sustained it during the 1960s. The American cinema was undergoing a crisis of its own and living through a period of structural change. The enormous success of *The Sound of Music* in 1965 had lured the studios into a big-budget 'blockbuster' phase which 'led to a number of very costly mistakes and a cycle of overproduction that nearly bankrupted several of the major companies' (Maltby, 1995: 74). In addition, a number of the majors had been, or were in the process of being, absorbed into conglomerate companies. The rejuvenation of the American film was to be achieved in the late 1960s with the success of moderately budgeted films such as *Bonnie and Clyde* (1967), *The Graduate* (1967) and, an extremely successful low-budget picture, *Easy Rider* (1969). Such films ushered in a somewhat parsimonious phase in the financing of Hollywood films before the 'blockbuster' syndrome reasserted itself in the mid-1970s after the success of films such as *The Godfather* (1972) and *Jaws* (1975).

There was much talk of crisis in the British industry, although John Boulting took a somewhat different line on the prospects for production in the changed financial situation following the US withdrawal:

> I take a different view to others on this so-called crisis. I don't believe it *is* a crisis, in a sense. In the same way that if a human being lives in a fantasy world, ignoring reality for five to seven years, and then emerges from the fantasy – that is the first step in a cure, not a crisis. (Mayne, 1970: 203)

Events were returning the British production industry to a realistic situation in which the rebuilding of the industry would have to be based on indigenous efforts rather than the external investment that had sustained the industry during the 1960s. The replacement investment was to come from Elstree, as Walker had noted, together with a newcomer to film from the world of television. The conglomerate movement in America was echoed in the British film industry with the EMI group's take-over of the Associated British Picture Corporation while the other major – Rank – had begun the process of diversification earlier. There were new names among the most influential executives particularly the brothers Lew Grade and Bernard Delfont. Delfont was head of EMI's film division during the 1970s while his brother, Lew Grade, was the force behind the film production programme of ATV, the largest of the regional commercial television stations, which had owned studio premises at Elstree since 1962. These companies were, at different times in the decade, to mount ambitious production programmes aimed at the international market, and, as was usual in the industry, to become entangled in various ways with the American industry. Despite John Boulting's hint that the new conditions of the 1970s prompted by the withdrawal of US finance would bring a new realism to the industry, the shaping force remained transatlantic, even if more of the finance was generated internally. The traditional goal of the large British production company – penetration of the American market – was to reassert itself, especially in the second half of the decade. At the same time, the prospects for the independent film-maker deteriorated somewhat with various ownership battles over the independents' flagship British Lion and its Shepperton studio. The company was run by Michael Deeley and Barry Spikings in the difficult years of the early 1970s and in 1976 it was taken over by EMI primarily to enable the company to obtain the business skill and acumen of its management duo (A. Walker, 1985: 142). In the British film industry, a determined ambitious assault on the American market seems to be an inevitable consequence of industrial reconfiguration. The establishment of the large combines following the 1927 Quota Act led to the bold Gaumont British programme of the 1930s, the emergence of the Rank group led to the mid-1940s attempt to challenge Hollywood and the restructuring of the industry in the late 1960s, with the EMI take-over of ABPC and the shift from television to film by the Grade interests, led to further attempts to create a British cinema with international ambition. In 1978, the two companies jointly established Associated Film Distributors to handle the American distribution of a promised twenty-plus films per year for a four-year period (A. Walker, 1985: 201). Previous attempts at breaking into the American market by Gaumont British and Rank had also involved the setting up of distribution companies in America.

By the time that he embarked upon international film production, Lew Grade had established substantial credentials in the media world based on the success of ATV and of ITC, the company set up by the Associated Communication Corporation for the production of television series. He had already acquired plenty of experience of selling television programmes to the Americans, including major successes such as *The Saint* and *The Avengers*, and, in Alexander Walker's words, used 'the TV-based corporation in the same way as a Hollywood studio used its production record' (1985: 106). Grade's television track record was used as a means of persuading investors that his film production ventures were based on sound and proven business expertise in the entertainment industry and his television activities enabled a relatively straightforward transition to international US-orientated film production. As Jeremy Tunstall has suggested:

> Lew Grade increasingly from the later 1960s used his ATV commercial licence and his own previous American experience to become an 'offshore' production company for American network television – these shows used American stars, American production styles and (as a result of, or in anticipation of, American sales) American sized-budgets. (1977: 101-2)

Over the decade, Grade was involved in the production of around one hundred films, including *Moses the Lawgiver* (1975), *The Return of the Pink Panther* (1976), *The Cassandra Crossing* (1976), *March or Die* (1976), *The Medusa Touch* (1978), *Escape to Athena* (1979), *Green Ice* (1981) and *Raise the Titanic* (1980), using a range of American and European stars such as Burt Lancaster, Ava Gardner, Ryan O'Neal, Roger Moore, David Niven, Sophia Loren, Omar Sharif, Richard Burton and Alec Guinness. Critical opinion of the films has been hard, with one writer describing them as 'rootless productions of no relevance to any nation, lacking purpose or passion' (J. Walker, 1985: 45). In addition to his production and associated distribution activities, Grade also acquired the Classic cinema chain, creating a vertically integrated combine to compete with the EMI and Rank groups, though it was a short-lived venture which was effectively dismantled in 1981. The *coup de grâce* was delivered by the failure of *Raise the Titanic*, with the name of the ill-fated ocean liner providing journalists and commentators with 'a general metaphor for the fate of Lord Grade's huge communications empire' (A. Walker, 1985: 203).

EMI began the 1970s with a number of production strands and a less focused policy, and looked to experience within the film industry itself for its management team. Film director and actor, Bryan Forbes was appointed to organize a production programme of modestly budgeted 'quality' films, while a subsidiary company, Anglo-EMI, was responsible for TV spin-offs such as *On the Buses* (1971) and *Steptoe and Son* (1972). EMI-MGM productions was set up in conjunction with the American company when they closed their British studio. Forbes left the company in 1971, with responsibilities for the entire production schedule shifting to Nat Cohen, head of Anglo-EMI. It was Cohen who produced the Agatha Christie adaptation *Murder on the Orient Express* (1974), a box-office hit both in Britain and America which encouraged the company to set its sights on the American market; it was, however, the management team of Deeley and Spikings, brought to EMI with the take-over of British Lion in 1976, that supervised the company's strategic attempt to break into the American market. In addition to part-financing from American sources, some of the films made by EMI, such as *The Deer Hunter*, *Convoy* and *The Driver* from their 1978 schedule, were actually made in America and, indeed, were American films from the cultural perspective. In fact, this strategy was seen as paving the way for a more sustained indigenously based production programme underpinned by American finance. As Michael Deeley suggested to Alexander Walker:

> We are now more heavily committed to making movies in America than some of the traditional powers of Hollywood like MGM or Warners are just now. Our show of strength will increase the willingness of Americans to come in on films we shall soon be making in Britain. (1985: 195)

EMI had run into serious financial difficulties by this time. *Honky Tonk Freeway* (1981), which started life as a low-budget project, had escalated in the production process to a $26 million film. It was not quite the $34 million of *Raise the Titanic* but the impact was similar, contributing to the industry abandoning 'the attempt to beat Hollywood at its own game' (Hill, 1999: 40). However, the experience did not quite quell the international ambitions among relative newcomers to the industry and the subsequent decade saw the rise and fall of Goldcrest, *Chariots of Fire* (1981) with its four Oscars and what some saw as a renaissance in the British film, partly in terms of the intermittent success of 'heritage' pictures in the international market, including *Chariots of Fire* itself, and a number of films from the Merchant Ivory production team, such as *A Room with a View* (1985). The targeting of the American market seems a constant in British thinking about the role of cinema after around one hundred years of American audiences responding positively to the occasional British film, but, like their British counterparts, preferring the Hollywood product for their regular entertainment experience. However, if the British film has not always fared well in America, there is a sense that British life and culture, the country's literature and history, have found a positive response among American audiences, especially when filtered through the conventions of the American film. The next two chapters will consider this phenomenon.

6 Adaptation: Literature, History, Film

Although British or English films have made an intermittent impression on American audiences, sometimes capturing large audiences, sometimes circulating through specialist cinemas, more often than not they have been seen as failing to provide the entertainment qualities of the Hollywood picture. A 1930s memo from Warner Bros. New York sales manager to Jack Warner about a film with English subject-matter may be taken as indicative:

> The reaction to the title *The Private Lives of Elizabeth and Essex* is extremely bad. I am getting letters of protest from every part of the country and my own people tell me that wherever they go exhibitors are objecting to this title. They say it smacks of Alexander Korda and that in the south, mid-west and small towns particularly, it will be confused with an English picture, which as you know do very little business especially in small towns. (Behlmer, 1986: 100)

The fears of the executive centred upon the possible association with the 'English picture' in general, through its echoing of the Korda titles such as *The Private Life of Henry VIII* (1933) and *The Private Life of Don Juan* (1934). Yet the problem was not with the English subject-matter. Indeed, British culture – its literary heritage, aspects of its history – was eagerly embraced by Hollywood film-makers as a rich storehouse of material for adaptation to the Hollywood film. Although 'British' and 'English' are frequently used interchangeably in discussion of the cultural sources drawn upon by Hollywood, the range of material used by the studios, especially during the 1930s when many of the 'Hollywood British' films were made, embraces English, Scottish, Irish and Welsh literature and history. 'British' subject-matter, then, has formed the basis of many very successful pictures from the early days but subject to the transforming processes of Hollywood film production, subject to a logic that derives from the nature of a large-scale industrial institution producing mass and popular culture for Americans in the first instance, but for an international audience as well, an international audience within which Britain had a key place.

Adaptation and narrative

The early cinema in America and elsewhere, the 'primitive cinema' as it is sometimes called, was characterized by a range of genres – actualities, travel films, trick and comic films, visual newspapers, war reconstructions, sporting events – based on the documentary capacities of the medium. There were also brief story films based on scenes from plays, on crime incidents, on historical episodes, on popular song lyrics and on traditional fairy and folk stories. These early 'narratives', which constituted only a small part of the overall production profile, depended for their intelligibility on the audience's prior knowledge of their subject-matter through familiarity with 'well-known stories, comic strips or popular songs'. Apart from some notable exceptions such as the films of Méliès, they did not have the 'self-sufficient' character of 'most contemporaneous literature and theatre, where it was assumed that audiences had no foreknowledge of the narrative's plot, characters, etc.' (Musser, 1990b: 257-8). Other strategies, such as the spoken accompaniment from a lecturer, could be employed to render the early narratives comprehensible, but their relationship to their familiar source material was of considerable importance. However, as Robert C. Allen has noted, the generic profile changed substantially in the period from around 1904 to 1908:

> Prior to 1904, American movie screens were shared by a number of different types of films: news films, reproductions or recreations of news events, trick films, travelogues, comic vignettes and dramatic narratives. By 1908, however, the narrative film, especially the dramatic narrative, had all but pushed documentary films out of the nickelodeons and vaudeville houses, a remarkable change in the functional orientation of American cinema. (1977: 12-13)

In the context of the shift to narrative, the adaptation of pre-existing material drawn from popular literature, drama and painting, the Bible, newspaper stories, history, folk-tale and myth was soon to become commonplace as a strategy for film manufacturers seeking to meet the increasing demand for film entertainment. The actuality-based picture was relegated to the margins of the new film-based entertainment industry although, in the eyes of many historians, it had made a substantial contribution to the development of the film narrative and, in particular, to film editing (see, for example, Bottomore, 1990: 104-13). The development of the 'story film' into the characteristic product of the new industry is linked with the increase in demand for film entertainment and, in particular, with the advent of the nickelodeon around 1905 which established the film as the central feature of a new entertainment and leisure experience – 'going to the pictures'. Prior to this, films had circulated through a variety of venues as an aspect of the general amusement programme of the fairground and the circus, or as an element of the modular vaudeville show. The nickelodeon placed film at the centre of the stage and, as Eileen Bowser has suggested, 'it was the emergence of the story film, in 1904-1906, that drew people to the nickelodeons. Even though greater numbers of actuality films were still being produced at that time, many more copies of story films were sold' (1990: 53). The daily change of programme soon adopted by the nickelodeons generated a voracious demand for new product and the main American companies responded. The Biograph Company, 'the first in the United States, if not the world, to make the decisive shift toward fiction "feature" films' (Musser, 1990: 375), embarked upon a production programme of story films in 1904. Others followed and, although innovations such as stars and the long feature film did not become established until the years of the First World War, the industry quickly settled into the production of the fictional story film as its primary activity.

Explanations for the shift to the story film and to different forms of narration are various, embracing a range of social, cultural, moral and economic reasons. It has been argued that the increasingly varied ethnic origins of the urban population, the result of immigration, meant that the nickelodeon audience lacked the common frame of reference constituted by fairy tales and popular songs from the indigenous culture, which gave 'primitive cinema' its fund of subject matter. This prompted a move towards the 'self-sufficient' narrative characteristic of classical cinema with its accessibility, its repetitions, its high level of signifying redundancy, which made it suitable for a broad audience with diverse cultural frames of reference (Bowser, 1990: 54). Other historians have drawn attention to the cinema's quest for respectability in these early years. The narrative templates drawn from theatre and literature appeared to provide a measure of respectability and maturity for a form of entertainment which had become associated with the chronic ills of city life and with the impoverished urban working classes. The shift has been related to the industry's attempts to attract a middle-class audience and, as Tom Gunning has suggested, one way of achieving this was to shift to a different source material for narrative films:

> The narrative structure of the films would have to be brought more in line with the traditions of bourgeois representation. One of the clearest signs of this is the films made in 1908-9 based on famous plays, novels and poems. Before 1908, the primary sources for films seem to have been vaudeville and burlesque sketches, fairy-tales, comic strips and popular songs. These forms stressed spectacular effects or physical action, rather than psychological motivation. Although still in an elementary form, film now looked towards more respectable narrative models and the problems they entailed. (1990: 339-40)

Yet, the shifts in the form, style and subject-matter of the films have to be set within the significant structural changes that the industry underwent during the years immediately before the First World War consequent upon the formation of the Motion Picture Patents Company in 1908 and the stabilization of the industry. Film exchanges had replaced the less efficient outright film sales methods of the earlier period, and the nickelodeon had established itself as the characteristic venue for film entertainment. The demand for film was considerable and, in order to meet the increasing demands of the exhibitors with their daily programme changes, the manufacturing branch of the industry was obliged to put film-making on to a rational basis and to move to the 'systematic mass production' of narrative films (Bordwell *et al.*, 1985: 130). The narrative film, based on the continuity principles associated with film-makers such as

Porter and Griffith, might be seen as one method of achieving a regular, controlled and predictable approach to the supply of films which could be centralized and managed according to factory principles. Actualities depended upon chance events and required mobile camera forces scattered throughout the country and, indeed, the world, making planning and control difficult from the business point of view. In the competition between film modes for primary place in the evolving world of cinema entertainment and the nickelodeon, the narrative film, as Charles Musser has argued, was adopted for many reasons, including the raising of the cultural status of the industry, but 'standardization, narrative efficiency, and the maximization of profits were among the most crucial determinants' (1990b: 272). The precise form of narrative which developed drew upon artistic qualities such as character individuation and varying perspectives and viewpoint on the pro-filmic material, that is to say strategies which may be linked to pre-existing literary and dramatic forms. As film form evolved features such as spectacle, drawn from the countervailing artistic trends of the 'primitive' cinema, blended with the literary qualities to produce the variable narrative form known as 'classical cinema'. Also important in the promotion of literature as cinematic source-material was the advent of the 'feature film' – the long picture – and the 'evidence overwhelmingly supports a connection between the famous play, novel, and story adapted into film and the increasing length of the product' (Bordwell *et al.*, 1985: 131). Adaptation of one sort or another became an integral part of the system of production as the industry developed from the cottage industry of the early years to the big business of Hollywood's 'golden age'.

Hollywood, adaptation and mass culture

The Hollywood feature film is a major constituent of mass art, a cultural phenomenon which has been defined by Noël Carroll in terms of three key characteristics. Firstly, mass art enjoys the status of 'art' in terms of most conventional definitions of the term; secondly, mass art is produced and delivered to audiences by mass-media technologies; and, thirdly, mass art is designed in form and content to ensure ease of comprehension and accessibility to a 'indefinitely large, undifferentiated' audience (1998: 184ff.). The Hollywood film is a work of art in the sense that it possesses many of the qualities associated with generally acknowledged artistic practices and, indeed, can be seen as clearly aligned in certain respects with traditional art forms such as literature and drama. Although Hollywood films are often denied the status of 'art' by critics working within evaluative models of cultural production, as Carroll has suggested, 'there is no question that mass art would count as art in terms of the leading *classificatory* approaches' (1998: 197-8, emphasis in original). The second characteristic – production and delivery through mass-media technologies such as cameras and projectors – is uncontentious; and the third – ease of comprehension and accessibility – enables a distinction to be drawn between different kinds of film art which share the technological delivery base. For example, an avant-garde film from Derek Jarman or Peter Greenaway, although sharing the technological production and delivery base of a Hollywood film, would not count as a work of mass art because it is addressed to a minority audience familiar with the conventions of the 'art' cinema and the particular histories of art to which such films belong.

Hollywood films, by contrast, are characterized by a tendency to adopt forms and themes that can be readily comprehended by a mass audience. As Victor Perkins has written:

> The dialogue and action of each of them is fully understandable without specialized knowledge of political mechanisms, sociological jargon, philosophical concepts or historical facts. None of them employs a form so radically new as to require a substantial re-adjustment of the spectator's attitude. There is nothing in the plot or presentation to baffle anyone who keeps pace with the developing conceptions of mid-century, mid-Atlantic popular culture. (1972: 162)

Yet, within the confines of a commercialized cinema, the early 'quality' film movement of around 1908-10 and the 'prestige' film developments in the 1930s indicate that the American or Hollywood film has, at times, sought an accommodation with 'high art' as a specific commercial strategy. The search for accessibility did not preclude a degree of cultural ambition. In the 1930s, for example, it might be suggested that Hollywood producers were seeking 'middlebrow' status for their products with the innovation of the prestige picture; that they were seeking to establish a stratum of their art which would occupy a position in between modernist and avant-garde art, with its specialized minority appeal, and the highly conventionalized genre films – gangster films, Westerns, melodramas – which were designed for a mass audience. The concept of 'middlebrow art', as John Baxendale has pointed out, emerged in the interwar period as an alternative to both the culture of modernism – Joyce's novels, serial music, Cubist painting – that was demanding and restricted to a coterie, and the commercial technologically produced cultures of Hollywood, radio and popular music, with their mass circulation and appeal (Baxendale and Pawling, 1996: 49). The audience for middlebrow art was educated and discriminating but neither patient with the specific demands made by modernism and the avant-garde, nor satisfied with the populist character of the commercial culture of the time. The re-cycling of canonical literature from the nineteenth century and before, and the historical biographies which formed the bases of many prestige films, can be seen as satisfying a need for elevated entertainment with appeal for a 'middlebrow' audience.

Also, the performance of many of the prestige films indicated that cultural ambition and commercial viability were not necessarily at odds with each other. A number of the films deriving from British literature or drama enjoyed considerable critical acclaim and performed well at the box-office. Oscars of one category or another were won by *Cavalcade* (1932), *Mutiny on the Bounty* (1935), *A Midsummer Night's Dream* (1935), *Wuthering Heights* (1939) and

Pride and Prejudice (1940), and many of the 'British-derived' prestige films were included in the various annual 'top ten' lists, based on critical and box-office performance, compiled by trade papers such as *Variety* and *Film Daily* (Balio, 1993: 405-12). However, many cultural critics argue that the process of adaptation, the passage from the 'high art' of literature to the 'mass art' of cinema, required substantial mutilation of the source-texts and a subordination of the qualities which gave them artistic status to the demands of accessibility and the box-office.

By the 1930s, with the massive increase in production schedules and the concomitant appetite for literary and dramatic source material, the actual process of turning a 'property' – novel, play, short story – into a film began in the studio's story department staffed by specialist readers. Janet Staiger has outlined the process as follows:

> The reading staff would prepare ten- to seventy-five-page synopses which the editorial staff analysed and assessed in a one-page summary. Extensive files with cross-checking by 'plot structure, the dramatic possibilities, and the characteristic comic or tragic elements of the story' covered almost everything published. If a studio purchased a 'property', the other studios kept track of it in case they decided to buy it later. In the early- or mid-1930s, story conferences started, with verbal discussions of the stories before treatments were made. (1985: 322).

The subsequent activity of adaptation, the passage from novel to film as managed by the studio through its teams of writers, the translation from treatment and story outline to scenario and shooting script, was a complicated and somewhat opaque process, often with many interventions and many contributions, evidenced in the numerous films with multiple writing credits. Furthermore, although adaptation is sometimes constructed in terms of a simple medium-to-medium transaction, it is a complex process of adapting a cultural product produced at a specific time and in a specific context to the demands of a radically distinct form of cultural production with its own conventions and practices, and to the character of contemporary tastes and preferences. The process of adaptation, especially of familiar, revered texts from literary history, is sometimes regarded as a matter of finding visual equivalents for the 'essence' of the literary text, a process of identifying key elements of the source-text and then finding cinematic equivalents for them. However, it may be better understood as 'a complex reconciliation of the interrelated demands between fidelity to material, practices of the medium, and expectations of the audience' (Sconce, 1994: 141-2).

For the 'prestige' production, a degree of fidelity to the original was required, not so much in terms of the preservation of the novel's 'essence' or 'spirit', but rather in terms of the 'quality' element which provided the motivation for such adaptations. 'Prestige' status required that the film retained some of the qualities of the original novel that would confer upon it a degree of distinction by association; at the very least, the original title was necessary to achieve this.

In this way prestige pictures were to be distinguished from the ordinary generic films – the Westerns, the gangster films, the routine musicals – which characterized Hollywood's output. Yet, the American cinema as well as evolving a portfolio of genres also had established a set of conventions for narrative itself. Audiences were attuned to these and expected elements, such as stars, romantic themes, visual spectacle, linear narrative organization and closure, as part of the normal experience of watching a film, even one with prestigious credentials. Recruiting distinguished novelists and dramatists to work on important literary material was one way in which the studios sought to sustain the elevated level of the original source through the adaptation process. However, Hollywood practice, mindful of the need to reconcile literary achievement with Hollywood convention, was to pair distinguished writers with Hollywood professionals whose grasp of screencraft gave direction to the process and guaranteed that the transformation of original novels was governed by Hollywood's narrative codes and conventions. The writers recruited by Hollywood had an approach to their work formed in the different and less aggressively commercial context of the literary world. As Sam Goldwyn put it in a characteristically blunt appraisal of the potential problem:

> The great trouble with the usual author, is that he approaches the camera with some fixed literary ideal and he cannot compromise with the motion-picture viewpoint. He does not realize that a page of Henry James prose, leading through the finest shades of human consciousness, is absolutely lost on the screen. (Quoted in Fine, 1985: 52)

Most studies of adaptation are based on assumptions about narrative transferability. Both the novel and the mainstream fiction film are forms of narrative art convergent at some level in terms of story, discourse, event, situation, setting and character. The critical language of 'equivalents' between the two mediums at the level of narrative, however, tends to neglect the fact that the Hollywood mainstream film is more than simply story. As Richard Maltby has suggested:

> narrative functions as part of the provision of pleasure in cinema entertainment, not as the point of it. Story-telling helps ensure that the movie can be consumed as a coherent event, but it holds no privileged place among the pleasures a movie offers. At the most familiar level, we may enjoy the chase scenes in an action movie, the songs in a musical, or the performance of a particular star, while remaining disengaged from the over familiar or repetitive plot-line. It is every bit as hard to imagine a movie without spectacle or performance, without special effects or a star, as it is to imagine a movie without a story. (1995: 324)

Performance and spectacle, stars and action, are the kinds of qualities expected of a Hollywood film; they are part of Sam Goldwyn's 'motion picture viewpoint' and Sconce's 'practices of the medium, and expectations of the audience'. The reconciliation of literary sources to Hollywood practice is a complex matter but, in Ruth Vasey's words it is the values of the Hollywood film industry which predominate:

> A motion picture may be set in New York or ancient Rome, but if the movie is a product of Hollywood we know that the fiction will be governed by a set of narrative and representational conventions that will override the social, geographic, and historical characteristics of its nominal locale. (1997: 3)

Although passing a revered novel through the elaborate filter of Hollywood practice is frequently seen in terms of falsification and the traducing of original text and author, it might be more fruitful to see it in terms of the production of a completely new text with its own conventions and protocols. A text related in some way to the source, but possessing a different character and set of qualities by virtue of being a Hollywood film. Critical judgement upon it can then be conducted in the context of Hollywood values rather than in the context of literature.

Adaptation and history

The American film industry's appropriation of British culture was not confined to literary traditions; selected episodes and events from British history, the lives of prominent historical figures, together with a range of material more properly described in terms of historical myth and legend, have also provided significant sources for Hollywood's entertainment cinema. The themes and subjects derived from the nineteenth-century classic novels of Austen and Dickens, the horror stories of Mary Shelley and Robert Louis Stevenson and the detective fiction of Conan Doyle were supplemented by themes derived from British history, legend and folklore. In addition, Hollywood's literary films often converged with the historical picture in so far as a period dimension was also involved, at least in terms of setting and costume if not in the detail of character and event. The latter may have been largely fictional whereas setting and costume could be subject to the demands of period verisimilitude. In fact, many of the Hollywood films which are discussed under the rubric of 'the historical picture' derive from literary sources including, for example, *The Charge of the Light Brigade* (1936), which acknowledges Tennyson's poem of the same name as its source; films set in India deriving from the writings of Rudyard Kipling, such as *Wee Willie Winkie* (1937); and *Ivanhoe* (1951) and *The Adventures of Quentin Durward* (1956), adapted from the novels of Sir Walter Scott.

According to many commentators it was 'the American success of Alexander Korda's British-made *The Private Life of Henry VIII* released in 1934, which suggested that British subject matter could be commercially viable' (Wollen, 1998: 129), although Mark Glancy also draws attention to the influence of an earlier 'American-British' film – *Cavalcade*, terming it 'probably the most imitated of all 'British' films' (1999: 72-3). Indeed, the 1930s and 1940s are conventionally regarded as the period when Hollywood concentrated upon

British subject-matter and it has been noted that more than 150 'Hollywood British films' were made during this period (Glancy, 1999: 1). Yet, the use of British historical subject-matter can be traced to the earliest days of the American film and the Edison company's *The Execution of Mary, Queen of Scots*, a brief film made in 1895 for the Kinetoscope which used the stop-motion technique to render the decapitation (Custen, 1992: 5, Musser, 1990, 86-7). Through the 1910s and the 1920s American film-makers turned periodically to British historical subject-matter drawn both from fact and legend sometimes based upon literary sources, and Hollywood pictures have continued to feature historical subjects from the medieval epics of the 1950s, many of which were made in Britain as 'runaway' productions, to films of the 1980s such as those based upon the Robin Hood legend.

At one level, of course, history and folklore constituted just another storehouse of subject-matter from which the film industry drew in the context of the voracious demand for narrative films which developed in the early days of the industry. As the film business moved from the 'cottage industry' status of the early years to the large-scale volume production industry of the 1930s and 1940s, the various genres which emerged sedimented themselves into the system, partly because of their appeal to audiences, but also because of the investment in the raw material – costumes, period props, standing sets – and in the cultivation of performing and writing skills suited to particular genres. Once a studio embarked upon an elaborate historical drama, the material residue left after completion of the production and the developing skills of the personnel involved was a compelling reason for further exploitation of the genre.

The use of historical material as the basis of entertainment cinema raises relational issues similar to those raised in connection with literature. However, the film and literature relationship is symmetrical in kind, one which operates between different kinds of imaginative and fictional practice. Judgements on the viability, suitability or appropriateness of the relationship set up between, say, a classic novel and its film adaptation are frequently determined by cultural evaluations of the respective mediums, with the prestige of literature forming a substantial regulatory context within which such judgements are made. Films based upon classic literature are often criticized for failing to adhere to the source-text, despite the inability of critics to provide adequate definitions of 'fidelity', but the conventional typologies of the potential relationships usually position 'fidelity' in a spectrum including more distant relationships in which the novel-source simply provides raw material for the film. In addition, such typologies can be regarded as a set of neutral alternatives for the film-maker working from the basis of a literary work without evaluative and hierarchical implications. Many critics have rejected the regulatory frameworks of traditional cultural hierarchies, constructing an alternative culture in which texts (films, novels, plays) intermingle in various ways within a spectrum which includes both 'copying', as in Gus Van Sant's version of *Psycho* (1998), and looser forms of adaptation, as in Hitchcock's *Psycho* (1960), derived from the Robert Bloch novel, a work which itself was inspired by the documented case history of an actual murderer. Fictional film-makers do not work *ex nihilo* but the world of imaginative convention is regarded as infinitely more malleable than the world of historical actuality, and liberties taken with artistic convention and precedent are frequently expected of the artist.

The relationship between film and history is more complex. 'History' can, of course, be defined in textual terms as the contents of the history section of a library – books, journals – which address the past through description, interpretation and commentary. Indeed, 'history' in this sense carries its own prestige when contrasted with the cinema and may well constitute a regulatory context for the assessment of historical films. However, the direct adaptation of historical texts is unusual in mainstream cinema where the characteristic adaptive relationship is with fictional works. History in the sense of 'that which has been written/recorded about the past' (Jenkins, 1991: 6) plays a more distant role in the construction of the historical film, usually to provide information on the detail of historical events, as well as that of costume and setting, to prepare for their transformation into narrative fiction and to contribute to the verisimilitude and realism of the picture. The factor which distinguishes historical from literary adaptation is the 'the past itself' (ibid.), a notion of history which conforms to the lay understanding of the term. While historical films may well be derived from a range of sources including historical literature, both factual and fictional, a key relational factor for the genre is the existence of this other sense of history as 'the past' – events which happened, institutions which existed, human beings who lived and died – as distinct from the descriptions of them, the commentary upon and the analysis of them which constitutes the other sense of the term. For Pierre Sorlin, whose book is subtitled 'Restaging the Past', it is this relationship to 'history' – an external factor – which defines the historical film genre distinguishing it from other film genres which, he argues, 'developed within the world of cinema'. By contrast 'historical films . . . are defined according to a discipline that is completely outside the cinema' to which, for many commentators, an allegiance is owed, over and above the usual criteria by which entertainment cinema is judged (1980: 19-20).

The idea of 'the past itself' – something which exists, or existed, independently of historical books and articles – constitutes a separate category in the relationship between the film and its sources, even if the immediate source of a film is a history text of some sort, academic, popular, or, as is most likely, fictional. While it may be possible to adapt the relational schemas used for literary adaptation for the many historical films based upon poems, novels or written historical accounts, that relationship is inevitably more complicated, involving as it does, the additional relationship between the fictional film and the actuality as represented by 'the past itself', a category which has no obvious equivalent in the relationship between film and literature. A Hollywood historical film such as *The Charge of the Light Brigade* may have as its immediate source a Tennyson poem, but its subject-matter involves it in a complex network of relationships with contemporary accounts of the battle in the newspapers of the time, subsequent historical writing on the Crimean war including the biographies of figures such as Lord Cardigan and Lord Raglan, as well as the conceptually distinct notion of a set of events from British history which actually happened at the battle of Balaclava in 1854.

A literary critic might inveigh against Hollywood's cavalier approach to the adaptation of a nineteenth-century novel. The 1939 Hollywood production of *Wuthering Heights* jettisoned a substantial part of Emily Brontë's novel, including Catherine's death halfway through the story, in order to achieve a neatly closed text which resolved the narrative of Catherine and Heathcliff in tragic terms. Such an approach to adaptation, in which elements of the original are used selectively, can impact dramatically on the source-text determining its public image, creating for it a profile which may be at odds with its form and meaning. As one critic has suggested:

> People who have never read the novel feel that they know its central theme, epitomized by the famous still from William Wyler's 1939 film showing Laurence Olivier and Merle Oberon as Heathcliff and Catherine, silhouetted against the sky, their arms full of heather. Yet, no such scene appears in Emily Brontë's novel; the lovers are never together out of doors after their childhood. (Stoneman, 1998: vii)

Yet, it is possible to mount a defence of the film in terms of 'fidelity to the spirit of the novel', or to argue that that the novel was simply used as a 'loose source' for the new fiction, or provided an inspiration for a reworking of its central themes, or made aspects of the revered original available to a mass audience and thus justifying the alterations and amendments. At bottom, there is no ultimate arbiter in an argument between a literary critic troubled by a particular example of adaptation and a film critic anxious to defend the use of literary sources, or, more neutrally, to specify the relationship between film and novel in an analytical spirit. A film based on a novel may be trivializing, unfaithful to the detail or spirit of the source-text, tasteless, fanciful or whatever, but it remains in a relationship which can only be judged in subjective ways.

In contrast to this, it may be argued that the historical film can be 'wrong' in both serious and trivial ways, and that concepts such as 'truth' and 'verifiability' can be used to measure a film against the 'history' to which it alludes. Historian Robert Rosenstone writing on *Reds* (1982), Warren Beatty's film about the American journalist and revolutionary, John Reed, draws attention to the way in which the film fails to 'fulfill many of the basic demands for truth and verifiability used by all historians'. The film, he suggests, 'indulges in overt fiction – to give just two examples – by putting John Reed in places where he never was or having him make an impossible train journey from France to Petrograd in 1917' (1988: 1174). Yet, such licence with fact and incident does not represent the gravest charge to be levelled at the historical film:

> Far more unsettling is the way each compresses the past to a closed world by telling a single, linear story with, essentially, a single interpretation. Such a narrative strategy obviously denies historical alternatives, does away with the

complexities of motivation or causation, and banishes all subtlety from the world of history. (Ibid.)

This is of major social concern for, as Rosenstone suggests, films and television programmes now constitute 'the chief source of historical knowledge for the majority of the population' (ibid.). As he argues, this 'criticism of history on film might be of no importance if we did not live in a world deluged with images, one in which people increasingly receive their ideas about the past from motion pictures and television, from feature films, docudramas, mini-series, and network documentaries' (ibid.). What is at stake is the source of a nation's historical consciousness, which, of course, carries in its wake implications for national identity. Professional historians have long been concerned with the implications of the popular media delving into their territory and Rosenstone quotes an American academic writing in the 1930s:

> If the cinema art is going to draw its subjects so generously from history, it owes to its patrons and its own higher ideals to achieve greater accuracy. No picture of a historical nature ought to be offered to the public until a reputable historian has had a chance to criticize and revise it. (1995: 45-6)

Yet, by the end of the 1920s, the major Hollywood studios had established research departments and libraries staffed to provide accurate background information on film subject-matter, including period detail for set and costume designers, biographical and other information on historical personages and material on customs and etiquette. 'The overall job of the department', as Custen states, 'was to answer specific questions from writers, directors, art directors, producers, and other personnel concerning any and all aspects of production' (1992: 113). The endeavours of such departments were gathered into research guidebooks prepared for each film which provided authoritative guidance on matters of historical accuracy for its production and became known as 'bibles' in the industry (ibid.: 114). However, as with the Bible itself, the prescriptive material in the guidebooks was not always followed by the film-makers and the regulatory force of the information was often tempered by other pressures on the production process, such as the conventions of narrative and genre and notions of entertainment and audience pleasure.

The 'bibles' contained extensively researched pictorial material on the various aspects of the period which might have some reflection in the production and included, for example, details of the costume of the period; yet, in the course of production a film originating in one period could be transposed to another to secure enhanced production value. Edward Maeder discusses the adaptation of Jane Austen's *Pride and Prejudice*, a novel set in Regency Britain:

> *Pride and Prejudice* (1940) is set in the first decade of the nineteenth century, but the costumes are actually in an 1830s style. The designer, Adrian, persuaded the director, Robert Leonard, to place the story out of its time frame. . . . He chose an 1830s style so that the costumes could be more excessive and

decorative than the style of the earlier period, the classic revival, best known for the long tubular Empire dress. (1987: 12-13)

In addition, in the translation to the screen, meticulous period costume information, often the results of extensive and painstaking research, was frequently mixed with an awareness of contemporary fashion. As Maeder suggests, 'movies rarely replicate the exact look that prevailed; instead the costumes take elements from past styles and combine them with aspects of contemporary fashion'. He refers to the men's suits in *Gone With the Wind* (1939) which 'reflect the late-1930s cut with broad shoulders, a fullness across the upper rib cage, and a narrower cut over the waist and hips. The style and cut of the lapels are strictly contemporary, although the scale is similar to those worn in 1860' (ibid.: 9-10).

Of course, there is a broader definition of 'history' than that constituted by history in the academy, and modern industrial culture incorporates a wide and complicated network of historical representation, including the dramatic fictional material based on history. The historical feature film should be positioned in relation to what some historians have termed the 'public theatre of history', through which the population in general makes sense of its past. This public theatre – 'the field of public representations of history' – includes the representation of institutions such as Parliament, the monarchy and the military through the displays of state pageantry involved in 'jubilees, royal weddings, state visits, state funerals and commemorative events'; 'historical recreations' such as the re-enactment of the battles of the Civil War; 'the whole world of museums, art galleries, record offices, the Department of Environment's official preservation orders, the "National" Trust, the "National" Theatre, and in general the sphere of history as "cultural policy" '; the definitions of history in the educational context of the schoolroom; 'historical tourism'; radio, television and the press; mass publishing, including 'popular fiction and the modern form of the illustrated documentary book' and the popular historical biography; and the network of local amateur associations, historical and archaeological societies, oral history groups and the like (Popular Memory Group, 1982: 207-9). This is a complex network of historical representation with a range of involvement, from the formal agencies of the state to the voluntary associations in the local community, from the official to the informal. In one sense it is a world which sits beneath the world of history in the academy, not exactly in thrall to 'basic demands for truth and verifiability used by all historians' but, at least in its discursive forms – popular historical writing and cinema – not entirely exempt either. It does suggest, however, that the representation of history is not simply a matter of recitation of fact but rather that history is a complex 'way of seeing', capable of a range of inflections and crucially related to the world of politics and ideology.

The historical film is part of 'public history', to use Custen's term, with an efficacy as a provider of historical insight resident in its wide reach and appeal compared to written history, even the genre of popular history produced outside the academy. In addition to the factor of popular reach and appeal, multiplied since the advent of television, it has been argued that such media are 'better suited than written discourse to the actual, representation of certain kinds of historical phenomena – landscape, scene, atmosphere, complex events such as wars, battles, crowds, and emotions' (White, 1988: 1193). Tracking the accuracy of the historical film against the documented and verifiable accounts of history written by professional historians is understandable, yet films do not really compete with professional history in the formation of a popular historical consciousness. Rather, the historical film runs alongside state pageantry and display, the museum and the contents of the popular best-seller lists, the accessible though imperfect sources of historical awareness for most people.

Historical films and genre

Although, as has been suggested above, distinctions can be drawn in principle between adaptations from literature and 'adaptations' from history, many literary adaptations have an historical dimension, while many historical films are adaptations from literary accounts of the past. The reference point for the definition of 'the historical film' is, of course, some notion of 'history' itself, or of 'the past', as a tangible and stable index to which a particular film can be related. 'Like other genres,' suggests Marcia Landy, 'the historical film has a specific identity and employs a number of conventions and codes that define its character. These films take history as their subject, foregrounding it conspicuously and self-consciously, employing it for propaganda, spectacle, or analysis' (1990: 53).

A number of writers on the subject seek to construct typologies based on such relationships between a film and, to use Sorlin's terms, the 'discipline that is completely outside the cinema' – history (1980: 20). One such is outlined by Landy as follows:

> Historical films, according to Jean Gili, are of three types: those that feature the lives of famous individuals, those that tie fictional protagonists to a specific historical context by dramatizing the socialization of the individuals and their assimilation into the collectivity, and those costume dramas that use fictional characters in indeterminate historical settings. (1991: 54)

Yet. the extent to which concepts such as 'history' and 'the historical' provide a stable notion of 'the past' and provide a simple candidate for an oppositional pairing with the terms used in discussion of Hollywood films generally – 'fiction', 'entertainment', 'spectacle' – is open to question. As Maria Wyke has suggested, 'since the 1970s, a new self-consciousness about traditional conceptions of history and the rhetorical conventions for its presentation have collapsed the formerly clear boundaries between history and fiction' (1997: 12). 'History' as envisaged by postmodernist writers such as Hayden White is a discourse about the past conceptually distinct from the past itself though related to it in a range of ways. In constructing the historical film genre, writers on film usually elide the two senses of 'history' – the discourse and the actuality – implicitly utilizing a notion of a knowable past to which films can be related. Material from both academic history and the less formal 'public theatre of history' – historical personages, past events and institutions, eras and epochs – can be recounted, signalled and hinted at in various ways in the course of translation into the fictional world of the Hollywood feature film. Along the lines suggested by Gili, historical individuals – kings, queens, politicians, explorers, inventors, military and naval figures, even 'ordinary people' – can be positioned in the context of documented historical events; or they can be located in fictional events. They can also be located in events with a basis in historical documentation but incorporating a good deal of speculative licence in the detail of events. Documented historical events can be populated with fictional characters; fictional though identifiably historical events – events clearly set in the past – can be populated with historical personages or with fictional characters; or, as frequently happens, historical events are mixed with fictional events and fictional characters are mixed with historical individuals. There is also the matter of characters from legend whose historical status is the subject of debate and conjecture. Cinema audiences have long been acquainted with the events and personages of British history from the twelfth century, such as the Crusades, Richard the Lionheart and King John; more often than not, however, these elements are to be found in films which centre upon the legendary figure of Robin Hood. The precise extent of the intermingling of 'history', legend and fiction, the balance of elements, can be used to distinguish between different kinds of historical film.

In defining the historical picture, both Sorlin and Landy allocate a central role for the use of historical material related to ideas of nation and national identity. As Sorlin writes:

> In the case of the historical film, what are the signs by which it can be recognized as such? There must be details, not necessarily many of them, to set the action in a period which the audience unhesitatingly places in the past – not a vague past but a past considered as historical. The cultural heritage of every country and every community includes dates, events and characters known to all members of that community. This common basis is what we might call the group's 'historical capital', and it is enough to know that it is watching an historical film and to place it, at least approximately. (1980: 20)

It is a definition which stresses the 'national' nature of the historical picture. Such a genre, it has also been argued, is 'deeply intertwined with myths of the nation' and the specific historical subject-matter appropriate to the genre in its national context is drawn from 'moments in the history of the nation that are considered central to the formation of national identity' (Landy, 1990: 53). It is a definition, however, with a somewhat problematic fit to the American cinema, which has mobilized aspects of the histories of numerous nations in its address to a transnational audience. A cursory glance at the 1930s 'prestige' films reveals historical subject-matter as diverse as ancient Imperial Rome in *The*

Sign of the Cross (1932) and *Cleopatra* (1934), the French Revolution in *Marie Antoinette* (1938) and Tsarist Russia in *The Scarlet Empress* (1934) and *Rasputin and the Empress* (1932), as well as the numerous titles based upon British history. Sorlin's use of the concept of 'historical capital' might suggest that what constitutes a readily comprehensible historical film for one audience may not work for a group with a different storehouse of 'historical capital'. However, it could also be argued that some histories, such as those of prominent European powers significant for the development of world history, do have an international currency, rendering them suitable for adaptation to the popular Hollywood picture. Sorlin does extend the definition of 'historical film' to include those dealing with historical times less familiar to particular audiences which, he suggests, can compensate for gaps in the audience's knowledge by emphasizing 'the historical nature of what is shown' through the period detail and other means which 'stress the historical nature of events' (1980: 20). The stress on the historical nature of events is perhaps a clue to the difficulties posed by attempting a singular definition of any genre; 'stress' implies a balance of elements tipped in a particular direction to which we can affix a generic label. The historical film is one in which the elements of history have a prominence either through familiarity of detail for an indigenous audience, the notion of shared 'historical capital', or through a deliberate elaboration of historical information related to material likely to be unfamiliar to a particular audience. In terms of Hollywood's appropriation of British history, a sense of common heritage and language might explain the ways in which the history and associated legend and folklore became firmly established as accessible subject-matter for the various cycles of historical films which came from the major studios.

'History' of one sort or another and from a range of national and geographical sources has provided material for a substantial segment of Hollywood's output, including genres which can be defined in terms which, though including 'history' in some way, have other defining, and in many cases more important, characteristics as well. In a discussion of the most prominent of Hollywood genres, Jim Kitses has suggested that 'First of all, the western is American history' (1969: 8). Yet, history has a variable presence in the genre. *My Darling Clementine* (1946), with its historical personages – the Earps and the Clantons, Doc Holliday – and events such as the gunfight at the O. K. Corral blends a sense of history with other elements of the genre such as the revenge motif. *Rio Bravo* (1959), by contrast, uses entirely fictional characters and offers no specific clues as to precise historical time or place, and focuses upon specific generic elements such as revenge, law and order, as well as the typical Hawksian attention to the male group. There are many genres which use history in particular ways. The costume picture, by definition, roots its appeal in the spectacular *mise en scène* offered potentially by the history of dress and fashion; the epic implicitly mobilizes the history of heroic human achievement, often with a religious inflection; the biopic and the adventure film have often based themselves on historical figures and events though both genres can accommodate very recent and contemporary figures and events as well. Such genres have used a wealth of historical material – institutions, events and personalities both fictional and real – from the past, together with the pictorial opportunities offered by settings from the past; in addition, Hollywood's numerous adaptations of nineteenth-century literature have added to the ways in which 'historical' elements such as setting and costume have woven themselves into Hollywood cinema as a whole. In some respects, *pace* Landy, the permeation of Hollywood's subject-matter by 'history' makes it difficult to identify a distinctive generic strand which might be called 'the historical film'. 'History', like romance, might be considered a staple component of the Hollywood system of genres, sometimes playing a background role in a film dominated by other concerns, sometimes foregrounded as the principal theme of the film.

Richard Maltby has suggested that, in the Hollywood system, 'history' is best regarded as a 'production value' (1995: 311). Accuracy, either in terms of actual historical event or the details of costume and setting, could provide authenticity and verisimilitude for romantic and other narratives; the dramatic episodes of history, the land and sea battles, the coronations and public executions, could be turned into spectacular events for the screen, as could the settings of castle, cathedral and stately home. Historical subject-matter, as well as classic literature, could confer 'prestige' on a film and attract greater numbers into the cinemas, including the educated classes whose resistance to the medium was bound up with assumptions about its relative cultural worth. Indeed, in 1938 *Variety* carried an article headlined 'Historical Pix to up B. O.', commenting on Will Hays' belief in 'the possibilities of swelling the customer ranks by adding a classroom tinge to celluloid fare without detracting from the entertainment value' (20 April 1938: 7). However, as with the classics of literary history, the events and personalities of history were obliged to submit to the fictionalizing processes of Hollywood, to conform to the commercial and aesthetic requirements of the studios. The features of the historical picture which alarmed Rosenstone, the compression of 'the past to a closed world' and 'telling a single, linear story with, essentially, a single interpretation', are key characteristics of the Hollywood narrative film. As Maltby suggests 'Hollywood films are . . . fictions before they are histories' and are 'shaped by a set of narrative and generic conventions' (1995: 309).

British literature both 'classic' and 'popular', and certain aspects of British history, have been mobilized frequently in the service of the Hollywood classical film, a form with broad determining parameters covering formal matters of narrative structure and stylistic choice, the performance dimension implied in the star system, the role of spectacle, as well as thematic desiderata such as the romance and action. Whatever the standing of the original novel or the detail to be found in academic historians' accounts of the historical event, the Hollywood system tended to absorb material and subject it to the norms and conventions of its typical product – the feature-length narrative film. The treatment of literature as source was not entirely cavalier as part of the logic of the prestige picture in particular was to sell itself using the 'aura' of the original work – Shakespeare, Dickens, etc. – to attract an educated audience. Yet the values of entertainment and accessibility were paramount and both literary prestige and historical accuracy had to accommodate the demands of popular appeal. The process of adaptation was to the presumed levels of tolerance and understanding of the mass audience. The next chapter explores the scope of British literature and history which reached the screen.

7 British Culture and Hollywood

The most prominent of the early story films shown in America – Edwin S. Porter's *The Great Train Robbery* (1903) – drew its title and basic story from a late nineteenth-century play (Musser, 1990: 352). Other early story films drawn from pre-existent literary sources included the 1903 versions of the popular nineteenth-century novel *Uncle Tom's Cabin* by the Edison Company and by Sigmund Lubin, and the fairy tale adaptations from the Selig Company – *Pied Piper of Hamelin* (1903) and *Scenes from Humpty Dumpty* (1903). There were some early adaptations from British literature both classic and popular. Vitagraph imported a Méliès adaptation of Defoe's *Robinson Crusoe* (1902), and made one of the early Sherlock Holmes films, together with an E. W. Hornung adaptation, based upon the Raffles character. It was, however, the 'quality' film endeavour from 1908 onwards that prompted the major borrowing from British and European literature and drama and began a practice of adaptation from the classics that the American cinema continues to this day. The adaptation of elevated literature and drama was one strategy, along with historical pictures and films based upon biblical stories, adopted in the prominent national cinemas of the time to construct an 'art' cinema. Several firms, including Film d'Art in France, Autoren Film in Germany, Cines in Italy, Vitagraph in America, Nordisk in Denmark and the Hepworth company in Britain, made a number of films adapted from the classics of European literature during this period (Neale, 1981).

Shakespeare, in particular, enjoyed a considerable vogue in the American cinema in the years leading up to the First World War, reflecting the status that the dramatist enjoyed in American culture of the period. John Ford's Western, *My Darling Clementine* (1946), contains a sequence in which a travelling actor entertains, or fails to entertain, an audience in a saloon with a rendition of the soliloquy from *Hamlet*. The unruly Clanton gang berate the actor's efforts but are silenced when Doc Holliday insists upon listening to the performance and, indeed, completes the speech when the actor's nerve fails him. The sequence condenses the history of Shakespeare within American culture, indicating the presence of the playwright's work in nineteenth-century frontier America and its familiarity to the audience. The cultured Doc Holliday appreciates the performance and is familiar with the details of the play, while the unruly outlaws play the groundlings and hurl abuse at the actor. Scholarly accounts of the period endorse Ford's thumbnail sketch of a pervasive cultural phenomenon. As Lawrence Levine has written, the 'theater, like the church was one of the earliest and most important cultural institutions established in frontier cities. And, almost everywhere the theater blossomed Shakespeare was a paramount force' (1984: 38). During the nineteenth century, according to Levine, Shakespeare had become an ingrained element in a broad public culture, not a coterie taste, nor a badge of distinction associated with specific classes in the community.

Although there is some dispute about the precise role of Shakespeare and his work in early twentieth-century American culture, it is clear that some familiarity with his work was widespread and that film-makers could present condensed versions of the plays which would resonate in different ways with their audiences (Uricchio and Pearson, 1993: 67). In Europe, films utilizing fragments of Shakespeare plays began in the late 1890s with Herbert Beerbohm Tree's *King John* (1899). In France the duel scene from *Hamlet*, with Sarah Bernhardt playing the Prince, was filmed in 1900, scenes from *Romeo and Juliet* were filmed in the same year and, in 1907, Georges Méliès made a version of *Hamlet*. Charles Urban's filmed storm sequences for a Herbert Beerbohm Tree theatrical production of *The Tempest* were released as a film in 1905 and imported into America by George Kleine. Also in 1905, the American Mutoscope and Biograph Company made *Duel Scene from Macbeth*, shot by cinematographer Billy Bitzer (Ball, 1968: 26-36). However, it was not until later in the decade with the advent of the various 'film art' trends that Shakespeare adaptations begin to occupy a prominent position in the production schedules of the leading American and European companies. As Robert Hamilton Ball writes:

> 1908 was the key year, 1908 through 1911 the period, the United States led the way; with somewhat different impulses, Italy and France joined the parade. In four years, not counting minor adaptations and petty pilferings, almost fifty new productions of Shakespeare were on the screens in America, England and on the Continent. They included seventeen of Shakespeare's plays, seven of the tragedies, six of the comedies, two each of the dramatic romances and English histories. Most of them were in one reel, approximately a thousand feet of film; some spilled over into two; one anticipated the feature picture of a later era. (1968: 38)

A number of firms were involved, including Kalem, Selig, American Mutoscope and Biograph and the Thanhouser Film Corporation, but the most prolific producer of the playwright's work in the United States was the Vitagraph Company of America with titles such as *King Lear, Macbeth, Othello, Richard III, The Merchant of Venice, Romeo and Juliet* and *Twelfth Night*.

The most familiar explanation for the move towards 'high' culture represented by the Shakespeare adaptations and the various other borrowings from prestigious literature and drama has to do with what Eileen Bowser calls 'the industry's uplift movement' (1990: 43). Considerable concern about the moral tone and unsavoury subject-matter of early had culminated in censorship moves in many states and the closure of New York's nickelodeons in 1908. There were also concerns about the impact of films upon children and young people. Although the nickelodeon closure was short lived, the indications were clear; the film industry would have to raise the tone of its films if it wanted to avoid interference from outside organizations. It was felt that the social status of the cinema could be raised by association with high literature and drama, enabling producers and exhibitors to 'demonstrate that the motion-picture show was an appropriate place for children and that they were bringing high culture to the masses' (Bowser, 1990: 43). In the case of Shakespeare, films were taking advantage of a highly prestigious source embedded in the general culture but, as Uricchio and Pearson point out, there were other reasons for providing the brief versions of *King Lear*, *Macbeth*, and *Othello* alongside the quest for cultural respectability:

> . . . the industry had several good reasons to produce these particular films at this historical juncture. First, Shakespeare, although an English poet, was so revered in the countries of the European export market that adaptations of his work were guaranteed to sell. Second, in the wake of the 1907 *Ben Hur* copyright decision, studios were acutely aware of whether material was in the public domain and knew that Shakespeare was not only respectable but free. Third, . . . Shakespeare may have been far more accessible to a diverse spectrum of viewers than a late-twentieth-century perspective might suggest. Fourth, Shakespeare provided as many thrills – duels, illicit romances, murders – as the rankest cheap melodrama. And fifth, if critics accused filmmakers of the excessive depiction of duels and other unsavoury material, the industry could feign outraged innocence and wrap itself in the Bard's cultural respectability. (1993: 69)

In addition to the above reasons, the industry was facing an increasing demand for material and the vast store of European and American literature and drama of the past was available as a ready source of subject-matter for an industry constantly in search of fresh ideas and fresh stories. American and European companies made films based upon the works of Dickens, Tennyson, Charlotte Brontë, Walter Scott, Robert Louis Stevenson, Arthur Conan Doyle, Thomas Hardy, Oliver Goldsmith, George Eliot, Robert Browning and Mary Shelley (Low, 1949: 189). The work of many of these writers was to feature in various ways in the subsequent history of the American film. Sometimes, as with Shakespeare, the reasons had a lot to do with cultural respectability and the attempt to create American versions of an 'art' cinema; sometimes, however, the novels provided sources for key popular Hollywood genres and cycles, as in the case of writers such as Mary Shelley, Robert Louis Stevenson and Arthur Conan Doyle.

Shakespeare adaptations did not figure prominently after the hectic production activity of the Vitagraph company and others in the 'film art' period, although there was one high-profile production of *The Taming of the Shrew* in 1929 made by Mary Pickford's company featuring the silent star and her partner, Douglas Fairbanks. Two major Shakespeare films were made in the 1930s:

Warner Bros.' *A Midsummer Night's Dream* (1935), developed out of a lavish theatrical production of the play in the open-air Hollywood Bowl some three years earlier, and MGM's *Romeo and Juliet* (1936). Both films had above-average budgets of more than $1million, high profile casts and top production personnel. *A Midsummer Night's Dream* starred Dick Powell and James Cagney, and was directed by the distinguished Austrian theatre director, Max Reinhardt, with assistance from William Dieterle; *Romeo and Juliet*, an Irving Thalberg project, featured Norma Shearer, Leslie Howard and John Barrymore, and was directed by one of MGM's top film-makers, George Cukor. Both films attracted favourable reviews but both were deemed over-long by the critics. According to *Variety*, the Reinhardt picture cut 'by at least 20 minutes . . . would be greatly improved as entertainment' (16 October 1935: 22). *Romeo and Juliet* ran for two hours and ten minutes and although the same paper's reviewer wrote wearily that 'Toward the end it seemed like a long sit', it was suggested that the film would 'attract a new crop of cinema patrons from the arty, cultural, literati and dramatic bunch' (26 August 1936: 20). In that sense the film fulfilled the aims of the earlier American Shakespeare adaptations to raise the cultural quality and status of the medium. The reviews, though somewhat reverential in respect of the cultural ambition involved in adapting Shakespeare, were sceptical about the commercial prospects of the films. The scepticism proved to be justified and late in 1936 *Variety* proclaimed 'The Bard a B. O. Washout' and that 'Hollywood has passed up its option on William Shakespeare':

> Two major efforts enrolled the best production and acting talent which the film capital possesses, but now Shakespeare is on his own again. He'll continue to do all right, no doubt, with his job in the legit and public library circulation, but as a Hollywood writer he just didn't click.
> And, whatever hesitancy there has been about looking at the facts (which mean box office returns) squarely in the face after the public's reception of 'Midsummer Night's Dream' and 'Romeo and Juliet,' the lack of interest in 'As You Like It', British-made and recently released in this country, has resulted in cancellation of any plans for future Shakespearean adaptations. (9 December 1936: 3)

Prestige pictures and British literature

However, the discouraging example of Shakespeare notwithstanding, the strategy of adapting literary classics did grow in importance as the long feature film supplanted the short pictures of the early period and became central to the major companies' overall production plans from the twenties onwards. In the 1930s and 1940s, in particular, major studios such as MGM, RKO and Warner Bros. and some of the smaller concerns such as Monogram, presented adaptations of the work of Dickens, Emily and Charlotte Brontë, Thackeray, Mary Shelley and Bram Stoker, along with the work of European authors such as Tolstoy, Dumas and Hugo. Indeed, the literary adaptation was an important and central constituent of the 'prestige picture', which emerged as a key production trend in 1930s Hollywood (Balio 1993: Ch. 7).

Prestige films were defined both in material terms – the considerable size of their budgets – and, in cultural terms – the high status of their source material, drawn from the achievements of prestigious literature and drama, the lives of major scientists and political figures and the events of European and American history. British culture had considerable appeal for a number of reasons and, in addition to the various literary adaptations, aspects of British history including its imperial past, together with folklore and legends, constituted sources for a number of films. Taken together these films might be regarded as a distinctive Hollywood production trend – the American-British film – a sub-genre of the prestige film based on the adaptation of a national history and literature which, with its crucial ties of history and language, possessed a specific resonance for an American audience. The trend is signalled in an intriguing way by a 1937 *Variety* headline which read 'Best English Pix Are Made in U.S., Says Aussie Censor'. In the course of his annual report, the Commonwealth Film Censor, Creswell O'Reilly, had stated that 'the best British films are made in America' (31 March 1937: 14). In a similar vein, though in less provocative terms, Arthur Dent, director of the Associated British Picture Corporation, also writing in *Variety* suggested that:

> Some of the most successful American pictures of recent years have been based on British subjects and these indicate that audience interest is stimulated by the importation of ideas and stories from other countries. What is more logical than that these should come from Britain, a country that is closer to America in language, thought and ideals than any other in the world. (4 January 1938: 30)

Although some of the literary adaptations came from B-picture studios such as Monogram and the 'minor major' company, Universal, the best-known versions of the classic texts of British literature and drama fitted comfortably into the concept of the prestige picture outlined previously and defined by Tino Balio as 'a big-budget special based on a pre-sold property, often as not a "classic," and tailored for top stars' (1993: 179).

Many films were based on the nineteenth-century novel. Dickens was well represented with *Rich Man's Folly* (1931), a version of *Dombey and Son*, *Oliver Twist* (1933), *Great Expectations* (1934), *The Mystery of Edwin Drood* (1935) and *A Christmas Carol* (MGM, 1938). There were also the more prominent David Selznick 1935 productions of *David Copperfield* and *A Tale of Two Cities*. Selznick had joined MGM as a senior producer and his unit was responsible for some of the key prestige pictures from the studio most closely associated with the trend. In addition to the Dickens films, Selznick also produced *Dinner at Eight* (1933), with its galaxy of stars, and *Anna Karenina* (1935), with Garbo. *David Copperfield* cost just over $1 million to make; it featured W. C. Fields, Edna May Oliver and English child actor, Freddie Bartholomew, and was directed by George Cukor. *A Tale of Two Cities* was slightly more expensive at $1.2 million and had Ronald Colman in the leading role of Sidney Carton. High-profile adaptations of novels by Jane Austen and the Brontë sisters were also made. Sam Goldwyn produced a version of Emily Brontë's *Wuthering Heights* in 1939, directed by William Wyler and featuring Laurence Olivier and Merle Oberon as the doomed couple; MGM made *Pride and Prejudice* as part of their 'prestige' programme in 1940, also using Olivier in the role of Darcy and Greer Garson, the studio's leading female star of the time, as Elizabeth Bennet; Charlotte Brontë's *Jane Eyre* was filmed at Twentieth Century-Fox in 1944 with Orson Welles as Rochester, although the film was planned extensively at Selznick's independent studio by producer John Houseman and director Robert Stevenson, and was sold by Selznick to the major as a package which included 'the script, Stevenson, his production designer William Pereira, and the troublesome Joan Fontaine' (Thompson, 1993: 357). Other 'classic' British novels brought to the American screen in more modest fashion include another version of Charlotte Brontë's *Jane Eyre* (1934) and *The Mill on the Floss* (1939), from the novel by George Eliot, both made at the small Monogram studio, Wilkie Collins's *The Moonstone*, Kipling's *Captains Courageous* (1937) and *Wee Willie Winkie* (1937), Thackeray's *Vanity Fair*, brought to the screen as *Becky Sharp* (RKO, 1935), the first Hollywood feature film to use the recently developed three-strip Technicolor process, and two versions of Joseph Conrad's *Victory* from Paramount – *Dangerous Paradise* (1930) and *Victory* (1940).

British literature and Hollywood genre cinema

In both British and American culture 'high literature' enjoys a substantial status deriving from its perceived function as a repository of ethical and social values, as 'the best that is known and thought in the world', in Matthew Arnold's famous formulation. Such a status acts as a patrolling force when such literature is adapted for film. Many discussions of the relationship between classic literature and film seek to position adaptations in relation to respected source-texts, moving from a notion of fidelity to the original through various kinds of relationship which establish degrees of distance between source and adaptation. However difficult it is to define satisfactorily, Hollywood's treatment of classic literature required film-makers to operate with some notion of 'fidelity' to the Elizabethan plays and nineteenth-century novels frequently drawn upon. After all, part of the rationale for adaptation from such sources was to mobilize the cultural value inscribed in the works of Shakespeare, Dickens and others, to secure the 'prestige' category for the films which drew upon the literary classics. Popular literature provided a different potential, notably bound up with pre-established appeal as registered in best-selling novels, hit Broadway plays and musicals and the world of the popular paperback genre novel. 'Fidelity' to source seems less important in this context except in so far as the exploitation of popularity is concerned. Clearly, the adaptation of Arthur Conan Doyle's Sherlock Holmes stories required the films to replicate certain qualities of the original such as, for example, Holmes's rationality, the character of Doctor Watson and the mystery elements. However, when Universal acquired the screen rights to the stories in 1942, it embarked on a cycle of Sherlock Holmes films which transplanted the stories from Victorian Britain to the 1940s, enabling the great detective to pit his wits against Nazi Germany!

British popular literature has made a significant contribution to the American popular cinema with certain genres drawing extensively on a range of writing from various cultural levels. Crime, horror, the historical epic, the adventure film all in their ways drew upon such literature, although the impact was uneven and certain genres were more profoundly marked and shaped than others. For example, it has been argued that English crime literature had less of an impact on the American film than indigenous writing in the genre. In many respects the ratiocinative traditions and the often provincial class-bound character of the genre exemplified by the work of Agatha Christie made it somewhat unsuitable for adaptation to the proletarian action cinema of the crime genre in Hollywood. In a famous formulation, Raymond Chandler commented on the nature of the change to detective fiction brought about by the advent of the 'hard-boiled' American school of writing:

> The only reality the English detection writers knew was the conversational accent of Surbiton and Bognor Regis. If they wrote about dukes and Venetian vases, they knew no more about them out of their own experience than the well-heeled Hollywood character knows about the French Modernists that hang in his Bel-Air chateau or semi-antique Chippendale-cum-cobbler's-bench that he uses for a coffee table. Hammett took murder out of the Venetian vase and dropped it into the alley. (1976: 194)

Yet there were other kinds of English crime literature that did prove amenable to conversion into Hollywood cinema. The British crime and espionage story, in the shape of the work of 'Sapper' (Cyril Herman McNeile), E. W. Hornung, Leslie Charteris, Sax Rohmer and, most notably, the late nineteenth-century detective stories of Arthur Conan Doyle, together with material from the world of the boys' magazine, fed into the American crime cinema of the 1930s and 1940s, and particularly into the serial programme picture. Genre heroes from British crime fiction, including Bulldog Drummond, Raffles, the Saint and Sherlock Holmes featured on the American screen during this period, with Conan Doyle's legendary detective appearing in no less than fourteen films between 1939 and 1946. Subsequently, thriller writers with greater cultural status, such as Eric Ambler and Graham Greene, also featured as sources.

If British crime literature inserted itself into the genre in specific ways and at a tangent to the generic mainstream, British gothic and horror writing, by contrast, provided a richer store of material for Hollywood. Classic nineteenth-century novels from Robert Louis Stevenson, Mary Shelley and Bram Stoker formed a substantial basis for the horror genre which evolved in Hollywood during the 1930s in particular. Indeed the central icons of the genre, Victor Frankenstein, together with his monster, and Count Dracula can be traced back to the celebrated evening in the summer of 1816 at Lord Byron's Geneva retreat, the Villa Diodati. Byron, together with Percy Bysshe Shelley, Mary Shelley, her step-sister Claire Clairmont and Dr John Polidori, Byron's physician, set about amusing each other by writing ghost stories. Mary Shelley contributed the story of Frankenstein and Byron wrote the beginnings of a vampire story, an episode in literary history acknowledged by Hollywood in the prologue to *Bride of Frankenstein* (1934), a sequel to the original *Frankenstein* (1931). Mary Shelley's novel *Frankenstein* was published in 1818, though anonymously, and Byron's vampire story was published in 1819 in *The New Monthly Magazine* as 'The Vampyre: a Tale of Lord Byron'. In fact, the Byron idea had been completed by John Polidori, who based the central character on the figure of Byron, the decadent aristocrat enormously attractive to the opposite sex. It was this image rather than that of the medieval tyrant of history and folklore that influenced Bram Stoker towards the end of the nineteenth century and that was adapted for the theatre and the screen over a century after the Byronic gathering (Glut, 1975: 38-40; Hindle, 1985: 15-16).

It might be argued that distinctively British cultural and literary strands drawing on a wide spectrum of literature – from Mary Shelley's Gothic epistolary novel to Sapper's simple tales of xenophobic heroism – were channelled into the developing generic system in Hollywood with a dramatic degree of success in the case of the horror film. 'Prestige' films drew upon distinguished literature in order to enhance the cultural reception of Hollywood pictures and to heighten their appeal for the educated audiences; the use of Gothic literature and the popular thriller had other motivations, notably the mass appeal of the material that could be exploited by the film companies to satisfy the mass audience, the mainspring of Hollywood's economy. In Hollywood the phenomenon of adaptation, as Brian McFarlane has noted, operated 'between the poles of crass commercialism and high-minded respect for literary works' (1996: 7). While many prestige films drew overtly on the cultural prestige of their sources, often, for example, incorporating an image of the book itself into the opening sequence of the film, popular generic cinema simply drew upon whatever sources it was felt would provide the stimulus for a successful film cycle, regardless of their cultural status and position.

Crime and mystery: Sherlock Holmes and assorted heroes

Crime has been a staple element in American popular cinema since the earliest days of film and the influence of British crime films such as those of the Sheffield Photo Company and Walter Haggar has been noted as important for films such as *The Great Train Robbery*, made in 1903. Prior to this, however, the American Biograph and Mutoscope Company had drawn upon British crime literature producing the first Sherlock Holmes film – *Sherlock Holmes Baffled* – in 1900. Holmes had been introduced to American readers some years before. Indeed, the first Holmes novel – *A Study in Scarlet* – was set partly in America, and the second – *The Sign of the Four* – had been commissioned by the

American *Lippincott's Magazine*, in which it appeared some months before its London publication. Further films based on the exploits of Conan Doyle's character followed. In America, the Vitagraph company, soon to become better known for its Shakespeare adaptations, made *The Adventures of Sherlock Holmes* in 1905 and the Crescent Film Company made *Sherlock Holmes and the Great Murder Mystery* in 1908. These films represented an international trend in early cinema, with the Danish company Nordisk making several Holmes films between 1908 and 1911, a number of Italian versions, beginning in 1908 with *Rival Sherlock Holmes*, and in Britain a series of eight titles from 1912 made by the Franco-British Film Co.-Éclair.

After that and particularly during the 1920s the main Sherlock Holmes activity was in Britain, with three series of short films and two features from the Stoll company. There were, however, a few American productions during this period. In 1916 the Essanay company released *Sherlock Holmes* and during the 1920s there were two productions from major companies. Goldwyn Pictures produced *Sherlock Holmes*, featuring John Barrymore as the master detective, in 1922, and in 1929, Paramount produced *The Return of Sherlock Holmes* starring English actor, Clive Brook, and directed by Basil Dean. Apart from the adaptations of the original stories, a number of films used the Holmes figure for the purposes of comedy and parody including a Douglas Fairbanks picture – *The Mystery of the Leaping Fish* (1915) and a slapstick series from Mack Sennett (Hardy, 1997: 169). There were two American Holmes films in the early 1930s – *Sherlock Holmes* (Fox, 1932) and *A Study in Scarlet* (Worldwide, 1933) – but the upsurge of Hollywood interest in the detective began late in the decade with two films from Twentieth Century-Fox, *The Hound of the Baskervilles* and *The Adventures of Sherlock Holmes* (both 1939). The films were notable in particular for the introduction of Basil Rathbone and Nigel Bruce in the roles of Holmes and Watson.

Rathbone, though born in South Africa, was educated in England and established his acting reputation on the stage. He appeared in a number of silent films and achieved prominence as a supporting actor during the 1930s. His appearances during the decade, which included prestige pictures such as *David Copperfield*, *Anna Karenina*, *A Tale of Two Cities* and *Romeo and Juliet*, established a somewhat unsympathetic villainous image for him, epitomized in the role of Sir Guy of Gisbourne in *The Adventures of Robin Hood*. *The Hound of the Baskervilles*, released early in 1939, introduced a 'new' Rathbone which shed the connotations of his previous roles. The film was part of a second cycle of horror films which began in 1938 with the reissue of the early 1930s *Dracula* and *Frankenstein* as a double bill (Balio, 1993: 309-10). Indeed, Rathbone himself had appeared in some of the early films in the cycle. He played the title role in *Son of Frankenstein* (1939) and was Richard III in *The Tower of London* (1939), giving performances which lined up more coherently with his image as 'the best all-round villain the movies ever had' (William Everson, quoted in Shipman 1970: 454). In that context, his accession to the Holmes role is surprising, although his crisp and decisive clipped vocal delivery complete with English accent gave an authority to his performance; in addition, his 'erect guardsman-like bearing, with an extraordinary angular face, a long aquiline nose and a defiant jawline' rendered a physical image of Holmes not dissimilar to the graphic representations by Sidney Paget which illustrated the stories on their original publication in *The Strand Magazine*. Whatever the reasons, Rathbone's Sherlock Holmes acquired a definitive status along with Nigel Bruce's bumbling image of Doctor Watson. *Variety* hailed the picture as a 'strong programmer that will find many bookings on top spots of key dualers that attract the thriller-mystery patronage', and it described Basil Rathbone's performance as 'a most effective characterization of Sherlock Holmes' (29 March 1939: 14). The film was successful and this encouraged Twentieth Century-Fox to produce a sequel, *The Adventures of Sherlock Holmes*, which was released in August 1939. Whereas *The Hound of the Baskervilles* followed the original novel closely, the sequel was based loosely on an 1899 play written by William Gillette, an actor who established a reputation playing Holmes on stage. The play had formed the basis of a number of previous Holmes films including the 1916 Essanay version, the John Barrymore film made for Goldwyn in 1922 and the Fox company's *Sherlock Holmes*, made in 1932, with Clive Brook in the title role. The film featured Holmes's notorious adversary, Professor Moriarty, and a plot to steal the Crown Jewels, and in critical terms it is often regarded more highly than *The Hound of the Baskervilles*. *Variety*, for example, commented that it was 'about the neatest package in several attempts to make Sherlock Holmes exciting on the screen' and that it was 'considerably better than the last in this group and should prove a healthy buildup for others in this line of detective yarns' (6 September 1939: 14). However, the picture failed to repeat the box-office success of the earlier film and the studio decided to discontinue the series.

Variety was right about the film proving a healthy build-up for 'this line in detective yarns', however, and the characters were revived when Universal acquired the screen rights to the Conan Doyle stories from Twentieth Century-Fox in the early 1940s. Universal was a 'major minor' studio and specialized in the lower budget film and in cycles and series. The Sherlock Holmes stories, adapted to the budgetary constraints of the studio, formed the basis of a cycle of films beginning in 1942, running through twelve pictures and ending in 1946. The raw material was adaptable to two strongly established strands in the studio's output – the horror film and the espionage thriller – and the Holmes series was to become an important plank in the studio's wartime output, along with other horror and espionage films, Abbot and Costello comedies and costume epics with Jon Hall and Maria Montez (Schatz, 1989: Ch. 18). The first picture of the series – *Sherlock Holmes and the Voice of Terror* (1942) – opened with a title card proclaiming, 'Sherlock Holmes, the immortal character of fiction created by Sir Arthur Conan Doyle, is ageless, invincible and unchanging'. 'Ageless', to be sure, for the new series transplanted the Victorian detective to the present day which, in 1942, meant the midst of the Second World War. For Holmes's first case in the series, Nazi Germany was the adversary and the criminal deed was a planned invasion and occupation of Britain. Although in some respects aligned with programmer genres such as horror and crime, the Twentieth Century-Fox pictures had A-grade budgets and running times; by contrast, the Universal series aimed at the lower-half of the double bill and this was reflected most clearly in the running time of 65 minutes for *Sherlock Holmes and the Voice of Terror*. The subsequent films all ran for between 60 and 74 minutes, compared with *The Hound of the Baskervilles* at 80 minutes and *The Adventures of Sherlock Holmes* at 85 minutes. However, in addition to the story rights, Universal also purchased the Basil Rathbone and Nigel Bruce contracts, endorsing the common view that they incarnated Conan Doyle's characters with a great deal of credibility. The Twentieth Century-Fox pictures, though made during a year of gathering international tension in Europe, barely reflected the times. The opening film in the Universal series, however, made some months after America's entry to the war, used elements of a Holmes story – *His Last Bow* – set in 1914 around the time of the outbreak of the First World War. The story involved a German spy – Von Bork – engaged in the relaying of military secrets to Germany; a story which was simply forwarded in time to the Second World War. The elimination of the period costume, props and setting elements – Victorian dress, including Holmes's deerstalker hat, hansom cabs and so on – was a plus in budget terms for a B-picture project – but the setting of impending war with Germany resonated with contemporary audiences in both Britain and the United States. The story ends on an ominous, though optimistic note, with Holmes warning Watson that 'There's an east wind coming'. Watson interprets the comment in a literal way and disagrees, but Holmes continues:

> There's an east wind coming all the same, such a wind as never blew on England yet. It will be cold and bitter, Watson, and a good many of us may wither before its blast. But it's God's own wind none the less, and a cleaner, better, stronger land will lie in the sunshine when the storm has cleared. (Conan Doyle, 1981: 980)

The brief speech was retained verbatim for the film and, though written in the context of the First World War, the general sentiments were suitable for propaganda use in the midst of the Second World War. Subsequent films in the series also incorporated stirring codas – 'homilies' as Davies (1976) has termed them – which relate to the global political climate, together with references to the events of the war. The second film in the series, *Sherlock Holmes and the Secret Weapon* (1942), pitted Holmes against his legendary enemy, Professor Moriarty, who was working for the Nazis to obtain a bombsight mechanism smuggled out of Switzerland with its inventor and brought to England by Holmes. At one point in the film, when Moriarty and his henchmen have captured the inventor, a senior government official exclaims, 'Holmes, don't you realize what this means to England? We not only lose the bombsight but Germany gets it'. He continues, 'Coventry, Bath, Plymouth, London . . . all over again but with ten times the effect', alluding to key episodes of the German bombing campaign in Britain. Like its predecessor, the films end with a brief exchange between Watson and Holmes after the mechanism has been saved:

Watson: Thing are looking up, Holmes. This little island's still on the map.
Holmes: Yes. This fortress built by nature for herself.
       This blessed plot. This earth. This realm. This England.

The invocation of Shakespeare was not uncommon in British films of the time –
Jennings's documentaries, feature-film titles such as *The Demi-Paradise* and
This Happy Breed, Olivier's *Henry V* – and although the allusion is confined to
a couple of lines from *Richard II*, it provides a propagandist coda to the
adventure and mystery tale. *Sherlock Holmes Faces Death* (1943) also ends on
a pertinent propagandist note. The central female character renounces her land
inheritance to protect the ordinary people who live and work in the cottages,
villages and factories on the vast acres of land which she now legally owns. The
final sequence of the film has Holmes commenting to Watson on the
significance of this with a brief speech about the changing moral climate in
which greed and avarice are being replaced by more co-operative sentiments:

> There's a new spirit abroad in the land. The old days of grab and greed are on
> their way out. We're beginning to think of what we owe the other fellow not
> what we are compelled to give him. The time is coming, Watson, when we
> shan't be able to fill our bellies in comfort while other folk go hungry, or sleep in
> our beds while others shiver in the cold. When we shan't be able to kneel and
> thank God for blessings before our shining altars when men anywhere are
> kneeling in either physical or spiritual subjection.

Although somewhat sentimental, the impulses towards a more caring attitude,
the socially based sense of collective responsibility was part of the fabric of
British social thinking of the time. *The Scarlet Claw* (1944), although set in the
present, is a conventional horror/mystery with a monster and a series of murders
on the marshy moorland surrounding a village. It is set in Canada but the Devon
of *The Hound of the Baskervilles* seems an obvious reference point and indeed
the case of the 'hound' is mentioned in the film. Holmes solves the mystery and
unmasks the human being behind the 'monster', but contemporary events do
surface at the film's coda. Holmes delivers a brief speech extolling Canada as
'the lynch pin of the English-speaking world' and an important binding force
between the USA and the British Commonwealth of Nations.

Sherlock Holmes was not the only figure from British crime and mystery
fiction to feature on the Hollywood screen, although more films were based
upon Conan Doyle's 'great detective' than on other fictional figures. Characters
such as Bulldog Drummond, an early version of James Bond, Raffles, the
gentleman thief, and Fu Manchu, an oriental villain, deriving from crime fiction
of the 'golden age' did make occasional screen appearances in American films.
Sapper's Bulldog Drummond, a creation of the 1920s, had featured in some
silent British pictures before appearing on the American screen in an early
sound film – *Bulldog Drummond* (1929) – produced by Sam Goldwyn with
Ronald Colman in the lead role. Colman, one of the leading male stars of the
day, was an Englishman who had emigrated to America in 1920, and had built a

star career in silent pictures appearing opposite leading female stars of the time such as Lillian Gish and Vilma Banky. He repeated the Drummond role in Twentieth Century-Fox's *Bulldog Drummond Strikes Back* (1934) but his star status meant that he was used more frequently for prestige films than for genre pictures. In the late 1930s, Paramount launched a B-series featuring the character. Colman also played Raffles, the 'amateur cracksman', a character created by E. W. Hornung and conceived of as 'a criminal inversion of Sherlock Holmes' (Hardy, 1997: 282). Like Conan Doyle's stories, the Raffles tales were published in the *Strand* magazine in the 1890s and they soon became material both for the stage and for the early cinema. Vitagraph produced *The Adventures of Raffles, the Amateur Cracksman*, and this was followed by the inclusion of the character in some of the Danish Nordisk company's Sherlock Holmes films between 1908 and 1911. American silent pictures featuring Raffles appeared in 1917 and in 1925, both titled *Raffles, the Amateur Cracksman*; the first Raffles sound film was a Samuel Goldwyn production entitled simply *Raffles* (1930), with Colman, a picture which was remade by Goldwyn in 1940 with David Niven replacing Colman as the gentleman thief. Dr Fu Manchu, a master criminal bent on world domination, was the creation of Sax Rohmer (Arthur Sarsfield Ward) and first appeared in a series of short stories published in *The Storyteller* magazine from 1912 onwards. Although there were some short film series featuring Fu Manchu from British companies in the 1920s, the character came to prominence in the late 1920s and early 1930s with two American feature films – *The Mysterious Dr Fu Manchu* (1929) and *The Mask of Fu Manchu* (1932) – from Metro-Goldwyn-Mayer, with Boris Karloff in the lead. Subsequently, in 1940, the B-studio Republic made *Drums of Fu Manchu*, a serial in fifteen parts.

Gothic literature, horror cinema

The Hollywood crime genre, conceived broadly, accommodated the characters of British fiction at its margins, drawing upon various detectives and villains for the odd feature in the A-category, but confining even as popular a figure as Sherlock Holmes mainly to the B-feature series film. The central vigour of the genre during the 1930s and 1940s came from indigenous variants such as the gangster film and the film noir, from the recent history of gangsterdom and from the pulp fiction of Hammett and Chandler. The influence of British literature on the horror genre is more marked and, it may be argued, has shaped the contours of the genre in significant ways as compared with the marginal influence of British crime literature on the crime genre. Although, in the case of the crime film, the literary-cum-dramatic origins lay in popular fiction, the horror genre drew upon what might be termed 'classic sources'. Both, however, often arrived at the cinema by way of their adapted forms in the theatre. The horror genre, although now associated with the somewhat disreputable regions of popular culture, derives from rather more respectable cultural sources traceable to the Romantic poets, to Gothic literature and to the late nineteenth-century writing of Robert Louis Stevenson and Bram Stoker. Mary Shelley's novel, *Frankenstein*, published in 1818, Byron and his circle and their obsession with the vampire myth, the Dracula portrayed in Bram Stoker's novel and Robert Louis Stevenson's *Dr Jekyll and Mr Hyde* comprise a formidable set of literary antecedents which were transformed into a cinematic genre covering a spectrum of cultural levels from the popular genre film to the prestige picture. It did, however, take some time for the American cinema to embrace the Gothic heritage fully and to construct the horror genre as an important dimension of its generic profile. The early silent period saw American versions of *Frankenstein* (1910 and 1915), *The Vampire* (1910), inspired by a Burne-Jones painting, films based on Stevenson's *Dr Jekyll and Mr Hyde* in 1908 and 1912, and, loosely related, *A Fool There Was* (1915), the film which introduced the female 'vamp' figure in the person of actress, Theda Bara. Horror and fantasy formed the basis of a distinctive film trend in Europe during the 1920s, especially in the German cinema. Yet, this trend did not register in the American film industry and there 'was no horror or science-fiction genre in films of this period, although pulp fiction of this kind was already prevalent' (Koszarski, 1990: 184). What emerged was, in Koszarski's terms, 'a generalized "thriller" genre', although towards the end of the 1920s, the influence of the German cinema made itself felt in films such as *The Bat* (1926), *The Cat and the Canary* (1927) and *London After Midnight* (1927), which had a vampire theme of sorts. However, as Koszarski has suggested, it was not until the Universal cycle of the early 1930s that the horror and fantasy genre, a genre which constituted 'a significant departure from established thriller conventions of the silent period' actually emerged (1990: 186).

The Universal *Dracula* which effectively inaugurated the prolific cinema career of the most famous vampire of all, was also the beginning of a new genre. As David J. Skal has suggested, the character of Dracula 'has been depicted in film more times than almost any fictional being, with the possible single exception of Sherlock Holmes' (1990: 4). Though the Dracula myth stands at the apex of a popular genre recycled in countless variations in a low-budget film context, the Universal version released early in 1931 was conceived of as a prestige picture in some respects, and as a way for the studio to break into the first-run cinema circuits. The studio had owned a circuit of some three hundred subsequent-run theatres but these had been sold in the late 1920s to avoid the expense of converting them to sound and to raise finance for a programme of first-run films. Without a significant circuit of its own the studio needed a distinctive quality product to sell to the cinema chains controlled by the powerful majors. Among the first of Universal's prestige pictures aimed at the first-run audience was *All Quiet on the Western Front* (1930), directed by Lewis Milestone. With its budget of $1.45 million and its pre-sold subject-matter drawn from a best-selling novel, the picture fitted comfortably into the prestige category but the studio's economy could not sustain such expensive production. *Dracula*, also part of the studio's first-run strategy, fulfilled some of the criteria for a prestige film, particularly its immediate basis in a Broadway play and its classic novel origins, but its budget of $355,000 was more in line with the economy of a cost-cutting studio (Schatz, 1989: Ch. 6). *Dracula* did not enjoy the critical success of the Milestone picture, which won best picture and best director awards at the Motion Picture Academy ceremony for 1930. However, it provided a blueprint for the studio and started the Hollywood horror cycle of the 1930s, which remains identified with Universal, although such films were made at other studios including majors such as MGM and Paramount as well.

In some ways, the horror cycle anticipated the more extensive use of British cultural subject-matter that swept through the studios from around 1934 onwards. The Byron/Polidori story can be seen as originating the British version of the Dracula myth but Stoker's novel also reflected the influence of 'penny dreadful' writer Thomas Preskett Prest's *Varney the Vampire* and fellow-Irishman Sheridan Le Fanu's *Carmilla*, as well as various European imaginative variants on the myth. It also reflected Stoker's knowledge of non-fictional material relating to the myth as part of middle-European history and folklore reaching back to the fifteenth century and the historical figure of Vlad the Impaler, a Hungarian military figure renowned for his feats of cruelty to his enemies, the Turks. Stoker himself was the first to adapt *Dracula* for the stage shortly after publication of the novel in 1897 but the film's immediate source – the Broadway play – originated in a stage version of the novel written by actor/producer Hamilton Deane. Deane's play – a simplified version of the novel which restricted the setting to London – was first performed in England in 1924. Perhaps its distinctive contribution to the legend was the idea of presenting the Count in full evening dress and, as Glut has noted, 'This image of Dracula with white tie and tails and the long bat-like cloak, soon became the one the public identified with the character' (1975: 80). The American *Dracula* which opened in New York in 1927 was a revised version of the British play written by Deane in collaboration with the American playwright, John Lloyd Balderston, who was to work as a screenwriter on a number of the early horror films, including *Frankenstein*, *The Mummy* (1932) and *Bride of Frankenstein* (1934). Apart from Balderston's role in the stage adaptation, other non-British influences were also at work as Stoker's story made its way to the screen. Although a number of British writers had given the legend and the character a distinctive inflection and had devised the 'decadent aristocrat' image of Dracula which translated to the screen, it was Bela Lugosi, a Hungarian actor, whose performances both on the American stage and in the Universal film provided the popular image of Dracula. Its production team included the American director, Tod Browning, a horror film specialist who had directed MGM's *London After Midnight*, and German cinematographer, Karl Freund, whose background in the German cinema of the 1920s gave the film an expressionist inflection linking it to another set of cultural and artistic influences.

As with *Dracula*, the film version of *Frankenstein* was based on a stage play. The novel had been first adapted for the stage in 1823, a few years after its publication, to be followed by numerous nineteenth-century versions ranging in treatment from the dramatic to the comic. However, the immediate source for the film was a recent adaptation by an English writer – Peggy Webling – a member of the Hamilton Deane theatrical company. Webling's *Frankenstein*, a straightforward dramatic adaptation, was first performed in London in 1927, with Deane as the monster. During this period, the actor, well established as the stage *Dracula*, played both the vampiric Count and Frankenstein's monstrous creation, achieving the feat of 'performing the lead role of literature's two greatest monsters' on alternate nights (Glut, 1973: 44). Again, as with *Dracula*, the English stage adaptation was adapted by John L. Balderston for the American audience, and it was this 'adapted and embellished' version which Universal acquired for the planned film (Curtis, 1998: 127-8). Frenchman, Robert Florey, who had worked with writer Garret Fort on the script, was initially scheduled to direct *Frankenstein*, with Bela Lugosi to feature as the monster, though, eventually, neither were involved in the production. Direction was handed to the Englishman, James Whale, who had arrived in Hollywood a few years earlier after a career in the British theatre which had culminated in his production of *Journey's End*, the R. C. Sheriff play set in the First World War. Whale had come to America to stage *Journey's End* in a New York theatre but after this had signed a contract with Paramount and moved to Hollywood. He had signed with Universal in 1931 and was just completing work on *Waterloo Bridge* (1931), his first feature for the company, as pre-production on *Frankenstein* was beginning. After directing the film Whale was also to direct the sequel – *Bride of Frankenstein* (1934). Although the horror genre which developed from the early Universal pictures did involve contributions from different cultures, the key involvement of director Whale and stars such as Karloff, Colin Clive and Elsa Lanchester in the 'full-blooded Hollywood genre films whose cinematic and iconographic power has been unusually pervasive and enduring' (Barr, 1986: 9) underlines the importance of the British cultural contribution to Hollywood in the 1930s and, as Barr suggests, creates 'difficulties for the thesis that the British are "temperamentally unsuited" to cinema' (ibid.).

Hollywood's history of Britain

Both literature and history were seen as sources which could confer status upon the Hollywood institution and, as has been noted, British historical subject-matter was used by American film-makers from very earliest days of the cinema. By the 1910s the landscape of British history had found its way on to the American screen in a number of films with subject-matter from a range of historical periods. *The White Rosette* (1916) was set in the eleventh century, *Master Shakespeare Strolling Player* (1916), though set in the present, had flashbacks to Elizabethan England and the sixteenth century was also represented in an adaptation of Mark Twain's cradle exchange fantasy story, *The Prince and the Pauper* (1915). *Gretna Green* (1915), *Eugene Aram* (1916), *The Winning of Sally Temple* (1916) and *Sweet Kitty Bellairs* (1916) were all set in the eighteenth century and, in anticipation of later Hollywood trends, there were a number of films deriving from nineteenth-century British Imperial history. *The Campbells are Coming* (1915) and *The Leopard's Bride* (1916) were set in India, *The Four Feathers,* the first of the many versions of A. E. W. Mason's imperial novel set in the Sudan, was made in 1915 and *Second in Command* (1915) was about the Boer War. In addition, key figures from folklore and legend, such as Robin Hood and Ivanhoe, had featured in multi-reel films by 1913. The trend continued into the 1920s with the Elizabethan *Dorothy Vernon of Haddon Hall* (1924), featuring Mary Pickford, *The Fighting Blade* (1923) about the English Civil War, *The Amateur Gentleman* (1926), set in Regency times and a number of titles based on the Empire, including *The White Panther* (1924) and a second version of *The Four Feathers* (1928).

The 1920s also saw a number of films based on the recent history of the First World War centred upon British action of one sort or another and including *Havoc* (1925), *True Heaven* (1929), *Seven Days Leave* (1929) and the Anglo-US co-production *Journey's End* (1929). A number of the war films such as *Lilac Time* (1928) and *Midnight Lovers* (1926) featured the flying corps, as did two prominent titles from 1930, Howard Hughes's *Hell's Angels* and *The Dawn Patrol* directed by Howard Hawks. Biographical pictures (biopics) with British subject-matter – an important dimension of Hollywood's 'British genre' in the 1930s – were anticipated in two films about Disraeli. The first *Disraeli* was made in 1921, the second in 1929, with both featuring the British actor George Arliss in the title role, re-creating his American stage success of 1911 in the Louis Napoleon Parker play. The 1929 version was made at Warner Bros., a studio subsequently to be closely identified with both the 'biopic' genre and with British subject-matter across a range of genres. The 'Britishness' of *Disraeli* was part of the explanation for the success of the film and Warners had already released *The Divine Lady* (1929), based on the romance between Lord Nelson and Lady Hamilton. In 1930 the studio followed up with a number of titles which exploited the 'British dimension', including *The Green Goddess*, set in India during British rule, with Arliss as a Rajah, *The Man from Blankley's*, with John Barrymore playing a Scottish lord, *Sweet Kitty Bellairs,* a sound version of the Regency 'operetta-like romp' (Hirschhorn, 1986: 91), *The Flirting Widow*, derived from an A. E. W. Mason story, *Green Stockings*, and another Arliss vehicle, *Old English*, adapted from John Galsworthy's Victorian play (Altman, 1999: 40;). Although the best-known Hollywood British films – the literary adaptations and the historical pictures – were made subsequently, as Glancy has noted, 'Hollywood's taste for the most famous, traditional and antiquated aspects of Britain was already established at the beginning of the decade' (1999: 72).

The period most closely identified with British material is the 1930s and 1940s, with more than 150 'Hollywood British films' made during this time (Glancy, 1999:1). A good many of these were historical pictures and, as in the previous decades, historical personages, institutions and events from a number of distinct periods were depicted. Subjects ranged from Medieval kings and Tudor queens, Richard the Lionheart, Elizabeth the First and Mary, Queen of Scots, through maritime and military history, including the Crusades, the

Napoleonic wars, piracy on the high seas and the Crimean war, to nineteenth-century imperialist activities in India and Africa. There were also a number of films depicting the lives of prominent historical figures such as Disraeli, Clive of India, Florence Nightingale, the poets Elizabeth Barrett Browning and Robert Browning, and legendary characters such as Robin Hood. There were even films based upon the histories of august financial institutions such as Lloyd's of London and the Rothschilds. A number of the films with historical elements were derived from literary sources, though examples such as *Treasure Island* (1934) and *A Tale of Two Cities* (1935) put aspects of Britain's heritage on display as well as showcasing the literary achievements of Robert Louis Stevenson and Charles Dickens. Like their literary counterparts, many of the historical films were accorded 'prestige' status with high production values. Many of them featured the leading stars of the day in lavish period costumes in elaborate and carefully crafted settings.

Even Warner Bros. identified especially in the early part of the decade with contemporary subjects – gangster films and newspaper stories for instance – made a number of such pictures including some of the most significant of the British-orientated films. Indeed, it has been suggested by Nick Roddick that it was a British historical maritime picture – *Captain Blood* (1935) – that signalled 'a shift to more prestigious projects by the studio in the middle of the decade' (1983: 237), although, as has been noted above, the studio had worked in the historical genre previously with the George Arliss films at the end of the 1920s. *Captain Blood* featured Errol Flynn, who had started his Warners' career in their British studio working on a quota picture – *Murder at Monte Carlo* (1934) – and four of the studio's subsequent Hollywood-British films were built around his star persona. He starred in *The Charge of the Light Brigade* (1936), *Another Dawn* (1937), *The Private Lives of Elizabeth and Essex* (1938) and *The Adventures of Robin Hood* (1938), and made an appearance in *The Prince and the Pauper* (1937). The maritime subject-matter which proved successful at Warners also succeeded at MGM, the studio most closely associated with the prestige picture. *Mutiny on the Bounty* (1935) won the Academy Award for the best picture in a year when the nominations included a number of British-orientated films, some literary, some historical. In fact, the twelve nominations in the best picture category included five titles – *Captain Blood, David Copperfield, The Informer, The Lives of a Bengal Lancer* and *A Midsummer Night's Dream* – with explicit British affiliations, and a sixth, *Ruggles of Red Gap*, with a British – American culture clash theme of an English butler in the American West (Steinberg, 1981: 30-1).

MGM had already embarked upon the British theme in 1934 with its historical/literary picture, *The Barretts of Wimpole Street*, and with adaptations of Robert Louis Stevenson's *Treasure Island* and Dickens's *David Copperfield*. Subsequent 'British' pictures from MGM included more Dickens, *A Tale of Two Cities* (1935) and *A Christmas Carol* (1938), *Parnell* (1937), a biopic about the nineteenth-century Irish politician, and the three prestige films made in Britain – *A Yank at Oxford* (1938), *The Citadel* (1938) and *Goodbye Mr Chips* (1939). United Artists' activities were implicitly focused on prestige material and their link with British companies such as London Films and British and Dominions meant that a number of their releases during the 1930s were British pictures with British themes. Many of these were ambitious historical films. *The Private Life of Henry VIII* from Korda's company was followed by *The Scarlet Pimpernel* (1935), with its English Regency hero, together with the 1938 sequel, *The Return of the Scarlet Pimpernel*, the Elizabethan *Fire Over England* (1937) and the Technicolor Indian epic, *The Drum* (1938), while British and Dominions supplied *Nell Gwyn* (1935). Alongside the British-produced material, United Artists also released American-produced films with British historical subject- matter. These include two films from Darryl Zanuck's Twentieth Century company, *The House of Rothschild* (1934), about the origins of the London banking company, and the biopic of the eighteenth-century soldier and politician, *Clive of India* (1935); *Beloved Enemy* (1936) set in Ireland in 1921, from the Goldwyn company; and David Selznick's first independent production after leaving MGM , *Little Lord Fauntleroy* (1936), the tale of an American child who inherits an English title. Other studios also contributed to the Hollywood British historical film. The cycle of films set in Imperial India continued with Paramount's *The Lives of a Bengal Lancer* (1935), Twentieth Century-Fox's *Wee Willie Winkie* (1937) and RKO's *Gunga Din* (1939), which was that studio's most expensive picture of the decade. RKO also contributed to the Irish dimension of the trend with John Ford's *The Informer* (1935) and *The Plough and the Stars* (1937). The British strand continued into the war period with films such as *Forever and a Day* (1943), made by members of the British community in Hollywood as a contribution to wartime propaganda, consisting largely of episodes from British history; costume films with seventeenth-century settings, such as *Frenchman's Creek* (1944) and *Forever Amber* (1947), top box-office performers in their release years; and a number of literary/dramatic adaptations with period settings, including *Jane Eyre* (1944), *Gaslight* (1944) and *The Corn is Green* (1945). Although a small percentage of the films made during this period, the Hollywood British films of the time included many high-profile prestige films featuring the leading stars of the day such as Errol Flynn, Bette Davis, Cary Grant and Gary Cooper. Many of them have become Hollywood 'classics' noted in film-history books and frequently revived in repertory cinema and on television.

Historical material had proved ideal in the context of the 1930s prestige film, with its spectacular production values, and such values proved to be one of the weapons wielded by Hollywood in the face of the threat of television in the 1950s. The potential for spectacle in the historical film made it a key genre in the struggle for the audience, enabling producers to exploit the technologies of colour cinematography, the large widescreen presentation and stereophonic sound to the full with costume, action, crowd scenes and battles and exotic location shooting. It is no coincidence that the first CinemaScope film was the historical spectacle *The Robe* (1953), and that MGM's first CinemaScope picture was the British historical Arthurian epic, *Knights of the Round Table* (1954). The latter film, a 'runaway' production made at MGM's British studios at Borehamwood, was part of a distinctive generic trait focused on history and associated with the Anglo-US pictures of the time rather than indigenous production (Harper, 1997: 135-40). It appears in a range of guises including the Arthurian *The Black Knight* (1954), medieval adventure films such as *The Black Rose* (1950), *Ivanhoe* (1952), *The Dark Avenger* (1955) and *The Adventures of Quentin Durward* (1956), Regency films such as *Beau Brummell* (1954), naval and pirate pictures such as *Treasure Island* (1950), *Captain Horatio Hornblower R. N.* (1951) and *The Crimson Pirate* (1952), *The Mudlark* (1950), about Queen Victoria, two versions of the Robin Hood myth, *Rogues of Sherwood Forest* (1950) and *The Story of Robin Hood and His Merrie Men* (1952), and a number of Scottish-set films such as *The Master of Ballantrae* (1953) and *Rob Roy, the Highland Rogue* (1954). Some of these fell into the 'colossal division', as *Variety* termed it – expensive film production which Hollywood had resumed in the early 1950s. In Britain, the mantle of Korda and Gabriel Pascal as producers of big-budget spectaculars had passed to the Americans and the 'prestige' scale of these films certainly paid off in box office terms. British companies at the time, especially the Rank Organization, had retrenched, leaving the field clear for the Hollywood companies to exploit the spectacular qualities of the genre. Most of the historical films were in Technicolor and films such as *Knights of the Round Table*, *The Dark Avenger*, and *The Adventures of Quentin Durward* were made in the recently developed CinemaScope format.

American financing of British films continued into the 1960s, indeed it increased to as high as 90 per cent of the total production finance in the middle of the decade (Murphy, 1992: 258). Although the money went into a range of genres, including the more fashionable 'Swinging London' films, there were some large-scale prestige historical pictures which followed the traditions established in Hollywood in the 1930s and in the various American-supported British features of the 1950s. These included another version of *The Charge of the Light Brigade* (1968), more revisionist in temper than the Errol Flynn picture of the 1930s, and a number of films about medieval figures, including *Becket* (1963), *A Man for All Seasons* (1966), *Anne of the Thousand Days* (1970) and *Alfred the Great* (1969); the seventeenth century was represented by *Cromwell* (1970), and there was a revival of the nineteenth-century Imperial 'history' popular in the 1930s with *Zulu* (1963) and *Khartoum* (1966).

From the very beginnings of the American cinema, the classics of British literature, key events and personages from British history, together with mythic figures, have been transposed to the screen. The exact motivations have been variable: sometimes in the service of cultural elevation, exploiting the considerable prestige of English literature and drama from the Elizabethans to the nineteenth century; sometimes for the exotic and spectacular potential of location and setting; and sometimes for the inspirational and heroic possibilities inherent in the battles and romances of the past and in the colourful myths which have attached themselves to actual historical figures, such as Henry VIII and Elizabeth, and to the heroes of legend, such as Robin Hood.

8 Britain and Hollywood

The American film industry stands as the single most powerful and influential force in the history of the medium, setting standards to which other film-producing countries were obliged to aspire. Hollywood has systematically produced the bulk of films to establish a wide international circulation since the First World War and American films are, for most nations, more or less synonymous with popular cinema. As Andrew Higson has put it: 'The popular understanding of cinema is so closely based on the watching of American films that to offer something too different is almost to revolt against the very idea of cinema' (1995: 11). Britain, as an industrial country with a large urban population, was inevitably caught up in the movement towards the internationalization of the film industry under American hegemony and many of the reasons for Hollywood's particular success in the British market derive from the general explanations of its success in the global film market. Part of the explanation is economic – American films were able to cover their production costs in the large home market and this meant that exports could be priced to undercut competition from other national production industries. Part of the explanation is historical – at times the United States was able to take advantage of the decline of film production in a Europe preoccupied with international conflict, and to establish itself as the primary supplier of film entertainment in countries such as France, which had played a significant, indeed dominating, role in the international export market in the early years of cinema. Part of the explanation lies in the entrepreneurial skill and efficiency of the industry which began to organize itself along 'Taylorist' lines before the First World War and was in a position to take advantage of the market spaces opened up by the war, utilizing aggressive marketing strategies such as the block booking of films to exhibitors. The position has been well summarized by Acheson and Maule:

The Americans benefitted from the two world wars by creating during them an inventory of films available for release at the termination of hostilities and by attracting creative personnel from all corners of the world to reside and work in the United States. The United States was also the largest single market in the largest language market from a revenue perspective. At the same time, the United States had assimilated large blocks of viewers from different ethnic backgrounds. Films produced for this market had to cross cultural boundaries and therefore were easier to export. The American managerial and financial cultures were conducive to the development of contractual and institutional relationships that permitted the financing and distribution of films on a large scale. (1994: 293-4)

Part of the explanation, as the writers indicate, shifts from history and economics to the cultural, to a conceptualization of the American audience as representatives of a range of cultures, and especially of peoples from Europe, in the context of their mass immigration to the United States in the nineteenth and early twentieth centuries. In addition to the cosmopolitan domestic audience, the film-makers themselves – producers, directors, writers, stars – were recruited from the leading European film-making nations, including Britain. The fact that American films seemed to capture the public imagination in so many countries may be linked to their ability to synthesize different cultures, to devise genres for a wide range of ethnic communities, a requirement imposed by their domestic audience. In effect, Hollywood was exporting films designed to appeal to an 'American' audience constituted partly by relatively recent immigrant communities. A certain degree of the international was inscribed in the parochial, facilitating the circulation of such films on an international basis. As Geoffrey Nowell-Smith has suggested, the 'American cinema set out in the first place to be popular in America, where it served an extremely diverse and largely immigrant public. What made it popular at home also helped to make it popular abroad' (1985: 152). In addition, the Hollywood export machine displayed a sensitivity to foreign markets, drawing upon information about foreign countries supplied by government, and a readiness to modify the versions sent to specific countries in the light of local audience sensibilities (Vasey, 1997).

Britain was particularly affected by the flood of American films which started pouring into the country when the indigenous industry was attempting the reconstruction of a production industry after the privations of the First World War. Although the British film had been important in the early days of cinema, production had not developed as strongly as the distribution or exhibition sectors which had developed close links with the American industry. Prior to the First World War, London had become established as a distribution centre for American films, enabling US firms to reach the wide range of markets to which Britain as a major imperial power had access. British firms imported American films and re-exported them to various parts of the globe during the period when the American industry was still consolidating its position in its own domestic market. During the war, however, the American industry began to establish its global distribution system, opening offices in various countries, and London lost its key role as 'film clearing house of the world', although it did remain important as a centre for the European distribution of American films (Thompson, 1985: 29, 70). Britain's fast-expanding exhibition sector was an eager customer for American films but production was the 'Cinderella' wing of the industry starved of finance, unable to compete with the expensively budgeted films from America. American films, since the days of Griffith, have looked more opulent and more lavish than their British counterparts, and, it might be argued, have provided audiences with the spectacular qualities, the abundant visions, the expensive patinas which became woven into the very experience of cinema as an 'escape' of sorts from the humdrum realities of life for substantial sections of the populace. Ian Jarvie has argued that the pre-eminence of the American film derived from such qualities, which differentiated it from other cinemas and which consolidated its definitive position in world cinema:

> In early film trading, where many of the figures were expressed in footage, it seems to have been an axiom that one foot of film was equivalent to any other foot of film as product. This was not to be so for long, as genres, stars, films of different lengths, and spectacles introduced differentiation. In the pre-World War 1 period, much of film trading could be expressed in footage. My guess is that during the rapid changes of the war the U. S. product came to be*differentiated as such*, in addition to the differentiations *within* the American product. Certain qualities came to be offered by and expected from U. S. films, qualities that were highly salable in much of the world. Most notable of these qualities was that the films contained the work of popular stars, stars never remotely matched in numbers and drawing power by any other producing country. (Jarvie, 1992: 129-30; emphasis in original)

The Hollywood system enabled lavish expenditure upon stars and production values but the embrace of such definitions of the cinematic experience by a public negotiating this new form of entertainment was not simply achieved through commercial dominance. The specific features of the cinema which the Hollywood system created – long films with a forward narrative momentum, romance, action, stars and spectacle – engaged audiences regardless of the specific cultural detail in the story or in the *mise en scène*. The economic power of Hollywood is clearly an important factor in its success. The size of the American domestic market enables Hollywood to recover a substantial percentage of its production costs within the United States. This has enabled producers to export at highly competitive rates while still making profit, to flood overseas markets with lavish films at prices which undercut those required to sustain indigenous production on anything like the same scale. However, a simple economic explanation remains less than satisfactory in the face of the enthusiastic reception of Hollywood films throughout the world, which suggests that the success of American films 'arises not from their cheapness but from what the popular audience has obstinately continued to regard as the high quality of the American article' (Buscombe, 1981: 143).

Economic power needs to be linked to cultural appeal in order to understand the precise ways in which the Hollywood film located itself in the consciousness of the British and other publics frequently warned by cultural, moral and religious commentators about the dangers of succumbing to the values of a popular culture imported from America, often at the expense of the indigenous film. While it is true that the major American companies pursued many strategies to consolidate their position in the British market, establishing production units in Britain, investing in British companies, as well as luring key British actors and directors to Hollywood, the success of American films with British and other audiences was not simply a matter of imposition. Evidence for this can be drawn from trade paper surveys. For example, in 1937, *World Film*

News reported on a symposium on box-office appeal which indicated that the exhibition sector was satisfied that American films appealed to the widest audiences but considered that British pictures were not suitable for their working-class audiences, though they had some appeal for middle-class audiences in the Home Counties and on the south coast. A Scottish exhibitor commented at the time that British films were, in fact, 'more foreign to his audience than the products of Hollywood, over 6,000 miles away' and the superior appeal of the American film for the mass audience was confirmed by the Mass Observation survey of cinema-going in Bolton in the late 1930s (*World Film News*, February 1937: 6; Richards and Sheridan, 1987: 34).

Britain, despite the Scottish viewpoint, did share a more or less common language with the United States and an intertwined history and culture which provided Hollywood films with a high degree of accessibility for British audiences and made it more difficult for the indigenous industry to compete. The developing importance of cinema in Britain during the 1920s and after was based primarily on American rather than indigenous films. In many ways, this was of little consequence to the cinema owners, who could depend upon a regular and efficient supply of appealing and potentially profitable films provided by an industry which had begun to organize itself for the mass production and international distribution of films before the First World War. Similarly, the general cinema audience seemed quite happy with the Chaplin and Mary Pickford films, the spectacular films of Douglas Fairbanks, the Westerns of W. S. Hart and the serials which almost completely dominated the British cinema bills of the 1920s. By contrast, the Hollywood hegemony was of much consequence to the small British film-production industry, which found it difficult if not impossible to compete and which faced a very serious production crisis and the possible collapse of the industry in the mid-1920s (PEP, 1952: 41). It was also perceived as a serious matter by the political leadership and the cultural intelligentsia which understood a thriving national cinema in terms of national prestige and authority, cultural standing and importance.

Of course, Britain was not unique in the subordination of its own cinema to that of Hollywood. As noted above, the American cinema in the period following the First World War had become the dominant force in an industry which had been international from its beginnings, supplying films to Europe and Asia in such profusion as to threaten the economic viability of numerous indigenous industries as well as constituting an 'alien' cultural influence in the eyes of many commentators. Many European countries responded vigorously establishing protectionist measures which guaranteed home-produced films a share of the market. More significantly, countries such as Germany, France and the Soviet Union created powerful alternative traditions to the films coming from Hollywood and provided cinema with the great silent 'art' film trends – expressionism, impressionism, constructivism, the 'montage' school. Even the small Swedish cinema industry established a high reputation with films from directors such as Stiller and Sjöström and 'was recognised as the first major alternative to Hollywood to emerge after the war' (Thompson and Bordwell, 1994: 68). The British production industry produced no comparable movements or trends, only the odd film from Hitchcock and Asquith to set beside the prestigious cinemas from continental Europe.

The reasons for Britain's particular capitulation to American dominance are various. As well as the advantages of financial strength, high-production values and the efficient organization of production and distribution, the common language certainly meant that American films could circulate without inter-title translation during the silent period and without the dubbing or sub-titling necessary once dialogue had been added in the late 1920s. As well as the intrinsic advantages possessed by American films, as Rachael Low suggests, the potential competitor British films were subjected to critical vituperation and distributor/exhibitor indifference in Britain itself, leading to a kind of inferiority complex in the small British film-making community (1971: Ch. 8). In addition, by contrast to the position in some other European countries, the British government did not intervene to protect British films until the end of the decade and then only in terms of protectionist legislation in a desperate context in which the industry seemed 'well on the way to extinction' (PEP, 1952: 41). The German government, for example, had invested in the reconstruction of the German film industry after the war and introduced quota laws by the middle of the decade; the new Soviet state treated film as a uniquely important propaganda tool and fostered the climate in which directors such as Eisenstein and Pudovkin flourished; in France, although the state did not offer much in the way of support, the large commercial concerns – Pathé and Gaumont – created 'artistic' wings within their companies employing avant garde film makers such as Abel Gance, Jean Epstein and Marcel L'Herbier, and contributing to the resurgence of the French cinema of the time. The critically important 'art' cinemas of the period emerged from contexts more congenial to specialized indigenous production than was the case in Britain. Such countries also had to cope with the influx of the popular pictures from Hollywood but the development of 'art' cinemas in France and Germany, for example, was seen as a method of product differentiation and a strategy for creating a market for alternative forms of cinema.

Whatever the precise reasons for the American domination of the British screen, the interrelationships between the two industries have persisted from the earliest days of cinema and embrace both the economic and the cultural. The most public face of the relationship is, of course, the circulation of American films in Britain, sustained at a very high level since the silent period despite quota legislation, censorship and the state subsidy to the domestic industry. The enduring popularity in the face of certain forms of cultural resistance from critics and educators, politicians and clergymen, indicates the degree to which the Hollywood film has matched the aspirations and tastes of the British audience or substantial sections of it. The reverse traffic – British films in the USA – have not impacted sufficiently to provoke analogous discussion and, indeed, have often circulated in America through the small network of specialist 'art-houses' in the metropolitan centres and university towns (Roud, 1956/57: 119). That is to say they have circulated as films valued positively for their 'otherness' and their difference from the conventional Hollywood cinema programme, although the explanation for this is partly economic, as British films were usually regarded as not strong enough in box-office terms to warrant release on the national circuits. The contact between Britain and the American cinema has provided a varied set of relationships operating between the two industries and between the two cultures, with Hollywood holding the upper hand both in terms of economics and business and in terms of culture. American film companies have marketed their films with a great deal of success in Britain, while British films have enjoyed only intermittent success in the United States; American popular culture as relayed through the Hollywood film has exerted a great deal of influence in Britain, particularly among the working-class audience for the cinema, whereas British life and culture, as relayed through films from Pinewood, Elstree and Ealing, have had more of a niche impact on American culture. Subjects drawn from British culture and history, on the other hand, have exerted a more significant influence on American audiences when articulated with the conventions of the Hollywood film – narrative, spectacle and genre. The conquest of the British screen by the Hollywood picture achieved by the middle of the 1920s imposed a powerful framework of comprehension on the British public relating to what a film should look and sound like, and what the experience of cinema should be.

The Hollywood film and British film culture

A detailed critique of cinema in general, and American films in particular, took some time to evolve; it was not until after the First World War that the medium began to attract regular comment in the national newspapers, and that the practices of film criticism and reviewing became established. The cinema had become a central dimension of British popular culture, providing entertainment for the urban populations in particular, and its increasing importance in the early years of the twentieth century was registered in the emergence of trade papers and fan magazines incorporating commentary and information for both film exhibitors and film audiences. *The Optical Magic Lantern Journal* which started in the 1890s changed into *The Optical Lantern and Kinematograph Journal* in 1904. It then became *The Kinematograph Weekly* in 1907, to be joined in the following year by *The Bioscope*. Fan magazines appeared slightly later than the trade press, with *Pictures and Pleasure* and *Pictures and the Picturegoer* starting publication in 1913. By the 1920s, with the cinema established as a key feature of popular entertainment, commentators began to reflect on the significance of the medium for artistic and cultural production in a more general way. The emergence of 'art' cinemas in France and Germany, and the politicized artistic cinema of the USSR, stimulated interest among intellectuals whose endeavours were often focused upon differentiating film as a potential art form from the actual situation of a cinema in Britain dominated by the commercial culture of Hollywood. In addition to this, the crisis in British production of the mid-1920s occasioned much soul-searching among writers, artists and politicians about the significance of an indigenous cinema and its importance to the national cultural well-being. The lobby for the protection of the British industry from the power of the American industry, which culminated in the 1927 Cinematograph Films Act, operated at a number of levels – economic, political and cultural. The interest in film as an art form found a number of outlets, including the founding of the Film Society in London in 1925, the appearance of *Close Up* – a 'serious' film journal – in 1927 and the publication of Paul Rotha's *The Film Till Now* in 1930. Together with John Grierson's writings on cinema in general and his activities in the realm of documentary film, and the beginnings of 'serious' film reviewing in the broadsheet newspapers, these moves generated a particular set of attitudes to the new medium which were to sediment themselves into the minority wing of British film culture and provide an influential intellectual framework for subsequent debates on the medium. The 'ideology' of film represented by Rotha, the Film Society, *Close Up* and the documentarists had, at its centre, a range of negative perspectives on the Hollywood popular commercial film, running from suspicion to hostility, together with a reverence for the European 'art' film. The dichotomy of European art film/American movie was to become a cornerstone of thinking about the development of cinema in the minority film culture substantially unchallenged until the appearance of the journal *Movie* in the 1960s.

Rotha's book, written in the late 1920s, was an ambitious attempt to provide both a synoptic view of cinema's development to that date and a prescriptive commentary on the aesthetics of film. For a number of reasons, the American cinema represented 'the lowest form of public entertainment' (1967: 126). In some respects, Rotha's stance on Hollywood relates to the general attack upon the new technological and urban culture launched by Leavis and, somewhat later, the Frankfurt critics. The industrial structure, the commercial impetus, the volume production policies, the expensively produced spectacular films and the star system – 'a flagrant prostitution of creative intelligence and good film material' – led Rotha 'to regard Hollywood much as . . . a factory managed and owned by a number of astute business men, who seek only large financial returns from the goods they manufacture' (ibid.: 132, 127). However, Rotha's attack was not upon cinema *per se* but rather on the aesthetic qualities which Hollywood's films embodied – the 'realist–narrative' fictional cinema as it emerged from the American film industry. European films represented an alternative path for the medium and one which could elevate it into a high cultural position alongside traditional art forms. Rotha saw the photographic realism of the medium, its capacity to offer a credible representation of the world in its physical detail, 'the camera's misleading faculty of being able to record the actual', as a major obstacle to its maturing as an art form, to its evolution into 'film proper' (ibid.: 88). The task of the film-maker was to depart from the film's inherent photographic realism as obviously as possible and films were judged in terms of their degree of departure from the realism of the medium. Accordingly, in a hierarchy of cinematic forms, Rotha placed the abstract film at the head and the narrative fiction film near the bottom. The key developments for Rotha were in the German silent cinema, with films such as

The Cabinet of Dr. Caligari (1919) and *The Last Laugh* (1925), and the Soviet cinema, with directors such as Eisenstein and Pudovkin. German films, with their expressionist manipulations of *mise en scène* and cinematography, satisfied Rotha's interventionist aesthetic to perfection and he regarded *The Cabinet of Dr Caligari* as 'the first attempt at the expression of a creative mind in the new medium of cinematography' (ibid.: 94). Soviet films such as *Battleship Potemkin* (1925) and *The End of St. Petersburg* (1928) exemplified 'the most advanced forms of contemporary cinema' with their experiments in montage and their identification of editing as the crucial activity which elevated film from mere mechanical duplication to the status of creative art (ibid.: 105).

The principles behind Rotha's stance – the polarization of the commercial and art cinemas and their identification with America and Europe respectively – can also be detected behind the formation of the Film Society and the appearance of the journal *Close Up*. The Film Society had been formed specifically to bring the new European films to Britain, to provide an exhibition outlet for experimental films unlikely to secure distribution through the orthodox commercial channels. In effect, this meant non-American films. *Close Up* took up the cudgels on behalf of such films and, for the most part, maintained a stance of critical disdain for the endeavours of commercial cinema both in Hollywood and Britain with few exceptions. The journal saw its mission as speaking for a minority audience interested in film as an art form whose interests were not catered for by the prevailing entertainment cinema. As an editorial in the second issue of the journal put it:

> broadly speaking anything up to 75 per cent of modern films are at a certain level; they have moments, they reach a vast majority, they satisfy. But there is a minority of several million people to whom these films are tiresome, a minority that loves the film, but has too much perception, too much intelligence to swallow the dismal and paltry stories and acting set up week by week before it on the screen. This minority has got to have films it can enjoy, films with psychology, soundness, intelligence. (1927: Vol. 1, No. 2: 15-16)

The main objection to the American cinema was that it was not good enough; it failed to realize the enormous potential of the new art form. Part of the problem was the triviality of content – 'dismal and paltry stories' – but there was also an alleged aesthetic failure embodied in the evolving 'classical' style of cinema which restricted the artistic quality of the American film. *Close Up*, for example, included slogans such as 'We Want Better Films' and 'The Official Guide to Better Movies' on its cover to proclaim its commitment to promoting alternatives to the dominant Hollywood film (Donald *et al.*, 1998: 5-6). Its task was cultural education and, in addition to devoting much space to the various artistic currents in the best-known European cinemas, it provided background information and critical analysis of films from Argentina, Belgium, Czechoslovakia, The Netherlands, India, Japan, Portugal, Switzerland and Turkey. *Close Up* and Rotha shared the view that 'Hollywood movies are slick, facile, and well-finished. At the same time they display an absence of good taste, of intelligence, and, if the term is allowable, of culture' (1967: 140). John Grierson, though somewhat sceptical about commercial cinema and more committed to documentary, did offer a more nuanced view of the American cinema and a more measured understanding of the Hollywood picture than many of his contemporaries. In the 1920s, prior to his installation as leader of the British documentary cinema, Grierson spent some time in America and conducted research into Hollywood. His memorandum, 'Notes for English Producers', written in 1927 on his return from the United States, identified positive features of the Hollywood film based upon defining its popular appeal (Grierson, 1989). In certain respects, the orthodox position on the Hollywood film evolving out of the experience of the 1920s dismissed Hollywood's appeal in terms that were somewhat condescending to the mass audience. Rotha, for example, referred to 'a vacant-minded, empty-headed public, who flocked to sensations, who thrilled to sexual vulgarity, and who would go anywhere and pay anything to see indecent situations riskily handled on the screen' (1967: 130). *Close Up*, in a similar vein, conceded that the poor taste of the general public was beyond redemption and that 'as long as they desire eye-wash and bunk they must have it' (Vol. 1, No. 2: 15-16). For all his ultimate commitment to documentary cinema and his various reservations about the Hollywood film, Grierson was more detached in his analysis of popular American cinema, and he isolated its positive optimistic address as the key to its success.

The crucial factors for a successful film were 'that the outcome of a picture must be positive rather than negative, that it must concern itself with youth and achievement rather than age and disintegration, with matters that instil optimism rather than these that suggest a reason for pessimism' (Grierson, 1989: 315). Writing some years after Grierson, the American critic Robert Warshow also identified the commitment to 'a cheerful view of life' (1970: 127) as a key element in the social and political life of the United States, and one which was sustained in important ways by the positive and optimistic values embodied in popular culture in general. Grierson, in addition, also identified another quality of the American film which ran counter to the presuppositions of the minority film culture. Although Hollywood films were usually regarded as fantasy and dream, Grierson suggested that, despite a tendency to romanticize, American films did have their roots in the ordinary realities of American life and related more closely to the life of the 'ordinary American'. As he wrote:

> Hollywood has always had the good sense to loose an occasional salute to the common life. Behind its luxuries there has always been a suggestion of origin in Kanka Kee or Kalamazoo. Behind the gowns and gauderies there has been a frank allowance that the lady inside them started under honest parents as a shop girl. Tales of the Frontier or the Railroad and the Gangs and the War have remained faithful to the notion that rank was but the guinea stamp and a man was a man for a' that. (1966a: 86)

The populist character of the American film contrasted with the narrow social focus of the British film of the period, a focus which Grierson sought to shift in his efforts to construct the documentary film movement.

Subsequent attitudes to Hollywood pictures, especially amongst the intelligentsia, reflected the early deliberations, particularly in their negative form. Peter Stead has identified the areas of concern which prompted the anti-Hollywood stance among intellectual commentators, writers and critics, factors which had become embedded in the film culture after *Close Up* and *The Film Till Now*. Hollywood, it was suggested, had achieved its prominence through hard selling, through 'exploitation and manipulation' by entrepreneurs motivated by commercial concerns. Implicit in such a judgement was that the public's taste was not 'a natural and voluntary process', and that the popular success of the American film was achieved through skilful marketing in the pursuit of profit. In addition, this commercialism had both destroyed the developing art of cinema, especially after the introduction of sound, and impeded the development of film as an educational medium. There was also the concern about the content of Hollywood films, their fantasy qualities and their seductive portrayals of crime, sex and other staple themes of popular culture (Stead, 1981). Hollywood was, in short, commercial, anti-art and education, and peddled corrupt messages; the development of a robust film culture based on the documentary principles of 'realism', the stylistic qualities of the European 'art' film especially the Soviet cinema and a mixture of moral and education purpose was necessary to combat the forces of darkness coming from the other side of the Atlantic for the intellectuals who 'found it very difficult to come to terms with the mass popularity of American films' (ibid.: 25). For the intelligentsia the fact that the British public endorsed the Hollywood film with great enthusiasm was a matter of regret; that fact, though, was not lost on the politicians who adopted an 'arms length' principle in relation to the industry, assuming that the modest level of protection offered in the 1927 legislation and renewed towards the end of the decade was the most that the government could do in a free society. The public preference for American pictures was well-publicized and, in that light, 'British governments . . . never ever seriously considered measures to counter Hollywood's dominance' (ibid.: 22).

The 1940s saw something of a shift in the critical atmosphere, especially in relation to the domestic film previously dismissed in vituperative terms by the intellectual critical establishment. The success of the wartime pictures with both critics and the public brought a new confidence to the British cinema and critical activity became more concerned with the promotion of an indigenous cinema stimulated by the events of the war, which neither retreated into a narrow parochialism nor attempted to copy the Hollywood film. Dilys Powell, writing about *The Proud Valley* (1940) and *Convoy* (1940), made in the early days of the war at Ealing Studios, suggested that such films indicated new dimensions of subject-matter and approach:

> in these two modest productions, were the germs of a new movement in the British cinema: the movement towards concentration on the native subject, the movement towards documentary truth in the entertainment film. The war both

encouraged a new seriousness of approach by British producers and directors, and drove them to look nearer home than before in their themes. (1948: 78)

Critics wrote enthusiastically of a new kind of British film which blended the 'realist' aesthetics of the documentary movement with the narrative fictional structures of the classic feature film to produce the distinctive British 'quality' film of the period. The critical and commercial success of films such as *In Which We Serve* (1942) suggested a closer community between the intellectual critics and the public than was the case in previous times. However, the shift was not total and although there 'was a general optimistic support for British cinema provided it stayed true to its vocation of realism and quality' (Barr, 1986: 13), the critics were much less impressed with the prestige spectaculars such as Gabriel Pascal's *Caesar and Cleopatra* (1946) and the more Hollywood-like genre films – the costume films and melodramas, the crime pictures – which were also part of the British cinema of the 1940s.

Yet, if there was a partial shift in relation to the British film, the negative attitude towards the Hollywood film from previous decades continued. Peter Stead (1981: 29-30) suggests that British critical attitudes to the Hollywood cinema more clearly orientated to 'entertainment' were beginning to soften in the late 1930s even in the documentarists' journals such as *World Film News*; yet, the intellectual film culture of the 1940s as represented by Roger Manvell's influential book, *Film*, and the *Penguin Film Review*, which he edited, still took a somewhat lofty stance on the subject of the American film. The inaugural issue, which appeared in 1946, contained a number of articles which touched upon the Hollywood film and the familiar complaints were wheeled out. One article stated that the 'typical Hollywood film has given people all over the world an opportunity to slip away from the disappointments and inadequacies of their own lives to move for an hour or more in a world of half-truths and happy endings' (*Penguin Film Review* I, 1946: 59); the prominent critic, Richard Winnington, echoing *Close Up* and Rotha, wrote that American films were 'seventy five per cent. geared to the lowest tastes of a less matured and less experienced people' (ibid.: 27-8); a further article – 'The Seven Pillars of Hollywood' – referred to the 'mass of talent spoilt or destroyed by Hollywood' and 'the corruption of taste' embodied in its films. This sorry state of affairs, according to one contributor, was attributable to the industry being run by 'thirty ignorant merchants', together with the fact that 'the film is the only product of the United States which is not in the charge of experts, but is handled by people who have studied neither the theatre, nor music, nor history, nor even the European cinema' (ibid.: 94).

The post-war period, however, did see something of a critical accommodation to the American film developing somewhat slowly in Britain. There were some indications of a shift in attitude among some of the younger critics who began writing in the late 1940s for the short-lived magazine *Sequence*, and then for *Sight and Sound*, published by the British Film Institute. The journals represented alternative views to the orthodoxies established by Rotha and Manvell and, in particular, did not dismiss Hollywood but found merit in some

American pictures. *Sequence* published key articles on the films of John Ford and the American musical, and although it ceased publication in 1951 after 13 issues, Gavin Lambert moved to the editor's post on *Sight and Sound*, taking with him some of the ethos of *Sequence*. However, the major critical shift in attitude towards the American cinema in the post-war period came from France and a film culture far more receptive to Hollywood. Indeed, the positive attitude towards Hollywood associated with journals such as *Cahiers du Cinéma* and *Positif* in the 1950s can be traced back through the history of French film culture to the late 1920s. While Paul Rotha and *Close Up* were dismissing Hollywood, French film criticism was displaying a more even-handed treatment of both American and European films:

> Even a cursory examination of the contents of the *Revue du Cinéma* reveals a profile strikingly similar to that of the later *Cahiers*. In the 1929-31 period, more or less equal weight was being given to European 'art cinema' and avant-garde film (Pabst and Lang, Eisenstein and Pudovkin, Man Ray, Ruttmann and Bunuel, Dreyer) and American cinema (articles on Stroheim, Chaplin, of course, but also on Laurel and Hardy, Langdon, King Vidor, Hawks, Borzage, Sternberg, Lubitsch, Dwan). (Hillier, 1985: 2)

Similarly, the critics of *Cahiers* continued to write about a range of cinemas although it was their somewhat polemical championing of Hollywood films in general and, in particular, a spectrum of directors whose work was rarely taken seriously in British or American film criticism, that attracted attention. In addition, the aesthetics propounded in the course of their analyses tended to highlight *mise en scène* rather than montage as the central distinguishing feature of cinema as an art form, contradicting the assumptions about the centrality of montage that characterized British writing on cinema in particular. Their admiration for Hitchcock's *Vertigo* (1958), Hawks's *Rio Bravo* (1959) and the films of Douglas Sirk and Nicholas Ray differentiated them radically from the orthodoxies of Anglo-American film criticism in journals such as *Sight and Sound* although that did not involve a rejection of other kinds of cinema. At the end of the 1950s, as Richard Roud has noted, while both English and French critics shared the high valuation of certain non-Hollywood films such as Eisenstein's *Ivan the Terrible* (1945-58), Mizoguchi's *Ugetsu Monogatari* (1952) and the contemporary films of Truffaut, Bergman and Resnais, they were poles apart when it came to ranking the American cinema of the time (1960: 167ff.).

In the same period the editor of *Sight and Sound*, Penelope Houston, wrote a defence of the liberal humanistic criticism that now characterized the magazine, a critical stance which stressed content rather than form, another way in which the two film cultures differed in their approaches to the cinema. Houston argued that the task of the magazine was 'to examine the cinema in terms of its ideas, to submit these to the test of comment and discussion' and was sceptical about the formalism of the *Cahiers du Cinéma* group, regarding their concentration on *mise en scène* criticism seemingly at the expense of content as somewhat frivolous (1960: 164). It is a scepticism deeply ingrained in British film culture and traceable back to Grierson's strictures on Hitchcock written in the early 1930s. Although ready to acknowledge Hitchcock as 'the best director, the slickest craftsman, the sharpest observer and finest master of detail in all England', Grierson also considered that his films failed to engage seriously with social issues making him 'the world's best director of unimportant pictures' (Grierson, 1966b: 71-2).

The *Cahiers'* example, however, was taken up by other critical groupings in Britain. *Movie*, 'the most important pro-Hollywood journal outside France' (Elsaesser, 1979: 200), appeared in 1962 with a commitment to 'help remedy the unhealthy lack of reasoned disagreement about films in Britain', to quote from the brief editorial introduction to the first issue. The close analytical critical techniques and the catholic embrace of a range of cinemas, including classic Hollywood, 'art cinema', Japanese film-makers such as Ozu and the Italian peplum, provided an important antidote to the prevailing film culture and, in particular, to the influence of *Sight and Sound*. The journal's negative attitude to the British cinema, however, was redolent of Rotha and *Close Up*, although the terms of condemnation were somewhat differently inflected and more 'reasoned'. The stultifying effects of a film culture which centralized content, neglected form and style and displayed a contempt for the low-budget genre film were identified as reasons for the failure of the British cinema to match the achievements of Hollywood. As Victor Perkins, writing on behalf of the editorial board in the first issue of the journal, put it:

> We know that we can't have a *L'Avventura* or an *A Bout de Souffle* under the present system. We are much more disturbed by the fact that we are not getting the equivalents for *Psycho*, *Elmer Gantry*, and *Written on the Wind*. (1962: 7)

Yet, if the attitudes towards the indigenous film, or the 'critically respectable' indigenous film, echoed the positions established in the 1920s, the attitude towards the Hollywood film was changing. The new critics associated with *Movie* offered alternatives to the sedimented attitudes towards Hollywood, alternatives which treated the American film seriously and subjected it to the kind of analysis and criticism previously felt to be appropriate for the more self-consciously artistic cinemas of Europe. It was also a criticism which reduced the gap between the critic and the public at least in its implicit manifestation of a respect for the taste of the 'masses'. The critics of *Movie* had been brought up on an American culture represented by Hollywood films in particular but also by popular music, jazz and crime literature which, together, constituted a collective counterweight to the staid hierarchical artistic culture in Britain. Although the journal's origins in a university journal reflected an elite educational setting, the ethos that *Movie* promoted derived more from the loosening of conservative attitudes towards popular culture which marked the postwar period.

The American cinema has been an important and determining framework dictating the parameters of the film culture within which the British cinema, a body of indigenously produced films, a 'national cinema', has had to develop. The nature of the relationship between the two cinemas has meant that the energies of those involved in the British cinema were usually focused upon negotiating Hollywood and its films in various ways spanning economics, art and culture. On the one hand, such negotiation has involved the problems of raising production finance and of obtaining distribution in highly competitive domestic and international markets; on the other hand, it has meant problems associated with artistic form and content, decisions about artistic identity, about conceptions of a national cinema in an international industry. British film-makers have had to make films for a domestic audience accustomed to film styles and genres forged in the cosmopolitan atmosphere of Southern California and successful to the extent of defining the experience of cinema itself for the British cinema-goer. However, the professional culture in which such film-makers worked has also been affected by notions of cinema developed by cultural elites with strong allegiances to the European Modernist cinemas developed in the 1920s and a marked hostility to the popular culture of the Hollywood film. British film-makers have had to work in a film economy dominated by the power of the dollar, which at times has directed British film-makers into low-budget 'quota' film-making, at other times into the provision of ancillary services for Hollywood 'runaway' film-making. The spaces created for more sustained production independent to an extent of American influences – Korda in the 1930s, Rank in the 1940s – have been short-lived with production invariably returning to its precarious state and British film-makers returning to their somewhat restricted roles as subordinates to the American industry. It has been argued that British film-makers have characteristically opted for either an imitative cinema based on Hollywood values but destined to fail in comparison with its American counterparts for both economic and cultural reasons, or to a highly parochial cinema built upon unexportable strands of indigenous popular culture such as music-hall comedy. In a perverse way this is confirmed by the performance of British films in America where big-budget films modelled on Hollywood have been rejected by American audiences and have failed to secure a consistent presence in American cinemas, and where more idiosyncratic films such as the Ealing comedies have secured a niche position as 'art cinema' valued for their difference, for their 'parochial' qualities.

Attempts to understand the contours of a British cinema formed in this climate have produced a national cinema defined in a number of ways. The specificity of indigenous popular culture, the vigorous underlife of horror, low comedy, crime and melodrama, have produced a cinema defined in terms of 'films with an allegorical or poetic dimension' (Barr, 1972: 21); the films of David Lean, Anthony Asquith and Alfred Hitchcock point to a cinema of 'self-reflexivity' which foregrounds 'the processes of looking, dreaming, and fantasising' (Barr, 1986: 19). There is also a cinema which derives power from 'emotional restraint' and which has devised distinctive ways of presenting emotion, passion and repression (Durgnat, 1971; Dyer, 1994; Medhurst, 1984); a cinema of narrative structures which stress display, especially of 'heritage material', and which adopt episodic as opposed to linear narrative strategies, group- rather than individual-centred narratives (Higson, 1995); and a cinema with a commitment to 'the social' together with 'a relative lack of interest in the individual or subjectivity' (Williams, 1996: 192). Some of the qualities cited derive from indigenous cultural factors while others can be considered variations from the American narrative models, yet this complicated set of influences has enabled British film-makers to create 'an extremely rich and critically under-rated cinema' (Nowell-Smith, 1985: 152), a body of films which may regarded as a considerable achievement in the face of the difficulties created by the presence of the American industry. As Alan Lovell has suggested, 'a cinema which can produce films as varied as *The 39 Steps, Fires Were Started, Black Narcissus, Henry V, The Ladykillers, Saturday Night and Sunday Morning, If . . . , Kes, Withnail and I, Distant Voices, Still Lives* and *Butterfly Kiss* deserves celebration' (1997: 242). Though others might construct alternative lists of films, the point made here is the diversity of output ranging from popular genres through drama-documentary and literary adaptation, to self-conscious 'art' cinema, achieved in the unpromising context of a film industry and film culture governed by polarized assumptions about cinema which set the vigour and energy of Hollywood narrative against the sophistication of the European 'art' cinemas, together with an ingrained tendency to elevate documentary-based modes and forms above both entertainment and art. The international character of the film industry established during its early history means that national cinemas acquire definition in the context of a balance between indigenous cultural influence – theatre, literature, history, myth, philosophy – and the paradigmatic status of the dominant international cinema from Hollywood. The complication with this context is the way in which Hollywood itself has appropriated national cultures, literatures and histories for its own cinema, providing a complex background against which other national cinemas seek definition. This is especially the case with British culture which has been an important source for the American cinema, confronting British film-makers with exemplars formed within the aesthetics of Hollywood but also deriving content from British novels and plays, and from British history, myths and legends.

References

Acheson, Keith and Maule, Christopher J. (1994) 'Understanding Hollywood's Organization and Continuing Success', *Journal of Cultural Economics*, 18: 271-300.

Aldgate, Anthony (1983) 'Comedy, Class and Containment: The British Domestic Cinema of the 1930s', in James Curran and Vincent Porter (eds), *British Cinema History*. London: Weidenfeld and Nicolson. pp. 257-71.

Aldgate, Anthony and Richards, Jeffrey (1994) *Britain Can Take It. The British Cinema in the Second World War*. Edinburgh: Edinburgh University Press.

Allen, Robert C. (1977) 'Film History: The Narrow Discourse', in Ben Lawton and Janet Staiger (eds), *Film: Historical–Theoretical Speculations: The 1977 Film Studies Annual (Part Two)*, 9-17.

Altman, Rick (1984) 'A Semantic/Syntactic Approach to Film Genre', *Cinema Journal*, 23 (3): 6-18.

Altman, Rick (1999) *Film/Genre*. London: BFI Publishing.

Anderson, Benedict (1983) *Imagined Communities*. London: Verso.

Anderson, Lindsay (1949) 'Alfred Hitchcock', *Sequence*, 9, 113-24

Anderson, Lindsay (1957) 'Get Out and Push', in Tom Maschler (ed.), *Declaration*. Port Washington, New York/London: Kennikat Press. pp. 137-60.

Anderson, Robert (1985) 'The Motion Picture Patents Company: A Reevaluation', in Tino Balio (ed.), *The American Film Industry* revised edition. Madison, WI: University of Wisconsin Press. pp. 133-52.

Andrew, Dudley (1984) *Concepts in Film Theory*. Oxford: Oxford University Press.

Andrew, Dudley (1995) *Mists of Regret. Culture and Sensibility in Classic French Film*. Princeton, NJ: Princeton University Press.

Armes, Roy (1978) *A Critical History of British Cinema*. London: Secker and Warburg.

Asheim, Lester (1951) 'From Book to Film: Simplification', *Hollywood Quarterly*, 5 (3): 287-304.

Atwell, David (1981) *Cathedrals of the Movies: A History of British Cinemas and their Audiences*. London: The Architectural Press.

Balcon, Michael (1969) *Michael Balcon Presents . . . A Lifetime in Films*. London: Hutchinson.

Balio, Tino (1976) *United Artists. The Company Built by the Stars*. Madison, WI: University of Wisconsin Press.

Balio, Tino (ed.) (1985) *The American Film Industry* (revised edition). Madison, WI: University of Wisconsin Press.

Balio, Tino (ed.) (1990) *Hollywood in the Age of Television*. Boston: Unwin Hyman.

Balio, Tino (1993) *Grand Design. Hollywood as a Modern Business Enterprise, 1930-1939*. Berkeley, CA: University of California Press.

Ball, Robert Hamilton (1968) *Shakespeare on Silent Film*. London: Allen and Unwin.

Barnes, John (1976) *The Beginnings of the Cinema in England*. Newton Abbot: David and Charles.

Barnes, John (1983) *The Rise of the Cinema in Great Britain: Volume 2, Jubilee Year 1897*. London: Bishopsgate Press.

Barnes, John (1996a) *The Beginnings of the Cinema in England 1894-1901. Volume 3. 1898*. Exeter: University of Exeter Press.

Barnes, John (1996b) *The Beginnings of the Cinema in England 1894-1901. Volume 4. 1899*. Exeter: University of Exeter Press.

Barr, Charles (1972) 'Straw Dogs, A Clockwork Orange and the Critics', *Screen*, 13 (2): 17-31.

Barr, Charles (1986) *All Our Yesterdays*. London: BFI Publishing.

Barr, Charles (1997) 'Before *Blackmail*: Silent British Cinema', in Robert Murphy (ed.), *The British Cinema Book*. London: BFI Publishing.

Barrow, Kenneth (1985) *Mr Chips. The Life of Robert Donat*. London: Methuen.

Baxendale, John (1996) 'In Search of the People: The Journeys of J. B. Priestley', in John Baxendale and Chris Pawling, *Narrating the Thirties*. London: Macmillan. pp. 46-78.

Bazin, André (1968) 'The Evolution of Film language', in Peter Graham (ed.), *The New Wave*. London: Secker and Warburg. pp. 25-50.

Behlmer, Rudy (ed.) *Inside Warner Bros. (1935-1951)*. London: Weidenfeld and Nicolson.

Bigsby, C. W. E. (ed.) (1979) *Superculture*. Bowling Green, OH: Bowling Green University Press.

Bluestone, George (1971) *Novels into Film*. Berkeley, CA: University of California Press.

Board of Trade (1944) *Tendencies to Monopoly in the Cinematograph Films Industry* (the Palache Report). London: HMSO.

Bordwell, David (1985) *Narration in the Fiction Film*. London: Methuen & Co.

Bordwell, David, Staiger, Janet and Thompson, Kristin (1985) *The Classical Hollywood Cinema: Film Style and Mode of Production to 1960*. London: Routledge and Kegan Paul.

Bottomore, Stephen (1990) 'Shots in the Dark – The Real Origins of Film Editing', in Thomas Elsaesser (ed.), *Early Cinema. Space Frame Narrative*. London: BFI Publishing. pp. 104-13.

Bowser, Eileen (1990) *The Transformation of Cinema 1907-1915*. Berkeley, CA: University of California Press.

Brown, Richard (1977) 'England's First Cinema', *The British Journal of Photography*, 124 (6100): 520-1, 530-1.

Brown, Richard (1998) ' "England is not big enough . . . " American rivalry in the early English Film Business: The Case of Warwick v Urban, 1903', *Film History*, 10 (1): 21-34.

Brown, Richard and Anthony, Barry (1999) *A Victorian Film Enterprise*. Trowbridge, Wiltshire: Flicks Books.

Burch, Noël (1990) *Life to Those Shadows*. London: BFI Publishing.

Buscombe, Edward (1981) 'Film History and the Idea of National Cinema', *Australian*

Journal of Film Theory, 9-10: 141-53.

Carroll, Noël (1998) *A Philosophy of Mass Art*. Oxford: Oxford University Press.

Chanan, Michael (1980) *The Dream that Kicks*. London: Routledge and Kegan Paul.

Chandler, Raymond (1976) *Pearls are a Nuisance*. London: Penguin.

Chapman, James (1998) *The British at War. Cinema, State and Propaganda, 1938-1945*. London: I. B. Tauris.

Christie, Ian (ed.) (1978) *Powell, Pressburger and Others*. London: British Film Institute.

Christie, Ian (1994) *The Last Machine*. London: BBC/BFI.

Coe, Brian (1981) *The History of Movie Photography*. London: Ash and Grant.

Conan Doyle, Arthur (1981) *The Penguin Complete Sherlock Holmes*. London: Penguin Books.

Cosandey, Roland (1996) 'Back to Lumière, or the Dream of an Essence: Some Untimely Considerations about a French Myth', in Christopher Williams (ed.), *Cinema: the Beginnings and the Future*. London: University of Westminster Press. pp. 82-94.

Crofts, Stephen (1993) 'Reconceptualizing National Cinema/s', *Quarterly Review of Film and Video*, 14 (3): 49-67.

Curran, James and Porter, Vincent (eds) (1983) *British Cinema History*. London: Weidenfeld and Nicolson.

Curtis, James (1998) *James Whale. A New World of Gods and Monsters*. London: Faber and Faber.

Custen, George F (1992) *Bio/Pics. How Hollywood Constructed Public History*. New Brunswick, New Jersey: Rutgers University Press.

Davies, David Stuart (1976) *Holmes of the Movies. The Screen Career of Sherlock Holmes*. London: New English Library.

de Grazia, Victoria (1989) 'Mass Culture and Sovereignty: The American Challenge to European Cinemas, 1920-1960', *Journal of Modern History*, 61: 53-87.

Dickinson, Margaret (1983) 'The State and the Consolidation of Monopoly', in James Curran and Vincent Porter (eds), *British Cinema History*. London: Weidenfeld and Nicolson. pp. 74-95.

Dickinson, Margaret and Street, Sarah (1985) *Cinema and State: the Film Industry and the British Government, 1927-84*. London: British Film Institute.

Docherty, David, Morrison, David and Tracey, Michael (1987) *The Last Picture Show? Britain's Changing Film Audiences*. London: BFI Publishing.

Donald, James, Friedberg, Anne and Marcus, Laura (eds) (1998) *Close Up 1927-1933*. London: Cassell.

Durgnat, Raymond (1971) *A Mirror for England*. London: Faber and Faber.

Dyer, Richard (1994) 'Feeling English', *Sight and Sound*, 4 (3): 17-19.

Ellis, John (1996) 'The Quality Film Adventure: British Critics and the Cinema, 1942-1948', in Andrew Higson (ed.), *Dissolving Views. Key Writings on British Cinema*. London: Cassell. pp. 66-93.

Elsaesser, Thomas (1979) 'Two Decades in Another Country: Hollywood and the Cinéphiles', in C.W. E. Bigsby (ed.) *Superculture*. Bowling Green, Ohio: Bowling Green University Press. pp. 199-216.

Elsaesser, Thomas (ed.) (1990) *Early Cinema. Space Frame Narrative*. London: British Film Institute.

Eyles, Alan (1997) 'Exhibition and the Cinemagoing Experience', in Robert Murphy (ed.), *The British Cinema Book*. London: BFI Publishing.

Fadiman, William (1962) 'Runaways', *Films and Filming*, July: 40-1.

Fine, Richard (1985) *Hollywood and the Profession of Authorship, 1928-1940*. Ann Arbor, MI: UMI Research Press Studies in Cinema.

Gifford, Denis (1986) *The British Film Catalogue*. Newton Abbot: David and Charles.

Glancy, Mark H. (1999) *When Hollywood Loved Britain: the Hollywood "British film" 1939-45*. Manchester: Manchester University Press.

Glut, Donald F (1973) *The Frankenstein Legend*. Metuchen, New Jersey: The Scarecrow Press.

Glut, Donald F (1975) *The Dracula Book*. Metuchen, New Jersey: The Scarecrow Press.

Gomery, Douglas (1992) *Shared Pleasures. A History of Movie Presentation in the United States*. London: BFI Publishing.

Gray, Richard (1996) *Cinemas in Britain: One Hundred Years of Cinema Architecture*. London: Lund Humphries.

Grierson, John (1966a) 'Hollywood Looks at Life', in Forsyth Hardy (ed.), *Grierson on Documentary*. London: Faber and Faber. pp. 86-100.

Grierson, John (1966b) 'Directors of the Thirties', in Forsyth Hardy (ed.), *Grierson on Documentary*. London: Faber and Faber. pp. 59-85.

Grierson, John (1989) 'Document: John Grierson on Hollywood's Success, 1927', *Historical Journal of Film, Radio and Television*, 9 (3): 309-26.

Griffith, Richard (1949) 'Where Are the Dollars? – I', *Sight and Sound*, December: 33-4.

Griffith, Richard (1950) 'Where Are the Dollars? – 2', *Sight and Sound*, January: 39-40.

Guback, Thomas (1967) 'American Interests in the British Film Industry', *Quarterly Review of Economics and Business*, 7: 7-21.

Guback, Thomas (1969) *The International Film Industry*. Bloomington: Indiana University Press.

Guback, Thomas H. (1985) 'Hollywood's International Market', in Tino Balio (ed.), *The American Film Industry* (revised edition). Madison, WI: University of Wisconsin Press.

Gunning, Tom (1990) 'Weaving a Narrative. Style and Economic Background in Griffith's Biograph Films', in Thomas Elsaesser (ed.), *Early Cinema. Space Frame Narrative*. London: BFI Publishing. pp. 336-47.

Hampton, Benjamin (1970) *History of the American Film Industry*. New York: Dover Publications Inc.

Harding, Colin and Popple, Simon (1996) *In the Kingdom of Shadows A Companion to Early Cinema*. London: Cygnus Arts

Hardy, Phil (ed.) (1997) *The BFI Companion to Crime*. London: Cassell.

Harper, Sue (1994) *Picturing the Past. The Rise and Fall of the British Costume Film*. London: BFI Publishing.

Harper, Sue (1997) 'Bonnie Prince Charlie Revisited: British Costume Film in the 1950s', in Robert Murphy (ed.), *The British Cinema Book*. London: BFI Publishing. pp. 133-43.

Hartog, Simon (1983) 'State Protection of a Beleaguered Industry', in James Curran and Vincent Porter (eds), *British Cinema History*. London Weidenfeld and Nicolson. pp. 59-73.

Hawkridge, John (1996) 'British Cinema from Hepworth to Hitchcock', in Geoffrey Nowell-Smith (ed.), *The Oxford History of World Cinema*. Oxford: Oxford University Press. pp. 130-6.

Hayward, Susan (1993) *French National Cinema*. London: Routledge.

Higham, Charles (1994) *Merchant of Dreams. Louis B. Mayer and the Secret of Hollywood*. London: Pan Books.

Higson, Andrew (1989) 'The Concept of National Cinema', *Screen*, 30 (4): 36-46.

Higson, Andrew (1995) *Waving the Flag: Constructing a National Cinema in Britain*. Oxford: Clarendon Press.

Higson, Andrew and Maltby, Richard (1999) *"Film Europe" and "Film America": cinema, commerce and cultural exchange*. Exeter: Exeter University Press.

Hill, John (1992) 'The Issue of National Cinema and British Film Production', in Petrie, Duncan (ed.), *New Questions of British Cinema*. London: BFI Publishing. pp. 10-21.

Hillier, Jim (1985) *Cahiers du Cinéma. The 1950s: Neo-Realism, Hollywood, New Wave*. London: Routledge & Kegan Paul.

Hillier, Jim (1992) *The New Hollywood*. London: Studio Vista.

Hindle, Maurice (1985) 'Introduction', in Mary Shelley, *Frankenstein*. London: Penguin Books. pp. 7-42.

Hirschhorn, Clive (1986) *The Warner Bros. Story*. London: Octopus Books.

Hjort, Mette (1996) 'Danish Cinema and the Politics of Recognition', in David Bordwell and Noel Carroll, (eds), *Post-Theory. Reconstructing Film Studies*. Madison, WI: University of Wisconsin Press. pp. 520-32.

Houston, Penelope (1960) 'The Critical Question', *Sight and Sound*, 29: 4, 160-5.

Hunningher, Joost (1996) 'Première on Regent Street', in Christopher Williams (ed.), *Cinema: the Beginnings and the Future*. London: University of Westminster Press. pp. 41-54.

Jarvie, Ian (1992) *Hollywood's Overseas Campaign. The North Atlantic Movie Trade 1920-1950*. Cambridge: Cambridge University Press.

Jenkins, Keith (1991) *Re-thinking History*. London: Routledge.

Jones, Dorothy (1951) 'Hollywood's International Relations', *Hollywood Quarterly*, 11 (4): 362-74.

Jowett, Garth (1976) *Film The Democratic Art*. Boston/Toronto: Little, Brown and Company.

Kelly, Terence (1966) *A Competitive Cinema*. London: The Institute of Economic Affairs.

Kindem, Gorham (1982) 'The Demise of Kinemacolor', in G. Kindem (ed.), *The American Movie Industry*. Carbondale and Edwardsville, IL: Southern Illinois University Press. pp. 36-45.

Kitses, Jim (1969) *Horizons West*. London: Thames and Hudson.

Knight, Arthur (1953) 'The Reluctant Audience', *Sight and Sound*, 22 (4): 191-2.

Koszarski, Richard (1990) *An Evening's Entertainment: The Age of the Silent Feature Picture, 1915-1928*. Berkeley, CA: University of California Press.

Kuisel, Richard (1993) *Seducing the French: the dilemma of Americanization*.

California: University of California Press.

Kulik, Karol (1990) *Alexander Korda. The Man Who Could Work Miracles*. London: Virgin Books.

Landy, Marcia (1990) *British Genres. Cinema and Society, 1930-1960*. Princeton, New Jersey: Princeton University Press.

Lafferty, William (1990) 'Feature Films on Prime-Time Television', in Tino Balio (ed.), *Hollywood in the Age of Television*. Boston: Unwin Hyman.

Lean, David (1947) 'Brief Encounter', *The Penguin Film Review*, 4: 27-35.

Leavis, F. R. (1930) *Mass Civilisation and Minority Culture*. Cambridge: Minority Press.

Le Mahieu, D. L. (1988) *A Culture for Democracy*. Oxford: Oxford University Press.

Levine, Lawrence W. (1984) 'William Shakespeare and the American People: A Study in Cultural Transformation', *American Historical Review*, 89: 34-66.

Lovell, Alan (1972) 'Notes on British Film Culture', *Screen*, 13 (2): 5-15.

Lovell, Alan (1997) 'The British Cinema: The known Cinema?', in Robert Murphy (ed.), *The British Cinema Book*. London: BFI Publishing.

Lovell, Terry (19870 *Consuming Fiction*. London: Verso Books.

Low, Rachael and Manvell, Roger (1948) *The History of the British Film 1896-1906*. London: George Allen and Unwin.

Low, Rachael (1949) *The History of the British Film 1906-1914*. London: George Allen and Unwin.

Low, Rachael (1971) *The History of the British Film 1918-1929*. London: George Allen and Unwin.

Low, Rachael (1985) *Film Making in 1930s Britain*. London: Allen and Unwin, 1985.

Macnab, Geoffrey (1993) *J. Arthur Rank and the British Film Industry*. London: Routledge.

Maeder, Edward (ed.) (1987) *Hollywood and History: costume design in film*. London, Los Angeles: Thames and Hudson and Los Angeles County Museum of Art.

Maltby, Richard (1993) 'The Production Code and the Hays Office', in Tino Balio, *Grand Design. Hollywood as a Modern Business Enterprise*. Berkeley, CA: University of California Press. pp. 37-72.

Maltby, Richard (1995) *Hollywood Cinema An Introduction*. Oxford: Blackwell.

Marshall, Norman (1931) 'Reflections on the English film', *The Bookman*, October: 71-2.

Mayer, Michael F. (1965) *Foreign Films on American Screens*. New York: Arco Publishing Company.

Mayne, Richard (1970) 'What's Wrong with the Cinema?', *The Listener*, 83 (2133): 203-5.

McArthur, Colin (1984) 'National Identities', in Geoff Hurd (ed.), *National Fictions*. London: BFI Publishing. pp.54-6.

MacCann, Richard Dyer (1962) *Hollywood in Transition*. Boston: Houghton Mifflin.

McFarlane, Brian (1996) *Novel to Film. An Introduction to the Theory of Adaptation*. Oxford: Oxford University Press.

Medhurst, Andy (1984) '1950s War Films', in Geoff Hurd (ed.), *National Fictions*. London: BFI Books. pp. 35-8.

Merritt, Russell (1985) 'Nickelodeon Theaters, 1905-1914: Building an Audience for the Movies', in Tino Balio (ed.), *The American Film Industry*. Madison, WI: University of Wisconsin Press. pp. 83-102.

Metz, Christian (1975) 'The Imaginary Signifier', *Screen*, 16 (2): 14-76.

Moley, Raymond (1945) *The Hays Office*. Indianapolis, IN: Bobbs-Merrill. (Reprinted in 1971, New York: Jerome S. Ozer.)

Moorhead, Caroline (1984) *Sidney Bernstein: A Biography*. London: Jonathan Cape.

Murphy, Robert (1983) 'Rank's Attempt on the American Market', in James Curran and Vincent Porter (eds), *British Cinema History*. London: Weidenfeld and Nicolson. pp. 164-78.

Murphy, Robert (1984) 'Coming of Sound to the Cinema in Britain', *Historical Journal of Film, Radio and Television*, 4 (2): 143-60.

Murphy, Robert (1992) *Sixties British Cinema*. London: BFI Publishing.

Musser, Charles (1990a) *The Emergence of Cinema. The American Screen to 1907*. Berkeley, CA: University of California Press.

Musser, Charles (1990b) 'The Nickelodeon Era Begins. Establishing the Framework for Hollywood's Mode of Representation', in Thomas Elsaesser (ed.), *Early Cinema. Space Frame Narrative*. London: BFI Publishing. pp.256-73.

Napper, Lawrence (1997) 'A Despicable Tradition? Quota Quickies in the 1930s', in Robert Murphy (ed.), *The British Cinema Book*. London: BFI Publishing. pp. 37-47.

Neale, Steve (1981) 'Art Cinema as Institution', *Screen*, 22 (1): 11-39.

Nowell-Smith, Geoffrey (1985) 'But Do We Need It?', in Martin Auty and Nick Roddick (eds), *British Cinema Now*. London: BFI Publishing. pp. 147-58.

Nowell-Smith, Geoffrey and Ricci, Steven (eds) (1998) *Hollywood and Europe*. London: BFI Publishing.

Optical Lantern and Cinematograph Journal, The (1905)

Olivier, Laurence (1986) *Olivier on Acting*. London: Weidenfeld and Nicholson.

O'Regan, Tom (1996) *Australian National Cinema*. London: Routledge.

PEP (1952) *The British Film Industry*. London: PEP (Political and Economic Planning).

Perkins, V. F. (1962) 'The British Cinema', *Movie*, 1: 2-8.

Perkins, V. F. (1972) *Film as Film*. Harmondsworth: Pelican.

Perry, George (1975) *The Great British Picture Show*. St Albans: Paladin.

Popular Memory Group (1982) 'Popular Memory: theory, politics, method', in Richard Johnson, Gregor McLennon, Bill Schwarz, and David Sutton (eds) (1982) *Making Histories: studies in history – writing and politics*. London: Hutchinson. Pp.205-52.

Porter, Vincent (1983) 'Creativity at Ealing Studios and Hammer Films', in James Curran and Vincent Porter (eds), *British Cinema History*. London: Weidenfeld and Nicolson. pp. 179-207.

Porter, Vincent (1997) 'Methodism versus the Market-place: The Rank Organization and British Cinema', in Robert Murphy (ed.), *The British Cinema Book*. London: BFI Publishing. pp. 122-32.

Powell, Dilys (1948) 'Films since 1939', in Arnold L. Haskell, Dilys Powell, Rollo Myers, and Robin Ironside, *Since 1939. Ballet Films Music Painting*. London: Readers Union. pp. 63-95.

Ramsaye, Terry (1926) *A Million and One Nights: A History of the Motion Picture*. London: Frank Cass & Co. Ltd.

Ray, Cyril (1947) 'These British Movies', *Harpers*, June: 516-23.

Ray, Robert (1985) *A Certain Tendency of the Hollywood Cinema, 1930-1980*. Princeton, NJ: Princeton University Press.

Report of the Committee on Cinematograph Films (Moyne Report) (1936). London: HMSO.

Rhode, Eric (1971) *A History of World Cinema*. Harmondsworth: Penguin.

Richards, Jeffrey and Sheridan, Dorothy (eds) (1987) *Mass Observation at the Movies*. London: Routledge.

Richards, Jeffrey (1997) *Film and British National Identity*. Manchester: Manchester University Press.

Richards, Jeffrey (ed.) (1998) *The Unknown 1930s: An Alternative History of the British Cinema, 1929-1939*. London: I. B. Tauris.

Robinson, David (1996) *From Peep Show to Palace: The Birth of American Film*. New York: Columbia University Press.

Roddick, Nick (1983) *A New Deal in Entertainment. Warner Brothers in the 1930s*. London: British Film Institute.

Rosen, Philip (1984) 'History, Textuality, Nation: Kracauer, Burch, and Some Problems in the Study of National Cinemas', *Iris*, 2 (2): 69-84.

Rosenstone, Robert (1988) 'History in Images/History in Words: Reflections on the Possibility of Really Putting History Onto Film', *American Historical Review*, 93: 5 (December), 1173-85.

Rosenstone, Robert (1995*) Visions of the Past. The Challenge of Film to Our Idea of History*. Cambridge, Mass., London: Harvard University Press.

Rosenstone, Robert (1995)

Rossell, Deac (1998) *Living Pictures The Origins of the Movies*. New York: State University of New York Press.

Rotha, Paul (1967) *The Film Till Now*. London: Spring Books.

Roud, Richard (1956/57) 'Britain in America', *Sight and Sound*. 26: 3, 119-23.

Roud, Richard (1960) 'The French Line', *Sight and Sound*, 29: 4: 166-71.

Saville, Victor (1974) *Shadows on a Screen*. (Unpublished memoirs held in the British Film Institute Special Collection.)

Schatz, Thomas (1989) *The Genius of the System. Hollywood Filmmaking in the Studio Era*. London: Simon and Schuster.

Sconce, Jeffrey (1994) 'Narrative Authority and Social Narrativity: The Cinematic Reconstitution of Brontë's *Jane Eyre*', in Janet Staiger (ed.), *The Studio System*. New Brunswick, NJ: Rutgers University Press. pp. 140-62.

Sedgwick, John (1996) 'Michael Balcon's Close Encounter with the American Market, 1934-1936', *Historical Journal of Film, Radio and Television*, 16 (3): 333-48.

Sedgwick, John (1997) 'The British Film Industry's Production Sector Difficulties in the Late 1930s', *Historical Journal of Film, Radio and Television*, 17 (1): 49-66.

Sedgwick, John (1998) 'Cinema-going Preferences in Britain in the 1930s', in Jeffrey Richards (ed.), *The Unknown 1930s: An Alternative History of the British Cinema, 1929-1939*. London: I. B. Tauris. pp. 1-21.

Segrave, Kerry (1997*) American Films Abroad. Hollywood's Domination of the World's Movie Screens*. Jefferson, NC: McFarland & Company.

Shipman, David (1970) *The Great Movie Stars. The Golden Years*. London: Hamlyn.

Sinclair, Upton (1933) *Upton Sinclair Presents Williams Fox*. Los Angeles: Upton Sinclair.

Skal, David J (1990*) Hollywood Gothic. The Tangled Web of* <u>*Dracula*</u> *from Novel to Stage to Screen*. London: Andre Deutsch

Sklar, Robert (1976) *Movie-Made America*. New York: Vintage Books.

Sorlin, Pierre (1980) *The Film in History: restaging the past*. Oxford: Blackwell.

Sorlin, Pierre (1996) *Italian National Cinema*. London: Routledge.

Staiger, Janet (1985) 'The Producer-unit System: Management by Specialization after 1931', in David Bordwell, Janet Staiger and Kristin Thompson, *The Classical Hollywood Cinema. Style and Mode of Production to 1960*. London: Routledge and Kegan Paul. pp. 320-29.

Stead, Peter (1981) *Film and the Working Class*. London: Routledge.

Stein, Michael and Parker, Gillian (eds) (1981) *The English Novel and the Movies*. New York: Frederick Ungar Publishing.

Steinberg, Cobbett (1981) *Reel Facts. The Movie Book of Records*. Harmondsworth, Middlesex: Penguin Books.

Stoneman, Patsy (1998) 'Introduction', in Emily Brontë, *Wuthering Heights*. Oxford: Oxford University Press. pp. vii-xli.

Storey, John (1993) *An Introductory Guide to Cultural Theory and Popular Culture*. New York and London: Harvester Wheatsheaf.

Street, Sarah (1985) 'The Hays Office and the Defence of the British Market in the 1930', *Historical Journal of Film, Radio and Television*, 5 (1): 37-55.

Street, Sarah (1986) 'Alexander Korda, Prudential Assurance and British Film Finance in the 1930s', *Historical Journal of Film, Radio and Television*, 6 (2): 161-79.

Thompson, David (1993) *Showman. The Life of David O. Selznick*. London: André Deutsch.

Thompson, Kristin (1985) *Exporting Entertainment. America in the World Film Market 1907-1934*. London: BFI Publishing.

Thompson, Kristin and Bordwell, David (1994) *Film History An Introduction*. New York: McGraw-Hill.

Thumim, Janet (1991) 'The "popular", cash and culture in the postwar British film industry', *Screen*, 32 (3): 245-71.

Truffaut, Francois (1978) *Hitchcock*. London: Paladin.

Tunstall, Jeremy (1977) *The Media are American: Anglo-American media in the world*. London: Constable.

Uricchio, William and Pearson, Roberta (1993*) Reframing Culture. The Case of Vitagraph Quality Films*. Princeton, NJ: Princeton University Press.

Uricchio, William (1996) 'The First World War and the Crisis in Europe', in Geoffrey Nowell-Smith (ed.), *The Oxford History of World Cinema*. Oxford: Oxford University Press.

Usai, Paolo Cherchi (1994) *Burning Passions: An Introduction to the Study of Silent Cinema*. London: BFI Publishing.

Vasey, Ruth (1997) *The World According to Hollywood 1918-1939*. Exeter: University of Exeter Press.

Walker, Alexander (1974) *Hollywood, England. The British Film Industry in the Sixties*. London: Michael Joseph.

Walker, Alexander (1985) *National Heroes. The British Cinema in the Seventies and Eighties.* London: Harrap.

Walker, John (1985) *The Once and Future Film.* London: Methuen.

Walsh, Michael (1997) 'Fighting the American Invasion with Cricket, Roses and Marmalade for Breakfast', *The Velvet Light Trap*, 40: 4-17.

Warren, Patricia (1995) *British Film Studios An Illustrated History.* London: B. T. Batsford.

Warshow, Robert (1970) *The Immediate Experience.* New York: Atheneum.

Watt, Ian (1972) *The Rise of the Novel.* Harmondsworth: Pelican.

Webster, Duncan (1988) *Looka Yonder.* London: Comedia/Routledge.

White, Hayden (1988) 'Historiography and Historiophoty', *American Historical Review*, 93: 5, 1193-9.

Wilcox, Herbert (1967) *Twenty-Five Thousand Sunsets. The Autobiography of Herbert Wilcox.* London: The Bodley Head.

Wilinsky, Barbara (1997) 'First and Finest: British Films on U.S. Television in the Late 1940s', *The Velvet Light Trap*, 40 (Fall): 18-31.

Williams, Christopher (1996) 'The Social Art of Cinema', in C. Williams (ed.) *Cinema, the Beginnings and the Future.* London: University of Westminster Press, 190-200.

Williams, Raymond (1965) *The Long Revolution.* London: Pelican Books.

Williams, Raymond (1976) *Keywords.* London: Fontana.

Williams, Raymond (1983) 'British Film History: New Perspectives', in James Curran and Vincent Porter (eds), *British Cinema History.* London: Weidenfeld and Nicolson. pp. 9-23.

Wollen, P (1998) 'Tinsel and Realism', in Geoffrey Nowell-Smith and Steven Ricci (eds), *Hollywood and Europe.* London: BFI Publishing. pp. 129-34.

Wood, Linda (1997) 'Low-budget British Films in the 1930s', in Robert Murphy, (ed.), *The British Cinema Book.* London: BFI Publishing. pp. 48-57.

Wyke, Maria (1997) *Projecting the Past: ancient Rome, cinema, history.* London: Routledge

Index